The Noughties in the Hispanic and Lusophone World

The Noughties in the Hispanic and Lusophone World

Edited by

Kathy Bacon and Niamh Thornton

CAMBRIDGE SCHOLARS

PUBLISHING

The Noughties in the Hispanic and Lusophone World,
Edited by Kathy Bacon and Niamh Thornton

This book first published 2012

Cambridge Scholars Publishing

12 Back Chapman Street, Newcastle upon Tyne, NE6 2XX, UK

British Library Cataloguing in Publication Data
A catalogue record for this book is available from the British Library

ISBN (10): 1-4438-4100-5, ISBN (13): 978-1-4438-4100-9

TABLE OF CONTENTS

Part Two: Cultural Memory in the Noughties

Part Three: New—and not so New—Beginnings

ACKNOWLEDGEMENTS

This book was born of many conversations before, during and after a Women in Spanish, Portuguese and Latin American Studies (WiSPS) conference in Dublin City University in 2008. Aware of the impending ten year anniversary of WiSPS and keen to celebrate it we threw around many ideas which would fit the decade. Claire Williams, the then president of the organisation, suggested the noughties. It seemed very apropos and we went with it. In a chat on a bus on the way into Dublin city after the conference we agreed to edit the volume as a worthwhile tribute to the range and strength of research that WiSPS members have engaged in over the last ten years. The subsequent call resulted in the current volume. So, first of all we must thank Claire for her idea. Next, we would like to thank the contributors, whose eagerness to embrace the topic resulted in the fascinating array of essays in this volume. This book is dedicated to the founding members of WiSPS, who saw a need to create an organisation that would support and mentor female colleagues as well as to provide a forum for feminist studies, and address the role of women in British and Irish Luso-Hispanism. We would also like to pay tribute to members new and old and to the contribution the organisation has made through its annual conference, study days, research fellowship and the supportive, engaging and lively exchanges that have taken place as a result of all these.

Niamh Thornton would like to thank Liz, as always, for providing invaluable feedback on the various drafts of the introduction and for her love and support, and to Dario for his occasional witticisms and stories which prove a welcome distraction from many hours in front of the computer.

Kathy Bacon would like to express gratitude to David for spurring me on, supporting me, and creating the emotional and practical conditions to make work possible, and to Chloe and Abigail for all the joy they bring.

INTRODUCTION

THE NOUGHTIES: FRESH START OR FALSE DAWN?

KATHY BACON AND NIAMH THORNTON

This volume is both inspired by and is a tribute to Women in Spanish, Portuguese and Latin American Studies (WiSPS). Since its establishment in the academic year 1999-2000 (see Severin 2008, ix-xi), WiSPS has witnessed the twenty-first-century noughties, completing its first decade and growing to become an established presence in Hispanic and Lusophone studies. All contributions in this volume are by members of WiSPS; some are papers given at WiSPS conferences, whilst others were written in direct response to our call for papers. The subject of the noughties was inspired by a suggestion from a former president of the association, Claire Williams, and we have been delighted by the range and scope of the chapters, which have provided a new perspective on their objects of study.

We are seizing the opportunity to study a time period that is both over and still happening as we write. The contributors have examined the noughties from a range of centuries. Some have had the advantage of distance, whilst others look at a time that is so recent it is still the present at the time of writing. It is this fascinating range of the historic and immediate that we have been eager to capture in this volume. It is not the same noughties that is being examined in each piece, yet there is significant resonance in the study of a particular, named decade. Whether in the distant past or the present, the advent of the noughties signals that the old century is over and the new has begun. While the notion of the *fin de siècle* has been well studied (see, for example, Showalter (1990), Teich and Porter (1990), Poyato (1997), and Richardson and Willis (2001)), the specificity of the noughties as a discrete period merits attention, which it has not always been paid.

As has been well catalogued by theorists (such as Toulmin and Goodfield (1965) and Whitrow (1989)) markers of time are arbitrary. Time is nonetheless rendered meaningful by calendars and clocks:

timekeeping is an invention that helps us organise society and is a tool to ensure the smooth running of both the public (workplace, industry, services) and of the private (home, friends, teams). It binds us to shared historical markers. Writing about century's end, Hillel Schwartz states that "nothing would be so foolish as to claim that all events of import occur at century's end" (1996, 10). Yet we ascribe to those events that do fall on particular dates a meaning that is all their own. Nature may not dictate what happens on a certain date, but it can be rendered significant by happenstance. Similarly, men and women can imbue a moment with a charged significance. As social, cultural and historical actors, individuals or groups aware of the mood of a time, and eager to make a date carry the weight of an event can make things happen because time has meaning beyond a simple arithmetical calculation.

The end of a century and—in the case of the twentieth century—of a millennium has its own mythos of the end of things. Some views of this ending are apocalyptic, in that they envisage a dramatic end of time, and others project forward whilst reflecting on what has gone before (see Showalter (1990, 1-18)). The beginning of a new millennium, century, and decade carries the weight of this end, on the one hand, and of the shining hopes of the coming of a new era, on the other. Schwartz sums up this tension between the time gone past of the old century and that which is yet to come, "[a]t century's end we are inevitably host to an oxymoronic time: the most desperate and the most exultant; the most constrained and the most chaotic" (1996, 6). When that century ends, whether on a note of *fin de siècle* ennui or glorious optimism, time continues apace and the turn of a century brings us onward into the future.

Some analysts of the noughties are optimistic, others pessimists. There may be disappointment in what has not come to pass or hope at what yet can be. Implicit in the metaphor of the forward march of time there can be a concomitant expectation of progress, which is not always delivered by lived reality. It is this Janus-faced dualism that many of our contributors are grappling with in this volume: traces and shadows of the past loom over the new decade that it is hoped will be put to rest, tackled or otherwise resolved, on the one hand; on the other, we find the taste of fresh, new beginnings, which, it is hoped, will bring a bright future. These dualisms are not always contradictory nor incompatible, but there can be tensions and difficulties which nuance our understanding of a specific context or narrative.

Decades can be framed by the events that take place. For example, the twentieth century did end with tales of impending disaster: newspapers were filled with fears about Y2K bugs that had the potential to bring electronic systems to collapse. It was predicted that planes would fall out of the sky and vital hospital equipment would stop. It didn't happen. Despite these fears, the decade began on a note of optimism. Subsequently, in the West the decade has been book-ended by two disasters: the attacks on the Twin Towers on 11th September 2001, an event which has had direct consequences on many non-Western states, and the 2007 banking crisis, which is still spinning its way through the financial sectors and has had detrimental effects on many international economies. It is easy to assume from a US and European perspective that these are global problems and that all countries are experiencing the reverberations from these events similarly. However, the picture is more complicated.

In order to grasp the nuances and divergences, consider a sampling of other stories that have predominated for Hispanic and Lusophone countries in the past decade. Brazil's positive outlook at the end of the decade is buoyed up by economic growth and their successful bids to host both the 2016 Olympic Games in Rio de Janeiro and the soccer World Cup in 2014. Spain has had its own terrorist attack on 11th March 2004, has experienced financial collapse, but also has been concerned with a tense debate over memory and the physical and metaphorical digging up of the past, as examined by Abigail Loxham and Lorraine Ryan in this volume. Mexico began the decade on an optimistic note when the *Partido Revolucionario Institucional* [Institutional Revolutionary Party] lost their 70 plus years of political dominance to the *Partido Acción Nacional* [National Action Party]. There was hope that the change would be positive. Change may have been needed, but Mexico is ending the decade deeply wounded by its dependence on the US economy, and with a near civil war between drug cartels resulting in thousands dead in the Northern States. This is a mixed picture. We cannot say that this has either been a wholly positive or negative decade. It is our aim that the reader comes away from reading this collection, not with a sense that there is a single noughties sensibility or mood, but that among the variety the similarities and contrasts may be illuminating.

The perceived newness of the noughties may be associated with a hope of progress, however that is defined. Feminist hopes of progress for women are variously addressed in this volume, in particular in the first section "Feminist Noughties?". It is clear from many of our chapters that feminism's job is not yet done. Some contributors have looked at the twenty-first century and considered the broken promises of the previous century in different Spanish-speaking and Lusophone countries. This has necessitated a look back to the twentieth century where a given cultural change has its origins. In chapter one María Donapetry looks at recent representations of women on screen. Providing a brief introduction to the long history of the nude in figurative art, Donapetry traces the trajectory of the *destape* era of the 1970s in Spain, and its persistent legacy of the objectification of women veiled in a discourse of liberation. She then examines films by Icíar Bollaín and Isabel Coixet in which women's nudity is represented on screen in ways that give them agency and do not compromise their subjectivity. There is a pessimism in the persistence of one form and its seemingly outdated representation of women, and an optimism in that there are those who are challenging the status quo.

The representation of female subjectivity is again addressed, this time in the context of theatre, by Susana Lorenzo-Zamorano in chapter two. She examines the ways in which female playwrights in Spain have negotiated their relationship with feminism since the transition to democracy. While she argues that in the 1980s most failed to present women in a subject position, she explores plays by Paloma Pedrero and Carmen Resino which deconstruct gender identities and question the roles traditionally assigned to women. Moving on to the the nineties and the noughties, Lorenzo-Zamorano examines the apparently contradictory situation in which there has been a rise in the number of women playwrights and plays in which a female perspective predominates, and yet such authors are still reluctant to admit the presence of a feminist (or any other activist) agenda within their works. Like Donapetry, however, Lorenzo-Zamorano posits that the twenty-first-century noughties may be witnessing productive challenges to the status quo, in the shape of radical feminist productions by all-female theatre companies such as Metadones, Margarita Borja's Sorámbulas and the Vacas Collective, and by the actress and playwright Angélica Liddell Zoo.

Just as the question mark in the title of this section is implicit in both Donapetry and Lorenzo-Zamorano's interrogations of feminism's successes and failures in Spain, in chapter three Paula Jordão's examination of Nélida Piñon's *Vozes do deserto* [Voices of the Desert] (2004) suggests that this novel represents a challenge to the status quo, this time in the Brazilian cultural context. Piñon's novel gives the ninth-century story, *The Thousand and One Nights*, a different interpretation by re-writing it. Her inclusion of different characters (Scherezade's sister), the attribution of new inspirations and settings for the story, and the foregrounding of the female voice, all reveal its twenty-first-century origins. Re-creations and new imaginings of long-established stories are common in late twentieth-century and early twenty-first-century women's writing. Jordão traces the distinctiveness of Piñon's novel, and how she has been influenced by contemporary feminist debates about women's place in both narrative and history in Brazil and beyond.

This sense of the noughties as a decade of progress for women in particular localities is explored by Laura Soler González, who argues in chapter four that the twentieth-century noughties "provided a specific historical framework for the emergence and development of feminism in Catalonia" (p. 59). She examines the importance of the writer Dolors Monserdà for this development, arguing that Monserdà's decision to write as a woman under her own name reflects her desire to open new pathways for women in writing and in society. The chapter considers Monserdà's involvement in social action, and her journalism and writings about women's condition. Soler González then discusses in more detail Monserdà's novel *La fabricanta*, showing how the novel addresses questions around modernity, public and private space, and the nineteenth-century "angel" archetype for women. While some have questioned whether this conservative Catholic writer can be considered "feminist" at all, Soler González strongly argues that Monserdà's fundamental contribution to feminism in Catalonia cannot be ignored.

By contrast, in chapter five, Susanne Meachem explores concrete economic conditions impacting negatively upon women in the noughties. For Argentina, the decade has meant financial troubles since December 2001 when it defaulted on its debts leading to a massive economic collapse that the country is still trying to fully resolve. The fallout from this collapse is explored by Meachem. She examines how the Argentine government is attempting to help the so-called "new poor" move out of poverty by using programmes that either deliberately or necessarily place women into a traditionally delimited role, and encourage them to stay out of the workplace in favour of facilitating male employment. Where time is associated with a notion of perpetual, forward moving progress this is a reminder that things have not necessarily improved for all women, in particular the poor, and that the rhetoric of womanhood is still bound up with a very particular role that makes parenting and the domestic sphere her responsibility. While the mythos of the inevitable modernisation brought about by time is consistently interrogated in this section, so too the hope for a better, more equal, future is heralded.

The noughties often has this dual pull: of being future-oriented and still bound to the past century. The legacy of the past is a recurrent theme in many of our chapters, and the second section, "Cultural Memory in the Noughties", focuses on such issues within Spain. In chapter six Lorraine Ryan characterises the twenty-first-century noughties as "the decade of memory in contemporary Spain" (p. 106), tracing how a new memory culture has arisen to challenge the hegemonic forgetting which presided after the Franco era. In the noughties, she argues, *la generación de los nietos* [the grandchildren's generation] have involved themselves in memory politics for reasons which are deeply personal, demanding that the Spanish Civil War and its aftermath be remembered, and challenging the official versions propagated under Franco. Ryan explores the importance and impact of the Law of Historical Memory which was passed in 2007, arguing both that it has been successful in raising consciousness about the experience of Republicans during the Civil War and the Franco era, and yet that much remains to be done for the fulfillment of its promises.

Continuing with the theme of memory, in chapter seven, Abigail Loxham examines a particular instance of this noughties remembering, looking at the traces of history in the present and how the ghosts of the past are represented in noughties Catalan documentary. The films by Carla Subirana and Albert Solé explore the effects of the collective amnesia or *ley-del-olvido* [law of forgetting] of the Spanish Transition through their own and their families' personal stories. It is a legacy of the late twentieth century that has been resurrected in the noughties by the children of those damaged by forgetting. In Spain, just as with many Latin American countries, such as Argentina, the new millennium has been a time for reflection on the past and a recovery of a new reading of its traces on the present.

Continuing this intersection of the private and public act of remembering, and spanning the twentieth- and twenty-first-century noughties, Alison Sinclair focuses our attention on the story of one child prodigy, and what we can learn from the ways in which he is represented and re-represented by different people and in different times. Pepito Arriola, as Sinclair argues in chapter eight, was in some sense a "trial run" at parenting a prodigy for his aunt Aurora Rodríguez, who was to become the mother and murderess of the prodigy and sexual reformer Hildegart. Competing versions of Pepito's childhood reflect the twentieth-century noughties' fascination with extreme phenomena such as prodigies and even the paranormal, perhaps in response to fears of decadence still lingering from the nineteenth century. A century later, at the anniversary of his birth, new stories about Pepito as a serious musician and composer reclaim him for Galicia and, in so doing, reflect the importance of cultural memory—in this case, what Sinclair calls "appropriations of excellence" (p. 157)—for the construction of national identities. We see in this section that significant relationships emerge between the noughties and previous time periods: the decade becomes an opportunity to look back in order to look forward, as all three chapters explore.

There is a return to the future in our final section, where it is both an opportunity for change and can work as a site for present-day anxieties. Our third section foregrounds “New—and not so New—Beginnings”, reflecting again the contrast between hopes for progress and wearisome repetitions. In chapter nine, Lesley Twomey argues that the eschatological perspective of a remade world casts a new light on misogynist discourse in Jaume Roig’s fifteenth-century *Espill*. This chapter firstly traces the misogynistic perspective undoubtedly present in the text, and the traditional good-evil dualism between the Virgin Mary and bad mothers (that is, all other mothers). But Twomey goes on to argue that there is a shift in perspective in Roig’s re-telling of Biblical parables towards the end of the text, focusing the narrator’s and our attention on the possibility of salvation at the final judgement. Women can indeed be saved in the new eternal order, and it is the narrator’s quest for a wife, not the wives themselves, which is leading him away from God. As Roig looks towards apparent apocalypse at a plague-ridden end of century, he focuses the reader on the new dawn of eternal redemption.

In chapter ten, Maria Manuel Lisboa also explores the new shape of the world following apocalypse, this time in twentieth-century incarnations. José Saramago’s *Ensaio sobre a Cegueira* [Blindness] (1995) is compared with works by John Wyndham and H.G. Wells, highlighting the way in which an apparent new order may in fact reflect the bad old days. Placing these chronologically separated texts in the context of recent millenarian preoccupations, this chapter explores the ways in which literal blindness and/or disease also function symbolically to lay bare disturbing patterns of power and violence. Hope for a utopian future turns out to share unsettling patterns with post-apocalyptic dystopias.

Finally, in chapter eleven, Margaret Clarke ends on a more optimistic note as she considers the search for new beginnings in Brazil in the context of the growth of the internet. Brazil is a nation that has experienced recent economic growth all the while having a large population living in poverty. As an entirely new phenomenon whose use and access is still being worked through, the internet was introduced in Brazil as recently as 1996. Conscious of the importance of access to technologies which have become indispensible in international business, creativity and communication, digital inclusion has been prioritised by the government. One of the ways those involved are attempting to cross the digital divide is through recycling, knowledge sharing and Open Source Software. Clarke explores how this is being carried out through governmental schemes, non-governmental organisations and the involvement of other social actors. The twenty-first century has been the dawn of a new era with the adoption of new technology going global. Clarke looks behind the often utopian discourse surrounding this new form of communication to see the practicalities of its dissemination amongst impoverished members of society. Twomey, Lisboa and Clarke are thus all considering both real and imagined futures from a noughties perspective.

Conclusion

The noughties is not a decade that has been weighed down with a qualified nomenclature. Therefore, we could encourage our contributors to analyse it with fresh eyes and without critical, cultural or historical frameworks that would limit their readings. Consider other decades whose adjectival complements determine meaning, such as the "swinging" or "radical" sixties, the "roaring" twenties, or the "greedy" eighties. All of these labels can be limiting and over-simplify, as well as ignore geographical (and other) differences. Not yet re-packaged and commoditised, the noughties can still be considered as a coincidence of events, moods, ideas, and creativity by the authors from a multiplicity of perspectives.

In addition, the very name noughties suggests an absence, a lack of any numbering system to fully classify it. A nought literally means nothing, yet its significance is truly redolent, as our contributors have explored. It is the gap that has been ignored, which further underscores its liminality. The noughties are a chronological border territory, similar to Mary Louise Pratt's cultural and linguistic "contact zone", which is "an attempt to invoke the spatial and temporal copresence of subjects previously separated by geographic and historical disjunctures, and whose trajectories now intersect" (Pratt 1993, 7). In this volume, we are interested in the temporal copresences, across different geographical terrains with linguistic and historical commonalities, and what we are confronted with by this inbetween-ness. Between the end of the nineties and the nascent century there are ten years of a temporal no-(wo)man's-land, which we are keen to map and explore.

The study of periods is more often the stuff of canonical and disciplinary evolution. For example, due to the extraordinary flourishing of creativity in Spain in the fifteenth to seventeenth centuries, it has been ascribed the moniker of Golden Age which has its attendant academic field. The Golden Age, like many other periods examined, is born of a coincidence of excellence which is then rendered meaningful retrospectively. Without contesting the validity of this approach, we instead aim to pick out a decade and consider its significance across a range of geographic and disciplinary areas. We have picked a defined period and its repetition over the centuries and sought to examine what is of particular interest during this time. This is not entirely at random. Aside from coinciding with the decade in which WiSPS was born, it is also one which deserves attention. It is variously overshadowed by *fin de siècle* ennui, squabbles over actual fixed beginning or end dates (is 2000 the end of an old century or the start of a new one?), and the absence of a well-established moniker. This lacuna is a gap which has proven worthy of study. The resultant volume has brought together apparently disparate authors, topics and geographical locations and revealed fascinating coincidences and divergences.

Works Cited

Poyato, José Calvo. (1997) *El desastre del 98*. Barcelona: Plaza y Janés.

Pratt, Mary Louise. (1993) *Imperial Eyes: Travel Writing and Transculturation*. London and New York: Routledge.

Richardson, Angelique and Chris Willis, eds. (2001) *The New Woman in Fiction and in Fact*. London: Palgrave.

Schwartz, Hillel. (1996) *Century's End: An Orientation Manual for the Year 2000*. New York: Barnes and Noble Books.

Severin, Dorothy Sherman. (2008) "A Brief History of WiSPS", in Ann Davies, Parvathi Kumaraswami and Claire Williams (eds), *Making Waves: Anniversary Volume: Women in Spanish, Portuguese and Latin American Studies*. Newcastle: Cambridge Scholars Publishing, ix-ii.

Showalter, Elaine. (1990) *Sexual Anarchy: Gender and Culture at the Fin de siècle*. London: Virago.

Teich, Mikulás and Roy Porter, eds. (1990) *Fin de siècle and its Legacy*. Cambridge: Cambridge University Press.

Toulmin, Stephen & June Goodfield. (1965) *The Discovery of Time*. London: Hutchinson of London.

Whitrow, G.J. (1989) *Time in History: Views of Time from Prehistory to the Present Day*. Oxford & New York: Oxford University Press.

PART I

FEMINIST NOUGHTIES?

CHAPTER ONE

THE "NOUGHTY" NUDE: NAKED WOMEN IN SPANISH CINEMA OF THE NOUGHTIES

MARÍA DONAPETRY

The female nude has been employed in Spanish film of the noughties as an unproblematic symbol of liberalism in Spanish film, which is a symptom of how little has changed in contemporary Spanish cinema since the Transition (1973-1982). This chapter considers four films from the noughties which raise issues regarding the representation of the female nude. *Los años desnudos* [The Naked Years] (Dunia Ayaso y Félix Sabroso, 2008) provides a contemporary starting point for reconsidering the aesthetics of the *destape* era (1970s) that persists insidiously in Vicente Aranda's *Juana la Loca* [Joan the Mad] (2001). By contrast, *Te doy mis ojos* [I Give You My Eyes] (Icíar Bollaín, 2003) and *Elegy* (Isabel Coixet, 2008) offer more enlightened alternatives to the prurient treatment of the female nude carried over into the noughties by such directors as Aranda. Bollaín and Coixet contest the kind of titillation associated with the *destape* aesthetics by, in one case, stigmatising the male who degrades the female body; and, in the other, by advocating a woman's choice over her nudity. The aim of my analysis is to explore the area where aesthetics and ethics overlap with regard to the representation of women's bodies on film.

In order to evaluate what is good and/or just, Paul Ricoeur suggests, we have no choice but to identify and distinguish ourselves and others as individuals, and to go from the moment "where the thinking subject claims to master meaning, to mutual recognition, where the subject places him or herself under the tutelage of a relationship of reciprocity" (2005, 25). This idea is linked to those of philosophers who write about the consciousness of the individual, such as Jean-Paul Sartre's reflection on the individual's identity (Cavallaro 1998, 116), and Fernando Savater's consideration of the humanity of the subject (1995, 27). Here, I want to explore the representation of female nudes in films made in the noughties in Spain, and determine from a feminist perspective how we can identify, acknowledge and distinguish the individuals we see on screen and the ethical meaning those images may encapsulate. I examine how these women become individuated subjects and not mere repetitions of a type.

What compels me to make an incursion into such a wide and complex field, in which ethics and aesthetics meet (and sometimes miss each other completely) is my will to recognise, identify, or identify with the representations of naked women on screen, and look for a meaning, if at all possible, that I may relate to as a woman, not only in the sense of understanding what I see on screen but also in the sense of exploring what I see as acceptable or degrading. In other words: I would like to discern the politics of the discourse and the images of female nudity in noughties cinema in Spain.

The female nude has been a consistent subject in art of all periods, most often as a spectacle which produces aesthetic pleasure in the observer. Both the technical abilities and the sensitivity of the artist as well as the capacity for judgement of the observer legitimise these representations. Nudity in figurative art is controlled and contained by the artist, the medium and the observers. Theoretically at least, painting a naked woman and observing the painting are not furtive acts. However, as John Berger has explained in *Ways of Seeing*, the legitimacy of this practice involves the objectification of the naked body: "The sight of it as an object stimulates the use of it as an object" (2008, 48). Cinema partakes of this kind of control and legitimacy. And yet, the realism conveyed by the movement of images, the sound and the actresses (live bodies) in cinema transforms the female nude into something different from that of a painting, a sculpture or a photograph. The relationship between spectators and a female nude on screen is socially and culturally contextualised in a different way to that of the still image, among other things because the film theatre (although it is a public space) fosters an illusion of intimacy impossible to replicate in a museum or in any open and illuminated space.[1] When the nude that appears on screen is or is supposed to be erotic, we enter into the murky area of unclear borders between what is artistic and what is pornographic (or pseudo-pornographic) or, as Lynda Nead puts it, "[between] pure and impure desire" (Nead 1992, 104). Morality comes into play as one of the key determinants as to whether a specific work is art or not. The fact that the intention of certain images is simply to sexually arouse the observer—to awaken "impure" desires in him or her, Nead seems to be saying—automatically disqualifies those images as art.

I do not completely agree with this binary as a method of distinguishing and recognising a work as art; even less so with regard to the sexual arousal of the observer/spectator, be it a woman or a man. The spectator's reaction, no matter how pure or impure his or her desires may be, does not determine the artistic quality of a work. No artist can predict or control the reaction of the observer. In fact, within Catholic tradition, there are several cases of paintings depicting "sinful" scenes intended to elicit rejection on the part of the observer, or depictions of celestial ecstasy intended to inspire the purest of thoughts, and in both cases the resultant reaction can be the opposite to the one intended. Bernini's sculpture of St Teresa in ecstasy, Hieronymus Bosch's *The Garden of Earthly Delights* or many of the representations of Saint Sebastian's martyrdom are cases in point.

An interesting phenomenon regarding female nudes in Spanish film was the barely disguised pornographic production of the mid to late 70s called the cinema of the *destape*.[2] These films had a transparent politics which responded to the recent disappearance of censorship (till then in the hands of the Francoist government and the Catholic Church), and, in addition, pandered to the perceived avid appetite of a male audience for "sinful" images. The fact that these films were sanctioned by a democratic government gave both filmmakers and audiences a sense of legitimacy. A cursory look at any film (and the promotional materials) of that period featuring such actresses as Nadiuska, Agatha Lys, María José Cantudo or the Estrada sisters, for instance, makes crystal clear the discursive intentions of this subgenre.[3]

Twenty years after the *destape* boom, Dunia Ayaso and Félix Sabroso in their joint venture *Los años desnudos* (2008), reflect critically and in depth on the implications of the legacy of the cinema of the *destape*. Since this film was made barely two years ago, I believe the directors intend to make clear that even now the *destape* mentality is still alive and well, and that there is a pressing need to "uncover" and critique it. The first scene of *Los años desnudos* shows starkly the dehumanising experience of being naked in a casting session for an actress: Sandra, played by Candela Peña (and by extension any actress in those circumstances) struggles to be recognised and acknowledged as a person. While completely naked and obviously uncomfortable, she asks the casting crew if they would like to hear her deliver part of a monologue from García Lorca's *Doña Rosita la soltera* [Doña Rosita the Spinster]. Her objectification is challenged by her demand to be seen beyond her physicality; she wants to show them she is capable of acting and not just of showing her body. The members of the crew, whom we hardly see, although obviously not interested, accept the offer and she starts reciting her monologue:

> ¿Y qué os voy a decir? Hay cosas que no se pueden decir porque no hay palabras para decirlas; y si las hubiera, nadie entendería su significado. Me entendéis si pido pan y agua y hasta un beso, pero nunca me podríais ni entender ni quitar esta mano oscura que no sé si me hiela o me abrasa el corazón cada vez que me quedo sola. (…) Sería el cuento de nunca acabar. Yo sé que los ojos los tendré siempre jóvenes, y sé que la espalda se me irá curvando cada día. Después de todo, lo que me ha pasado le ha pasado a mil mujeres. (…) No me agrada que me miréis así. Me molestan esas miradas de perros fieles. Esas miradas de lástima que me perturban y me indignan. (García Lorca 1935, Act 3)
>
> [And what can I tell you? There are things that can't be said because there are no words to say them; and if there were, nobody would get their meaning. You understand me when I ask for bread or water, even for a kiss, but you could never understand or take away this dark hand that freezes or burns my heart, I don't know which, every time I am alone. (…) It would be the neverending story. I know that I will always have young eyes, and I know that my back will become arched more each day. After all, what has happened to me has happened to a thousand women. (…) I don't like the way you look at me. Those faithful dogs' looks bother me. Those looks of pity that disturb and outrage me.][4]

The monologue has obvious resonances in this scene with the awareness of being looked at and judged. As she speaks, the camera goes from a wide shot where we see the crew's point of view to a close-up of Sandra's face. When she finishes, the camera zooms out to take in the crew's point of view. The delivery of the soliloquy in such an adverse setting, with the group of men as diegetic spectators, could easily stand as a manifesto for the actresses who have been undressed in film for no other purpose but the erotic titillation of male spectators. Since this titillation depends on the imaginary availability of the naked female body and the imaginary control by the spectator and his power to degrade her, Donã Rosita's complaint "I don't like the way you look at me" expresses the anger and the strength of the subject who has been literally divested of her humanity, of her individuality, but who states that the relationship between her and the crew is that of equals. If any kind of identification could take place between the extra-diegetic audience and the crew as a result of visual alignment, the statement would become an indictment difficult to ignore. The last words in the scene are Sandra's. While she picks up her clothes, she asks the crew who is going to pay for her taxi fare since "esto está a tomar po'l culo" [this (place) is in bumfuck]. We understand she means that the studio, or wherever they are doing the audition, is really far from the city centre; we also understand, though, the whole situation for her lacks any personal or vital reference. The location and the experience have little to do with the "factory of dreams" cinema is supposed to be for her.

The timeliness of *Los años desnudos* becomes particularly apparent against the backdrop of a proliferation of titillating female nudes in films made in the early noughties which sought to use them as the materialisation of all kinds of liberation for Spanish society and, in particular, for women. If during the Transition (1975-1982) women's representation on film went from subjugation to availability well within the most inflexible patterns of patriarchal thought, in the noughties there are film directors who conflate the female nude with women's freedom while objectifying the female characters. Just when we thought we were well beyond the knee-jerk reactions of the immediate post-Francoist period we find that a certain cinema *d'auteur*, instead of breaking the moulds in an avant-garde fashion, rehashes an insidious filmic discourse that reverts back both to popular predecessors of the *destape* and to the traditions of an already consolidated and canonised art. Susan Hayward explains the distinction between avant-garde and popular art thus:

> Mainstream art recodifies the dominant praxis—makes anew what is already there. In this respect it is heavily dependent on its immediate predecessor or else it harks back to earlier art forms…It serves to preserve the dominant ideology… Conversely, avant-garde, as its name suggests, is art before its time—art looking forward not backwards… attempting to break terrain with its implicit subversion of the old codes and conventions. (2005, 203)

There are many directors associated with the former discourse: Bigas Luna, Julio Medem and Vicente Aranda, amongst others, and all of them considered auteurs within the Spanish film industry and who have persistently represented women as objects to be looked at for the exclusive pleasure of the male gaze. For my purposes here, though, I will examine Aranda's film *Juana la Loca* [Joan the Mad] (2001) because it exemplifies in more obvious ways than others the insidiousness I am talking about.

When *Juana la Loca* was released, many critics described the film in terms of its authenticity and Aranda's ability to portray passion. Mateo Sancho Cardiel, for instance, summarises the essence of the film and its main protagonist thus:

> ¿Pasión? ¿Locura? ¿Obsesión? Lo que no cabe duda es que Juana, tal como se nos describe en la película, fue una persona que apostó por la autenticidad en la época en la que bajo pesados terciopelos los sentimientos morían ahogados, estuvo dispuesta a darse por completo, a humillarse, a perdonar todo por ese amor. Tenaz, visceral, soporta la carga de un reino entero sin ningún tipo de preparación ni interés, y *vive para dar placer a su marido*, Felipe el Hermoso. Un matrimonio que comienza como un choque de impulsos primarios, un sexo animal, pero pronto se convertirá en una pasión desgarrada, emotiva y escalofriante. Puede que sea locura, pero no cabe duda de que en ella arrastra al espectador, lo sumerge en una continua catarsis emocional hasta que lo deja sin aliento, pero con un sobrecogimiento que sólo se disipa aplaudiendo a rabiar al finalizar la proyección. (2001; emphasis added)
>
> [Passion? Madness? Obsession? There is no doubt that Juana, as described by the film, was a person who was committed to authenticity; in an era when feelings were drowned under heavy velvet gowns, she was eager to give herself completely, to humiliate herself, to forgive everything for love. Tenacious, visceral, she bears the burden of a kingdom without any preparation or interest, and *lives to give her husband Felipe el Hermoso pleasure*. A marriage that begins as a clash of primary impulses, animal sex, soon will become a searing passion, emotional and thrilling. It may be madness, but there is no doubt that it carries the spectator along, submerging him in a continuous emotional catharsis until it leaves him breathless, with an overwhelming feeling released only through furious applause at the end of the showing.]

In *Juana la Loca,* Aranda's version of Manuel Tamayo y Baus's theatre play (1885),[5] Juana's madness is explained in terms of a particularly feminine, relentless and uncontrollable sexual desire. That lack of control, according to Aranda, is what the court cannot understand and the reason why they declare her unfit to rule. Juana's character suggests a return to nineteenth-century theories about hysteria (i.e. the lack of control of the female sexual organs as the principal cause for madness in women) (see, for example, Showalter 1987). If what Aranda wanted to portray was a sexually "liberated" woman, misunderstood by her peers and ahead of her time, his film not only falls short in relation to giving Juana a modicum of subjectivity, but it also locks her tightly within a patriarchal straight-jacket. Aranda, though, is not satisfied with rehashing this particular character from Tamayo y Baus's play, and delights his audience with another *sui generis* recreation of a second female character, the Moor Aixa, who excites, beyond endurance, the libido of Juana's husband Prince Felipe el Hermoso (Phillip the Handsome), draws the jealousy of the queen and the voyeurism of male spectators.[6] Once again, we are witness to the "liberation" of a female character through her conversion into a tempting, seductive and dark body. The racialisation of her character is a matter that I do not have space to fully explore here, but that places Aixa in the role of other. This female body is not limited to insinuating an unrestricted sexuality, it also leads the unwary Prince to an abyss of sinful liaisons brought about by the exotic Satanism the beautiful Moorish woman practises. The ultra-fetishised Aixa embodies the image of woman defined by Freud as a dark continent.

In the cases of both Juana and Aíxa, what we understand is that Aranda identifies the independent woman with erotic excess. One of the problems with these erotic representations is that they are all visualised from an exclusively masculine point of view and for the voyeuristic satisfaction of the spectators. In spite of it all, I do not think these are motives to censor this or any other film by Aranda. I do think, though, that his representations of the female nude undermine in a fundamental way the possible intentions he might have had of making the historical episodes in the film more "modern" and more "authentic". If Aranda's idea of up-dating Tamayo y Baus's play is to include more naked bodies and more eroticism, it appears that Aranda has merely internalised the *destape* mode of thinking. That is, that showing more female nudes somehow guarantees freedom for both him as a director and for the female characters because they come across as uninhibited, and, in turn, for the audience, who can legitimately enjoy what is shown as expressions of that freedom. One could object at my excessive moral qualms. Aranda himself, though, insists on the moral aspects of the story he is telling: it is clear throughout the film that the declaration of unfitness of the Queen is subject to all sorts of immoral manipulations by King Ferdinand and Prince Felipe, who appear as men without scruples ready to victimise their daughter and wife, respectively, in order to establish or expand their power. If I kept a distance or just overlooked these moral concerns and focussed exclusively on the formal aspects of the film, I would be unable to properly critique the film, I would overlook the film itself.[7]

Not all directors treat the female nude in such a problematic manner, nor are all incapable of ridding themselves of the ethics and aesthetics of the *destape*. Although not exclusively, women directors seem to take issue precisely with the treatment of the naked female body and have implicitly challenged the *destape* legacy.[8] Icíar Bollaín in *Te doy mis ojos* (2003) and Isabel Coixet in *Elegy* (2008) are but two examples of the kind of awareness film directors can have of what showing a female nude on screen may mean aesthetically and ethically. Bollaín's film especially, because of its direct concern with domestic violence ("gender violence" or "violence against women" *tout court*), offers a scene which can be extrapolated to the general scope of this essay. At the beginning of the scene, Pilar, the battered wife and protagonist, is getting ready to go to Madrid for a job interview. When her friends come to pick her up, her husband—Antonio—gets upset because she is occupying her time in something unrelated to him, and starts tearing her art books apart. As his anger grows, he directs all sorts of abuse at her and proceeds to tear off her clothes until she is practically naked. While she tries to defend herself and keep her clothes on, Antonio pushes her to the balcony of the house so anybody in the street can see her naked. He eventually brings her back to the room and Pilar, paralysed by the horror of the ordeal and fear of him, wets herself. This physical loss of control reduces her to an infantile state of disempowerment. In this episode, Antonio does not undress Pilar in order to get sexual satisfaction but in order to degrade her even further. He undresses her as an act of personal violence and magnifies this act by dragging her to the balcony and exposing her nakedness in public. As spectators we understand that Antonio's intention to humiliate and dehumanise Pilar dehumanises him. While Aranda films women's bodies as objects for the consumption of an intra and extra-diegetic voyeur, the obviously violent and forced undressing of Pilar, her terror, and the dehumanisation of the perpetrator (Antonio) leave little or no room at all for any kind of erotic thrill.

In this scene Bollaín confronts how the female nude has been represented on film and in figurative art from a feminine and a feminist perspective. Pilar works in a museum and her job, among other things, involves explaining well-known paintings with female nudes: Titian's *Danae*, Ruben's *Orpheus and Eurydice* and *The Three Graces*. Pilar's understanding of these nudes is definitely different from that of her husband's. For Antonio the female nude is degrading and susceptible to degradation. Pilar, on the other hand, sees them as an acknowledgement of women's beauty, the kind of acknowledgement she would like to receive. Bollaín, through the dramatisation of Pilar's descriptions of the nudes, enacts the theme we are interested in here—the female nude—also in a dramatic way, i.e. in a double ekphrasis, and opts for a woman's position before that nude: a position which takes into account a woman's perspective when she knows she is being observed naked. This position, therefore, qualifies the politics of her filmic discourse as something in which the subject is interested and has an investment. As Arthur Danto puts it, "as far as showing the subject naked, the morality of that is altogether how the subject feels about [her]self as seen that way"

(Levinson 1998, 22). In *Te doy mis ojos* Bollaín is shedding the *destape* and exploring the female nude in a new and challenging way.

There is a single scene in *Elegy*, directed by Isabel Coixet, in which the protagonist bares her breasts to the camera. Consuela Castillo (Penélope Cruz) has had an intense affair with David Kepesh (Ben Kingsley) but, after he has shown his inability to integrate into her social sphere, she disappears for a while. One day she goes to see him. She explains that her estrangement had also to do with the fact that she has breast cancer and that she will soon have a mastectomy. Consuela wants David to photograph her with her breasts bare, that part of her body that stands for all the sexual pleasure and the emotional bond they had while they were lovers. In this sequence Coixet's camera focuses on Consuela's expression, and then on David's reaction at the news. Although her body has not been mutilated yet, the sense of loss and threat for both is what dominates the scene. In an essay about Coixet's film *La vida secreta de las palabras* [The Secret Life of Words] (2005), John Berger explains the kind of feeling I am referring to when talking about a scene in which the female protagonist also bares her breasts: "Tampoco se rinde en ella (*La vida secreta de las palabras*) culto alguno al dolor. Sencillamente se ofrece una visión de cómo a veces el sufrimiento conduce a una salvación compartida, que nunca es simple, que nunca es mera palabrería. Antigua. Algo que suelen descubrir quienes no tienen poder" (Andreu 2008, 95-6). [This film (*The Secret Life of Words*) does not pay homage to pain. The film simply offers a vision of how sometimes suffering is the means to a shared redemption, which is never simple, which is never just empty words. Timeless. Something that is usually discovered by the powerless]. After Consuela explains her motivations, David gets a camera and she poses for him, removing her top very slowly until her breasts are bare; then she looks at David looking at her. The film camera follows both characters' gaze forcing the spectator to align him or herself alternately with David and with Consuela, and eventually with both. They are sharing the pain as they shared the pleasure because in that sharing the humanity of both characters is at stake. This particular scene diverges crucially from the text on which it is based, Philip Roth's novel *The Dying Animal*. In the latter, David cannot help being aroused at the sight of Consuela's breasts. Coixet makes a strong point regarding this female nude: the naked body of a woman on screen is not there simply to give voyeuristic pleasure either to a diegetic male character or to the audience: there are other interpretative possibilities. Ignacio Vidal-Foch declares:

> Coixet es director de cine, no juez sentado en el trono de la moral; y en vez de dictar sentencias condenatorias o absolutorias, lo que hace es

> representar con elocuencia magistral la pavorosa carnalidad de Kingsley: esa calva con sus arrugas y ese labio superior fino como hoja de afeitar, por debajo de la cual salen las palabras "Estoy aquí…" o "Ecce Homo". (Andreu 2008, 12)

> [Coixet is a film director, not a judge sitting on the moral throne; instead of pronouncing sentences of approval or condemnation, what she does is to represent with magnificent eloquence Kingsley's terrifying carnality: that bald head with wrinkles and that upper lip as thin as a razor blade, beneath which the words "I am here…" or "Ecce homo" come out.]

I would add that David's carnality/vulnerability is paralleled by Consuela's. David's vulnerability has to do with old age; Consuela's with the threat of cancer, and both face the proximity of death. In general, I agree with Vidal-Foch: Coixet is definitely not a moral judge; but she is interested in the moral plight of her characters and lets the audience observe, understand, recognise and find (or not) the ethical value of the story she is telling and how she is telling it. David's holding a camera and taking a picture of Consuela at her behest reminds us that the decision to undress and to be looked at is all hers, and that she expects recognition, not objectification. Of course, there may be spectators whose reaction to this scene would not be very different from the one they would have watching an erotic or pornographic film. That, as I pointed out before, is not controllable by the director, no matter how clear and careful his or her intentions are.

In his *Invitación a la ética*, Fernando Savater explains that

> para la voluntad moral, no todo vale. En la vida—como en cualquier juego o en cualquier arte—hay cosas que no vale hacer, mientras que otras jugadas son excepcionalmente valiosas. Lo que no vale es lo que no *nos* vale; aquello que nos hace perder, lo que debilita nuestro juego o nos excluye de él. (1995, 63)

> [For the moral will, not everything goes. In life—as in any game or any art—there are things that are not acceptable, while other ways of playing are exceptionally valuable. What is not acceptable is what is not good for *us*; what makes us lose, what weakens our game or excludes us.]

As we have seen, there are many female nudes in cinema that cheat us, that are on screen with the sole purpose of corroborating that a woman's image exists as the object of pleasure for men. Those who make films of this kind count on the complicity of an audience which is either fully satisfied with what they see and consider it good, and/or perceives the images as "natural" and, therefore, consider them absolutely legitimate. Of course, such audiences do not question either the process by which the images are considered natural nor the implications of this naturalisation. On the other hand, as is the case in *Te doy mis ojos*, there are films which treat the female nude with the kind of realism in characters and situations that, as Gregory Currie suggests, "enabl[es] the sort of imaginative exercise that broadens rather than constricts our understanding of human possibilities of thought, feeling, and action" (Levinson 1998, 13).

The most basic principle of humanity according to Savater is that "el yo necesita, para ser plenamente yo, verse confirmado—esto es, reconocido—por otro yo" (1995, 27). [The I needs, in order to be I fully, to see itself confirmed—that is, recognised—by another I]. Feminism in its broadest sense works so that this principle is considered as valid for men as for women. The treatment of the female nude in cinema is one of many fields in which aesthetic reasons can function as "artistic" alibis for denying women that recognition. Ethics and aesthetics do not necessarily have to go hand in hand, no matter how much Ludwig Wittgenstein insists on identifying one with the other (1961, 6421). The conjunction of formal beauty with moral degradation is a possibility in art, but not at its best. In any case, we should be aware of that conjunction when it happens. There is arguably no point in even considering the possibility of imposing a certain "moral" code on the artist or the work of art since ethics has to do with what we want to be, what we aspire to be in order to become more human. "Art", says Elisabeth Schellekens, "is a means of expression—be it of emotions, political ideas or moral belief systems—and not a means of coercion" (2007, 90). However, every work of art, every film, has rules of engagement with its subject and with the audience. In the case of the female nude, because it affects women in the way we are recognised and identified as subjects through our naked bodies, those rules establish certain "condiciones de humanidad sin las cuales no sere[mos] admitid[as] como objeto[s] infinito[s] o se [nos] otorgará sólo el reconocimiento cruel de la violencia" (Savater 1995, 31) [conditions of humanity without which [we] will not be accepted as infinite object[s] or we will be given only the cruel recognition of violence].

Works Cited

Andreu, C. (2008) *Una mujer bajo la influencia: Isabel Coixet*. Madrid: Ediciones Autor.

Berger, J. (2008) *Ways of Seeing*. London: Penguin.

Castro García, A. (2009) *La representación de la mujer en el cine español de la Transición*. Oviedo: KRK.

Cavallaro, D. (1998) *The Body for Beginners*. New York: Writers and Readers.

García Lorca, F. (1935) *Doña Rosita la soltera*. *La insignia*, February 17, 2001. http://www.lainsignia.org/2001/febrero/cul_071.htm.

Hayward, S. (2005) *French Cinema*. London and New York: Routledge.

Levinson, J., ed. (1998) *Aesthetics and Ethics: Essays at the Intersection*. Cambridge: Cambridge University Press.

Nead, L. (1992) *The Female Nude. Art, Obscenity and Sexuality*. London and New York: Routledge.

Ricoeur, P. (2005) *The Course of Recognition*. Cambridge, MA: Harvard University Press.

Sancho Cardiel, M. (2001) Review of the film *Juana la Loca* (49º Festival de San Sebastián). http://www.cinencanto.com/crit_but/b_juana.htm. (accessed 22 September 2010).

Savater, F. (1995) *Invitación a la ética*. Barcelona: Anagrama.

Schellekens, E. (2007) *Aesthetics and Morality*. London: Continuum.

Showalter, E. (1987) *The Female Malady*. London: Virago.

Tamayo y Baus, Manuel. (1885) *La locura de amor*. Alicante: Biblioteca Virtual Miguel de Cervantes, 2000 (digital edition based on *Obras Completas*, Madrid: Fax, 1947, 391-475). http://www.cervantesvirtual.com/obra/la-locura-de-amor--0/.

Wittgenstein, L. (1961) *Tractatus Logico-Philosophicus*. London: Routledge and Kegan Paul.

Notes

[1] The current trend is that films are widely watched in DVD format or on a computer screen, so that the degree of intimacy is not so much an illusion as a reality.

[2] The *destape*, literally translatable as "undressing", is the term used to describe the cinematographic phenomenon of the Spanish Transition (1975-1983) when female nudes started appearing in films together with well known comedians such as Andrés Pajares, Fernando Esteso, Juanito Navarro, Antonio Ozores and others. *La trastienda* (Jorge Grau, 1975) is the first film showing a full frontal nude of the actress María José Cantudo.

[3] For a more detailed account of the *destape* see Amanda Castro García (2009).

[4] Translations, author's own.

[5] Manuel Tamayo y Baus's theatre play *La locura de amor* [The Madness of Love] (1885) is the textual basis for the films *Locura de amor* [Madness of Love] (1948) directed by Juan de Orduña, and *Juana la Loca* by Vicente Aranda.

[6] Aranda changes the original name of the Moorish woman in *La locura de amor* (Aldara) for Aixa. It is possible that his choice is based on the real historical character Aïsha bin Muhammad ibn al-Ahmar, mother of the king of Granada

Boabdil, and soul of the resistance against Isabella and Ferdinand during the siege of Granada. I believe, though, that a search for historical "authenticity" and legitimacy drove the director to make this particular change of names.

[7] I paraphrase Elisabeth Schellekens (2007, 89) here when referring to the possible appreciations of a film like Leni Riefenstahl's *Triumph of the Will.*

[8] As already pointed out, Félix Sabroso co-scripted and co-directed *Los años desnudos*. Benito Zambrano comes to mind, particularly in *Solas* [Alone] (1999), when thinking of male directors who do not treat the female nude as a vehicle for reducing the character to a mere object of pleasure.

CHAPTER TWO

FLUCTUATIONS IN FEMINIST COMMITMENT IN RECENT SPANISH FEMALE-AUTHORED DRAMA

SUSANA LORENZO-ZAMORANO

The shifting fortunes of feminism have always closely followed developments in the legal structures upon which power relations are based. The case of Spain presents some quite unique features as a result of Franco's forty years of dictatorship. After the dictator's death in 1975 women's rights rapidly began to gain ground in terms both of public acknowledgement and legal reform, one of the most important changes being the abolition of the so-called *permiso marital* in 1975 whereby women had to seek their husband's approval to take part in activities relating to family finances including employment, travel, and ownership of property.[1] Legalised gender inequality was thus abolished. However, in terms of the cultural scene, many ex-franquistas were participating in the newly appointed Democratic Centre government, which meant that culture and society were still under the weight of traditionalism with regard to freedom of expression and the social situation of women. In fact, ever since its formal beginning in 1975 the feminist movement in Spain has been characterised by its weakness, and "feminism" is a label that Spanish women have tended to reject at all costs, finding it particularly negative and ghettoising. This explains why, as Witte (1996, 7) points out in her comparison of Argentine and Spanish women playwrights, political commitment and the construction of a feminist perspective have traditionally been considered as separate issues. It should also be pointed out that political theatre has usually had negative connotations in Spain mainly because of its common association with a demagogic left wing and a lack of aesthetic quality. This deep-rooted prejudice has greatly contributed to slowing down feminist demands and has strongly affected Spanish theatre, as we shall see.

Generally speaking, the ebb and flow of Spanish feminism saw the initial relative enthusiasm of the late 1970s quickly turn into shyness and apathy in the 1980s[2] and to a false sense of achievement in the 1990s, when the promotion of the concept of the post-feminist era perhaps did little to help the cause of women's emancipation. Well into the second half of the 1990s, in fact, a distinct trend away from adopting openly feminist stances is noticeable in Spanish woman-authored theatre.[3] In a wider context, a similar decline in public interest in the question of women and the theatre may be seen, attributed by critics such as Jill Dolan to two factors: the backlash against feminism, and the way in which the 1990s "have shifted focus toward gay/lesbian/queer theatre and multiculturalism" (Shevtsova 1999, 99). One can thus see that the thematic preoccupations of Spanish theatre over the past twenty years have not been isolated from international trends. But the noughties also seem to witness a surge of female anger and a renovated feminist energy especially on the part of women's theatre groups or collectives that have now become part of the established scene. In this article I shall concentrate on those playwrights that somehow have gone against the current by making an important contribution to feminist critique with their works even if they are not strictly feminist or do not consider themselves as such.

The Eighties Generation

It was in the 1980s, when the efforts of liberal feminism were being channelled into reforming discriminatory legislation in Spain, that women as a category started to be acknowledged and women playwrights' historic exclusion from theatre corpora became a new focus for criticism.[4] In 1984 the theatre journal *Estreno* dedicated its autumn issue to women writing for the theatre in Spain at the time. In 1986 the *Asociación de Dramaturgas* [Association of Women Playwrights] was formed, and this body, in spite of its short lifespan (it would soon be swallowed up by the *Asociación de Autores de Teatro* [Association of Theatre Authors]), greatly contributed towards the creation of a female awareness that resulted in numerous debates, round tables and conferences on female dramaturgy. Finally, we must not overlook the publication of Patricia O'Connor's *Dramaturgas españolas de hoy* [Contemporary Spanish Women Playwrights] (1988), a key contribution towards the promotion and development of female-authored Spanish theatre. As a consequence, a considerable number of female playwrights emerged and began consciously to adopt a more woman-centred focus, although, as O'Connor underlines (1990, 377), they tended to avoid dealing with openly feminist themes or declaring themselves to be feminists. Indeed, one might, from a present-day viewpoint, find it surprising that the previous repression did not elicit a stronger reaction on the part of this new generation of women playwrights, as, by contrast, it did in the Southern Cone countries such as Chile or Argentina after the fall of their military regimes (Milleret 2004). Ann Witte has drawn attention to this lack of politically engaged theatre in the transition years:

> The transition from dictatorship to democracy, and the ensuing removal of the need to struggle against the institutionalised control of all sectors of political and cultural life, seem to create a vacuum for the committed playwright. (1996, 1)

From the standpoint of dramatic technique, Spanish women dramatists of the 1980s tended to write small-cast plays with linear narrative structures that deal primarily with the personal sphere (Witte 1996, 4). These plays do not usually foreground innovation in terms of plot or structure and generally fall within the limits of realism. In spite of their formal conservatism, some of these playwrights, such as Lidia Falcón (b.1936), also a lawyer and founder of the Feminist Party of Spain in 1979, and Pilar Pombo (1953-1999) produce theatre that is characteristically feminist. Falcón's *No moleste, calle y pague, señora* [Do not disturb, shut up and pay, madam] (1984), the title of which eloquently evokes masculine authority, and Pombo's two monodramas *Remedios* (1988) and *Isabel* (1987) are clear examples, to name but a few, of feminist theatre. Paradoxically, the plays of both these dramatists have received very little scholarly attention even on the part of those critics and researchers who have an interest in female-authored and/or feminist drama, and this would again seem to support the conclusion that overtly ideological theatre is not very popular in Spain.[5]

Generally most of the works produced at this time, while they may deconstruct sexual and gender identities, do fail ultimately to present the woman in a subject position. Despite this failure, it is undeniable that in this process of deconstruction the so-called first generation of the democracy blazed a fundamental trail.[6] One of the playwrights who has done so most effectively and openly and, in fact, the only one to have had her plays staged in mainstream commercial theatres is Paloma Pedrero (b.1957).[7] Herself an actress, she has made extremely efficient use of her plays' *mise en scène* to subvert and deconstruct traditional images of both men and women. Pedrero's dramaturgy abounds with metadramatic techniques, particularly ritualistic game-playing, which she mainly uses to disarticulate sexual identity and reinforce its precarious nature. Needless to say, Pedrero experienced great difficulty in having her work accepted, particularly by various male critics in the 1980s.[8] However, she is today cited as the most frequently staged Spanish-language woman playwright in the world (Zatlin 2001, 193), while several of her early works have found their way onto university syllabuses in many countries and achieved near-canonical status. One of these, *La llamada de Lauren* [Lauren's Call] (Pedrero 1999, 77-102), staged in 1985, focuses on Pedro and Rosa's married relationship, which is unsatisfactory, largely because he has not come to terms with his homosexuality. The irony comes from the fact that the result of this heterosexual masquerade is the cause of Rosa's own sexual dissatisfaction.

It is carnival time and Pedro persuades his wife Rosa, played by Pedrero herself in the original production, to engage in a role-swapping game through which he temporarily liberates himself from the sexual role imposed on him by society. But the illusion is broken when Pedro takes the game too far by asking his wife to wear a phallus. This leads to a scene of great dramatic tension in which Pedro summarises the newly conflictual nature of their own relationship, ultimately a microcosm of society's double standards, with the following words: "Yo no me puedo mirar y tú no me quieres ver" (Pedrero 1999, 97) [I can't bear to look at myself and you refuse to look at me].[9] A re-establishment of the previous order follows, and Pedro decides to slip out to join in with the carnival celebrations by himself, leaving Rosa at home in bed. In a significant gesture of resignation and acceptance, Rosa, who sees Pedro making his way out, goes to him and touches up his lipstick, leaving us with the impression that she now has simply to adjust to this lifestyle. Nevertheless, this sign of sexual liberation for the male, this shift away from heteronormativity, is only deceptive, as Pedro's homosexuality cannot be acknowledged in the outside world if it is not disguised.

Esta noche en el parque [Tonight in the Park] (Pedrero 1999, 149-158), from Pedrero's series of one-act plays *Noches de amor efímero* [Nights of Ephemeral Love] (1987-1989), has been judged by Lamartina-Lens to be Pedrero's most evidently feminist work (Podol 1995, 13). In it Yolanda confronts the married man who has seduced her but, unlike her, is not willing to pursue a relationship. The playful environment in which the couple have sex, namely behind a playground slide in a park, serves to reinforce Fernando's perception of Yolanda as a sexual object to play with. Yet in their second encounter she is the one that attempts to take on the mask of masculinity in order to get the orgasm she did not have the first time. Yolanda's aggressiveness is evident in this scene:

> ¡Siéntate en el columpio! ¡Vamos! (Fernando se sienta.) ¡Colúmpiate como la otra noche! ¡No se te ocurra hacer ninguna tontería! (Fernando se columpia.) Ahora me vas a decir la verdad. ¡No pares, colúmpiate más alto! Eso es. ¿Por qué no has contestado a mis llamadas? (Pedrero 1999, 154)

> [Sit down on the swing! Come on! (Fernando sits down.) Swing like the other night and don't you dare to fool around! (Fernando swings.) Now you are going to tell me the truth. Do not stop, swing higher! That's it. Why have you not answered my calls?]

In addition to the empowerment she derives from carrying a knife, her direct, strong language endows her with a subject status. However, her interference in the area of the subject in the symbolic order is doomed to failure and she ends up being killed by Fernando with her own knife. The symbolic setting of the park at night is important, as through it Pedrero makes it clear that transgressive relationships are necessarily transitional and elusive even in open and supposedly neutral spaces. This is significant when seen in relation to the work of the next generation of women playwrights, who generally fail to transcend the space of the home except when they resort to metaphorical and fictional spaces.

One of the very few examples of successful female agency is portrayed in Pedrero's *Resguardo personal* [The Voucher] (Pedrero 1999, 103-112; first performed in 1986), in which the capacity of the protagonist, Marta, for action is not impeded. Marta has just separated from her husband Gonzalo, a doctor who, excessively absorbed in his work, had disregarded his wife. Marta makes him believe that she has taken their dog to the pound and that it will be put to sleep if she does not collect it by a certain time. As she had anticipated, Gonzalo prevents her from retrieving the dog in order to make her pay for her behaviour and he leaves triumphant when in fact it is Marta who has deceived him. On this occasion, laughter is bound up with power and we can conclude that Marta's positioning herself as the "author" of a joke is subversive and dismissive of male authority. This kind of subversive use of laughter has been an important element in French feminist discourse, as for instance in Cixous's essay *The Laugh of Medusa* (1981), where the author suggests that a feminine text must pursue the following objectives: "to shatter the framework of institutions, to blow up the law, to break up the 'truth' with laughter" (258).[10]

Finally, the same playwright's *El color de agosto* [The Colour of August] (Pedrero 1999, 113-146; first performed in 1988) is particularly meaningful from a feminine perspective. The conflict arises when two women artists, María and Laura, are reunited after an eight-year separation apparently caused by Laura falling in love with Juan, a man she never marries but with whom she has maintained a love affair. As María has become very successful, she now wants to assist Laura financially. But we soon find out that through an emotional bond it is she who is dependent on Laura and that the latter is in fact the true inspiration behind María's talent. The text clearly suggests María's repressed lesbianism so various gender issues are brought together in this play, where the women's emotional conflict culminates in a violent scene in which both women symbolically paint each other's nude bodies. María finally ties Laura up, only to tell her that Juan is the man she is married to. The play thus illustrates women's right to sexual and emotional fulfilment, even if achieving it requires the betrayal of friendship.

One of the founding members of the aforementioned *Asociación de Dramaturgas* was the very prolific dramatist Carmen Resino (b.1941), whose works tend to be underpinned by a feminist approach in spite of her own rejection of the feminist label. Among them, *Nueva historia de la princesa y el dragón* [New Story of the Princess and the Dragon] (1989) questions, through the use of metaphor, the role assigned to women. The author's oblique technique uses the setting of feudal Japan, where Chinese Princess Wu-Tso is given in marriage to a weak Japanese prince. The contrast between Wu-Tso's fragile appearance and her inner strength defies our preconceived notions of masculinity and femininity (Witte 1996, 16). Wu-Tso dares, albeit in vain, to rebel and defy her father by telling him that she and not her brother should be the heir. But once in Japan the princess, although admired by the emperor, cannot survive in this extremely patriarchal system and symbolically dies on the emperor's throne.

It is interesting to follow the evolution of this group of playwrights over the years, as they seem to have been immune to the trend towards postmodern textual strategies which characterise a considerable number of plays during the nineties and noughties. Carmen Resino's recent play *La última reserva de los pieles rojas* [The Red Indians' Last Reservation] (2003) is a good example as it again falls within the limits of realism and traditional metaphor. Women are thus compared to the Native Americans whose territory was taken away from them by the white Americans. The protagonists of the play are two elderly women, Elena and Clara, who have dedicated their entire lives to satisfying the needs of their families, thus sacrificing their own identity, only to end up trapped in an old people's home. Elena, the rebellious one, tries to convince Clara to run away with her to a symbolic (and presumably fictitious) house she claims to have near the sea. However, in the third act she suddenly feels defeated whereas Clara develops a non-conformist attitude at the end, when her companion suddenly dies. The play has a profoundly pessimistic tone: "Antes, cuando éramos jóvenes, nos engañaban los maridos, los amantes… ¡ahora, los hijos!" [In the past, when we were young, our husbands and lovers cheated on us, now it is our own children!], says Clara (71), establishing a metaphor for alienation and diaspora, power and identity, in this ultimate failure to defy the cultural values that degrade ageing women.

Therefore we can conclude that this generation of playwrights focus on previously unexplored areas of gender relationships and start to question and draw attention to the traditional system of representation. However, it is important to note Candyce Leonard's remarks on the nature of their characters:

> The women characters no longer see subordination as their fixed position in the hierarchy. There is, however, a continued sense of restriction regarding women and power. The protagonists *vent their frustration, yet their rebellion is aborted*; although they do not usurp the male-dominated power, they are attempting to subvert it. That is, they haven't yet developed the strategies that would abolish the gender hierarchy in today's Spanish society; and it may be too soon for that. (1992, 252-253; emphasis added)

But has the following generation of playwrights yet developed these strategies? In order to answer this I will first outline the context in which this new group of dramatists was born. They are associated with the so-called "Bradomín generation", named after the Marqués de Bradomín Prize for playwrights under 30, which was awarded for the first time in 1985.

The Nineties and the Noughties

This period was dominated by the conservative Partido Popular (1996-2004), and the corresponding cultural shift to the right. This had an impact on theatrical productions, which became even less overtly political due to changes in the priorities of theatre funding introduced by the Aznar government. But the growing discontent with the Partido Popular led to a progressive awakening of the arts to a social commitment and a new period of consciousness-raising which reached its peak during the first four years of the twenty-first century, during which political theatre, in the broad sense of the term, can be seen to have made a comeback. Nevertheless, with a few notable counter-examples, it remains a man's world and a truly feminist approach is the exception rather than the rule. It is quite revealing, for example, that in a country where the increase in domestic violence is reaching alarming figures,[11] it is all but impossible to find explicit defences of women's rights in dramatic literature.

In terms of concrete policies, the last four years of conservative government in Spain (2000-2004) witnessed various manifestations of "censorship" in the arts and media that seriously put in question the validity of the democratic system and caused no little anger and mistrust in the progressive sectors of society. [12] In addition to this, despite overwhelming opposition to the war in Iraq by 90% of Spain's population, the governing party decided to send troops to support Bush's coalition.[13] Finally, when the Madrid bombings took place on 11 March, the Popular Party immediately blamed ETA and ignored the evidence that the bombings may have been carried out by a group linked to Al Qaeda. As a result, in the parliamentary elections held only three days after the terrorist incident, the Popular Party received 38% of the vote and was beaten by the Spanish Socialist Party (PSOE), with 43%.[14]

With regard to the theatre scene, in the 1990s the number of female dramatists increased due to various factors, including the new María Teresa León Award for women playwrights in 1994, and the creation for the first time in 1992 of a degree in playwriting nationwide. The same decade also witnessed a fundamental change in the creative process as many playwrights began to work alongside directors (Pallín-Vasco) or direct/perform their own plays themselves. Additionally, a new generation of gender-aware critics (Serrano, Ragué-Arias) emerged, who were more open to the unfamiliar. Consequently, new plays dominated by a female perspective that questions the male-dominated world were created. Nevertheless, not only have we found what could be considered a weak proportion of strictly "feminist" works but also a contradiction between the post-feminist discourse employed by many of these playwrights and the feminist critique found in their works.[15] One of the dramatists whose self-perceptions and views on her own writing best exemplify this position is Yolanda Pallín (b.1965), who has always been very reluctant to admit the presence of any activist agenda in her works. While she declares that women still need to achieve a better social position as various forms of discrimination prevail, she seems to locate her claims in the context of social justice and is very careful not to be associated with what she sees as the victim mentality of feminism (interview by the author, Madrid, 11 July 2001). As Mª José Ragué-Arias has pointed out:

> Ninguna de estas autoras de los 90, apenas ninguna de las generaciones anteriores, muestra demasiado interés por la especificidad femenina en la

> escritura dramática, ninguna pretende representar el género o la sexualidad. Su escritura y su temática no difieren substancialmente de la de los autores de su generación. Hay sin embargo en la temática y en los personajes de la mayoría de sus obras, un punto de vista femenino que busca la *identidad*, un rechazo implícito de la jerarquía masculina, un punto de partida que late en sus propias vidas. (1998b, 234; emphasis added)

> [None of these female playwrights of the 90s, hardly any of those from previous generations, shows much interest in the specificity of women's writing, none of them claims to be representing any particular gender or sexuality. Their writing and the topics they deal with do not differ substantially from those of their male counterparts. However, both in the subject matter and the characters of most of their works there is a feminine point of view that is searching for *identity*, an implicit rejection of the masculine hierarchy, a departure point located in their own lives.]

Being a "liberated" woman can also be counterproductive in terms of identity. The issue of split identities is indeed a typical theme of the cultural output of the 1990s. Pallín's *D.N.I.* (1996a; the acronym stands for National Identification Card) exposes the contradictions of a supposedly liberated woman who has shaped her life around three different men, namely her husband, her psychoanalyst and her boss. This woman finally decides to leave her three "monkeys", as she calls them, behind her and, significantly, forget about her lost identity card, which symbolised the imposition of patriarchal codes.

In order to represent a fragmented and confused sense of identity, women, and theatre practitioners in general, have moved away from traditional forms and resorted to non-naturalistic methods of representing male and female subjectivity. They write open-ended plays with more sophisticated, fragmented structures and explore the subconscious and the boundaries separating reality from illusion. These productions employ irony, parody, paradox and contradiction, are highly intertextual and play upon self-consciousness and reflexivity. All in all these plays, in stylistic terms, can be considered postmodernist, according to Geraldine Harris's definition of the term.[16] With regard to their content, however, not all of these plays present a sufficient degree of eclecticism to qualify as being truly postmodern.[17] Many women dramatists opt to dismantle the myths created by men by offering alternative versions to the androcentric accounts of history and widening their repertoire of affirmative female symbolisations. For example, Itziar Pascual (b.1967) draws upon classical mythology in *Fuga* [Escape] (1993), a variation on the Ulysses story, and *Las voces de Penélope* [Penelope's Voices] (1996). It is worth noting that Pascual, a vocal champion of theatre's artistic and political responsibility, is also one of the very few dramatists to have consistently declared herself to be a feminist.[18] In scene 16 of the aforementioned *Las voces de Penélope*, as Phyllis Zatlin has pointed out, the feminist voice is clearly represented by the Amiga de Penélope [Penelope's Friend], who "writes an essay on women dying in child-birth, from unsafe abortions, and from physical abuse" (2000, 11).

In contrast with the previous generation, plays from the 1990s onwards increasingly present a stronger assertion of individuality, a typically post-feminist construction of the self that nevertheless frequently turns out to be an illusion. The escape from the symbolic order into Lacan's imaginary is thus short-lived and representations of subversion ultimately reinscribe themselves in the very systems of representation that they set out to deconstruct. This is the case in *Memoria* [Memory] (1999), by Yolanda Pallín, where the female protagonist puts a fictitious end to her psychological dependence both on her father, with whom an incestuous relationship is suggested, and the married man she loves, by imagining the extinction of all men.

It should be added that this generation of playwrights develop a new approach to the mother-daughter relationship and do not simply focus on the father, as Patricia O'Connor (1998, 119) has remarked, referring to Spanish women playwrights such as Ana Diosdado and Paloma Pedrero in contrast to their American counterparts who, she argues, show a special interest in the mother. The mother/daughter relationship has in fact now become an important focus of Spanish women's writing, largely because of the daughter's rebellion against the limited role of her mother in a traditionally *machista* society. This runs in parallel with a certain pattern in Spanish society, which witnessed a dramatic fall in the fertility rate during the nineties, reaching its lowest value in 1998, and a very slow recovery during the first half of the noughties (Eurostat 2007, 16-17). Daughters now rebel against their mothers' lifestyles and increasingly panic at the idea of becoming their mothers thus developing an apparent "matrophobia" (Chodorow 1978, 236).

The theme of women's relationships has thus become increasingly important for Spanish dramatists. In the case of Laura in Pallín's *Los restos de la noche* [The Remains of the Night] (1996b), for instance, we confront a character who refuses to have children and is profoundly marked not just by her real mother but also by her spiritual counterpart, the Virgin Mary. Laura goes to church and, through a prayer to the Virgin, she offers a retrospective view of her repressed childhood that shows how her religious upbringing has acted as a burden on her psychological evolution:

Tú tienes la culpa, tú y los tuyos, María santísima / y la corte celestial. / Vale. / Cultivando la fe como una plantita y siempre se me mustiaba. / Como a *mi madre* las petunias que me daban tanta alergia. / Pues si no valgo para buena, os vais a enterar. / Y no. / Sólo sé que quería ser buena. (70; emphasis added)

[You are to be blamed, you and your own people, Holy Mother / and the celestial court. / Enough. / I tried to cultivate my faith as if it was a little flower, and it always withered. / Like *my mother*'s petunias I was so allergic to. / If I cannot be good, you will see. / And no. / I only know I meant to be good.]

The figure of the mother, however, to whom she refers on several occasions in her prayer, has not yet become separated from her, and this, according to Lacan (Moi 1985, 99-101), would prevent the shaping of her own ego and her opening up to the unconscious.[19] In this way both mothers would seem to be the locus of Laura's pathology.

Another important development in the 1990s was the growth in the number of all-female theatre companies with a clear and more radical feminist agenda, several of which firmly establish themselves during the noughties. This is the case for the *Metadones*, Margarita Borja's *Sorámbulas* and the *Vacas* Collective. The prolific *Asociación de Mujeres en las Artes Escénicas Marías Guerreras*, led by Itzíar Pascual, was created in 2001. One of their last productions, *No más lágrimas* [No More Tears] (2008), consists of a series of sketches analysing five different situations of women in contemporary society.

These women-centred productions, normally very experimental in style, can be considered a response to disillusionment and are certainly overtly political in their nature and a true expression of women's experiences. They tend to juxtapose different genres and intersperse the main text with poems, songs, dancing and movement. *Tres disparos, dos leones* [Three Shots, Two Lions] (1994), produced by *Teatro para el Instante*, thus combines texts from the Dadá Almanac with a Maori song, various fragments from African poems and the painting of Francis Bacon.[20] Another example of trans-disciplinary production, this time on a large scale, is *Toda la humanidad habla de Troya* [The Whole of Humankind is Talking about Troy] (1998), collectively created in the setting of the island of Tabarca off the coast of Alicante by *Sorámbulas*, *Q Teatro* and *Unidad Móvil*, which incorporates music, sculpture and philosophical and protest dialogue.

During the first decade of the twenty-first century, much critical attention has been devoted to the winner of the 2003 Innovative Theatre Prize Angélica Liddell Zoo, whose radical feminist work is admirably consistent in spite of a very much divided criticism. An experienced actress, like Pedrero, Angélica Liddell knows what works on stage and thus creates texts whose *mise-en-scène* stresses the connection between life and art, heavily drawing on visual material, including her own body. However, while Pedrero tends to respect the limits set by social taboos, Liddell breaks them completely in her highly innovative and experimental avant-garde texts and performances that can well be compared to English in-yer-face theatre in terms of their shock tactics.[21] She carries out a complete disarticulation of the family unit with the purpose of adulterating the complex ideological apparatus that affects and defines the politics of motherhood. In Liddell's case, the political unquestionably intersects with the personal, as can be seen from her own personal decision not to have children. One example of her turbulent world is the *Tríptico de la aflicción* [The Sorrow Triptych], made up of *El matrimonio Palavrakis* [The Palavrakis Couple] (2001), where a seven-year-old girl is not only abused by her father but brutally killed by her parents; *Once upon a time in West Asphixia* (2002), focused on a group of teenagers that want to control the world through sex; and *Hysterica Passio* (2003), in which the protagonist's schizophrenia stems from the sexual abuse he suffered as a child. Her dramatic works thus abound with torturers and tortured characters struggling to deal with their personal relationships, living on the borderline between a conventional reality and a world in which violence and sex abound. Liddell examines a society devoid of moral values from the perspective of the domestic microcosm and thus uncovers parallels and contradictions both at a national level and within the confines of the home.

Feminist manifestations throughout the last three decades show that, if bourgeois or liberal feminism dominated Spanish theatre in the 1980s, cultural feminism came to the fore in the 1990s and a limited number of radical feminist approaches to theatre have appeared in the noughties. Nevertheless, all in all we can conclude that in the Spanish female-authored theatre of the last thirty years the personal is not as political as it could have been and there is still an undeniable need for dialogue and debate. It should be noted that the female playwrights of the first generation of democracy continue to be under-represented in mainstream theatre and generally marginalised, proving that women dramatists have not yet reached equality. As for the next generation, works attacking *machista* attitudes and values still seem to be doomed to silence and relegated to alternative venues. In order to become more visible these dramatists either need to involve themselves in their own performances (Pedrero, Liddell) or create alliances (all-female theatre companies). Perhaps this is why most of them, particularly those associated with the so-called Bradomín generation, wishing to expose unfair power relations and challenge the reader/spectator's sign system, tend to do so in a diluted way that has to do with the aesthetics of postmodernism, where the final message reaches us more obliquely. Others have opted to avoid the treatment of such issues and, through their silence, have contributed to maintaining what Riane Eisler calls the "dominant system" (1991, 52).

This lack of unquestionably feminist theatre in Spain, frequently noted by Patricia O'Connor,[22] is in contradiction both with the current cultural situation and the historical background of the country and only partially reflects the effects of a globalised world on interpersonal relationships. Feminism, comprehending both universalistic and particularistic aspirations, is still necessary in today's society although as readers/spectators we are ultimately responsible for resisting the ideology that supports the object status of women in representation.

Works Cited

Amnesty International. (2004) "Spain: Government must live up to its responsibilities on protection of women's rights", July 5. http://www.amnesty.ca/resource_centre/news/view.php?load=arcview&article=1673&c=Resource+Centre+News (accessed 11 November 2010).

BBC News. (2004) "Spanish government admits defeat". http://news.bbc.co.uk/1/hi/world/europe/3511280.stm (accessed 11 November 2010).

Chodorow, N. J. (1978) *The Reproduction of Mothering: Psychoanalysis and the Sociology of Gender*. Berkeley & London: University of California Press.

Cixous, H. (1981) "The Laugh of the Medusa", in E. Marks and I. de Courtivron (eds), *New French Feminisms*. New York: Schocken Books, 245-264.

Davies, C. (1994) *Contemporary Feminist Fiction in Spain: The Work of Montserrat Roig and Rosa Montero*. Oxford and Providence: Berg.

Eisler, R. (1991) "Social Transformation and the Feminine: From Domination to Partnership", in C. Zweig (ed.), *To Be a Woman: The Birth of the Conscious Feminine*. London: Mandala, 43-54.

Eurostat. (2007) *Methodologies and Working Papers: Demographic Outlook: National Reports on the Demographic Developments in 2005*, European Comission. http://epp.eurostat.ec.europa.eu/cache/ITY_OFFPUB/KS-RA-07-001/EN/KS-RA-07-001-EN.PDF.

Falcón, L. (1984) *No moleste, calle y pague, señora*, *Estreno* X, 2, 26-33.
Falcón, L., & Gabriele, J. P. (1997) *El teatro breve de Lidia Falcón*. Madrid: Editorial Fundamentos.
Goodman, A. (2003) "Polls: 90 percent of Spaniards against war". Madrid: CNN. http://edition.cnn.com/2003/WORLD/europe/03/29/sprj.irq.spain/ (accessed 11 November 2010).
Harris, C. J. (1994) "Juego y metateatro en la obra de Paloma Pedrero", in John P. Gabriele (ed.), *De lo particular a lo universal: El teatro español del siglo XX y su contexto*. Frankfurt: Vervuert Verlag; Madrid: Iberoamericana, 170-180.
Harris, G. (1999) *Staging Femininities*. Manchester: Manchester University Press.
Hormigón, J.A., dir. (1996) *Autoras en la historia del teatro español (1500-1994)*. Madrid: ADE, vol. III, IV.
Immigration and Refugee Board of Canada. (2005) *Spain: Situation of and legal remedies for domestic violence, including provisions in the domestic violence law that was enacted in December 2004; whether the law mentions physicians' obligations to report domestic violence injuries (2003-2005)*. 6 October 2005, ESP100607.E. http://www.unhcr.org/refworld/docid/440ed6fb20.html (accessed 11 November 2010).
Instituto de la Mujer. (2002) "La mujer en el franquismo y la tradición española", Centro de Documentación. http://www.inmujer.migualdad.es/mujer/servicios/centro_documentacion/3.pdf (accessed 11 November 2010).
Leonard, C. (1992) "Women Writers and their Characters in Spanish Drama in the 1980s", *ALEC*, 17, 243-255.
Leonard, C. & Gabriele, John, P., eds. (1996) *Panorámica del teatro español actual*. Madrid: Fundamentos.
Liddell Zoo, A. (2004) *Tríptico de la Aflicción: Once upon a time in West Asphixia or Hijos mirando al infierno / Hysterica passio / El matrimonio Palavrakis*, *Acotaciones* 12, 67-170. The latter play also in *El Pateo* 7 (2001), and available from: http://parnaseo.uv.es/Ars/Autores/liddell/matrimonio/indomatri.htm (accessed 11 November 2010).
Lorenzo-Zamorano, S. (2008) "Corrupción, enfermedad y censura en el teatro español contemporáneo", in A. Davies, P. Kumaraswami and C. Williams (eds), *Making Waves: Anniversary Volume: Women in Spanish, Portuguese and Latin American Studies*. Newcastle: Cambridge Scholars Press, 25-42.

Milleret, M. (2004) *Latin American Women On/In Stages*. New York: State University of New York Press.

Moi, T. (1985) *Sexual/Textual Politics*. London: Methuen.

O'Connor, P. (1988) *Dramaturgas españolas de hoy: una introducción*. Madrid: Fundamentos.

—. (1990) "Women Playwrights in Contemporary Spain and the Male-Dominated Canon", *Signs* 15.2, 376-90.

—. (1994) "Mujeres de aquí y allá", in John P. Gabriele (ed.), *De lo particular a lo universal: El teatro español del siglo XX y su contexto*. Frankfurt: Vervuert Verlag, 158-169.

—. (1998) "Dramaturgas españolas y norteamericanas y la superación de fronteras", in L. Borràs Castanyer (ed.), *Reescribir la escena*. Madrid: Fundación Autor, 117-121.

Pallín, Y. (1996a) *D.N.I.*, in *D.N.I; Como la vida misma: IV Muestra de Teatro Español de Autores Contemporáneos* (Teatro Español Contemporáneo, 5). Alicante: Muestra de Teatro Español de Autores Contemporáneos, 9-28.

—. (1996b) *Los restos de la noche* (serie Literatura Dramática 15). Madrid: ADE, 49-101.

—. (1999) *Memoria*, in *Un sueño eterno: VII Muestra de Teatro Español de Autores Contemporáneos* (Teatro Español Contemporáneo, 9). Alicante: Muestra de Teatro Español de Autores Contemporáneos, 161-171.

Pascual, I. (1995) *Fuga* (Colección Nuevo Teatro Español, 15). Madrid: Centro Nacional de Nuevas Tendencias Escénicas, 11-26.

—. (1998) *Las voces de Penélope*, in *Premio Marqués de Bradomín 1997*. Madrid: Instituto de la Juventud, 101-135.

—. (2002) "Una posición política", in C. Oliva (ed.), *El teatro español ante el siglo XXI*. Madrid: España Nuevo Milenio, 281-284.

Pedrero, P. (1999) *Juego de noches: Nueve obras en un acto*, ed. V. Serrano. Madrid: Cátedra.

Podol, Peter L. (1995) "The Influence of Feminism on the Treatment of Sexual Transgression and the Double Standard in Contemporary Spanish Theatre", *Hispanófila* 114, 9-16.

Pombo, P. (1987) *Isabel: monólogo en un acto*. Madrid: Pliegos.

—. (1988) *Remedios: monólogo en un acto*, in P. O'Connor (ed.), *Dramaturgas españolas de hoy: Una introducción*. Madrid: Fundamentos, 129-141.

Ragué-Arias, Mª J. (1998a) "El lenguaje escénico de las mujeres: Aportaciones recientes", in K. Nigro y P. Zatlin (eds), *Un escenario propio/A stage of their own (I)*. Ottawa: Girol Books, 19-26.

—. (1998b) "La obra de algunas autoras españolas contemporáneas desde la perspectiva de la teoría teatral feminista", in L. Borràs Castanyer (ed.), *Reescribir la escena*. Madrid: Fundación Autor, 227-235.

Resino, C. (1989) *Nueva historia de la princesa y el dragón*. Madrid: Lucerna.

—. (2003) *La última reserva de los pieles rojas*. Madrid: AAT / Consejería de las Artes de la Comunidad de Madrid.

Rodríguez Richart, J. (2000) "El teatro feminista de Lidia Falcón", in H. Fritz & K. Pörtl (eds), *Teatro contemporáneo español posfranquista: Autores y tendencias*. Berlin: ed. Tranvía, Verlag Walter Frey, 89-105.

Shevtsova, M. (1999) "Bells and Alarm Clocks: Theatre and Theatre Research at the Millennium", *TRI*, 24.1, 98-108.

Stephenson, H. & Langridge, N., eds. (1997) *Rage and Reason: Women Playwrights on Playwriting*. London: Methuen.

Wandor, M. (1981) *Carry On, Understudies: Theatre and Sexual Politics*. London and New York: Routledge and Kegan Paul.

Weege, C. (1999) "El discurso femenino en la obra de Paloma Pedrero", in H. Fritz & K. Pörtl (eds), *Teatro contemporáneo español posfranquista: Autores y tendencias*. Berlin: ed. Tranvía, Verlag Walter Frey, 106-115.

Witte, A. (1996) *Guiding the Plot: Politics and Feminism in the Work of Women Playwrights from Spain and Argentina: 1960-1990*. New York: Lang.

Yudin, M. F. (1995) "Nunca he tenido tiempo para ser… yo: A Study of the Protagonists in Two Monodramas by Pilar Pombo", *Estreno* 21.1, 24-27.

Zatlin, P. (1980) "Theatre in Madrid: The Difficult Transition to Democracy", *Theatre Journal* 32.4, 459-474.

—. (2000) "The Theatre of Itziar Pascual", *Estreno* 26.1, 10-12.

—. (2001) "From Night Games to Postmodern Satire: The Theatre of Paloma Pedrero", *Hispania* 84.2, 193-204.

Notes

[1] Other important changes affecting women's lives were the repeal of the laws against adultery in 1978 and of the ban on the sale of contraceptives in the same year, along with the legalisation of divorce in 1981 (Instituto de la Mujer 2002).

[2] For more on this apathy and how the feminist movement petered out in the 1980s see C. Davies (1994 , 1-21)

[3] The 1980s were equally the decade of English women playwrights, including such significant figures as Caryl Churchill, Sarah Daniels, Pam Gems and Sue Townsend. In their introduction to their work (1997, xi) Stephenson and Langridge

make a similar comment on the situation in the UK: "The progress towards a more equal balance of male and female work which had been made (…) took a downward turn. 'Women writers who were prominent in the eighties were knocked out', says Vicky Featherstone, artistic director of Paines Plough, who also believes (…) that there's been a 'feminist theatre backlash'".

[4] On women playwrights' historic exclusion from theatre corpora see M. Wandor (1981).

[5] For more on these playwrights see Mary F. Yudin (1995), J.A. Hormigón (1996), L. Falcón and J. P. Gabriele (1997) and José Rodríguez Richart (2000).

[6] See Peter L. Podol (1995), who focuses his study on Paloma Pedrero's *Resguardo personal* [The Voucher] (1999) and *Esta noche en el parque* [Tonight in the Park] (1999), and Concha Romero's *Un maldito beso* [One Damned Kiss] (1989) and *¿Tengo razón o no?* [Am I Right or Not?] (1989).

[7] O'Connor (1998) also names Ana Diosdado and Mª Manuela Reina among the limited number of women playwrights who saw their plays staged in commercial venues in the 1980s. However, their plays do not break taboos or deal as drastically with gender issues as those of Pedrero's.

[8] For a fictional consideration of the difficulties that Pedrero has encountered in her career, see her autobiographical play *Yo no quiero ir al cielo (Juicio a una dramaturga)* [I Don't Want to Go to Heaven (A Woman Playwright is Judged)] (2004).

[9] All translations are my own.

[10] For more on the significance of laughter in feminine texts see G. Harris (1999, 49-53).

[11] According to Spain's Institute for Women's Issues, in 2002 "more than two million women suffered from physical and/or mental violence at the hands of their partners. According to the governing body of the judiciary, between 2002 and 2003, 131 women were murdered by members of their families—a 59 per cent increase in one year, which shows a clear lack of effectiveness of public policies to combat violence against women" (Amnesty International 2004). See also Immigration and Refugee Board of Canada (2005).

[12] On theatre and censorship and political theatre during the Aznar government see Lorenzo-Zamorano (2008) and also *Las Puertas del Drama* (*Libertad de Expresión I & II*), 18 & 19 (spring and summer 2004 respectively).

[13] See Goodman (2003).

[14] See BBC News (2004). On coming to power, the Socialist Party assigned half of its cabinet seats to women (8 altogether) and, among other initiatives, has legalised gay and lesbian marriages, passed the General Law of Measures for Integral Protection against Gender Violence, rationalised divorce proceedings through a new divorce law, and is now backing legislation to alter the current abortion laws.

[15] The term post-feminism is a contested one as on the one hand it suggests that there is no need for feminist activism any more but, at the same time, its aesthetics equally suggests that gender equality is far from having been reached and women's liberation is indeed an illusion. More specifically, post-feminist discourse acknowledges the fractured identity of the individual in the postmodern—and still predominantly masculine—society and examines the elimination of those dualisms

that have been used to explain reality i.e. self/other, male/female, reality/appearance, etc.

[16] Harris (1999, 7) defines stylistically postmodernist productions as "hybrids, both multimedia and fluctuating between various genres of visual and performing arts. They are eclectic in terms of borrowing from other, past texts and performances, employ irony, parody and pastiche, paradox and contradiction, and while they deliberately play upon intertextuality, they are also self-reflexive and self-referential. They eschew linear narratives, operating through juxtaposition and collage, and resist the production of fixed or single meanings or reading positions".

[17] In contrast with the Madrid scene, playwrights working in Barcelona tend to employ a higher degree of vagueness and imprecision in their characterisation and their portrayal of conflict. They also tend to use a more minimalist technique which reflects in a more naturalistic way all the contradictions and emptiness of everyday life. Lluïsa Cunillè's plays (b.1961), for instance, generally reflecting an absence of communication through minimal dialogue, can be termed postmodernist both in style and content.

[18] See Pascual (2002, 283), and Leonard and Gabriele (1992, 50).

[19] According to Lacanian psychoanalysis "it is only (…) when the father intervenes to break up the dyadic unity between the mother and the child, that the child can take up its place in the Symbolic Order, and thus come to define itself as separate from the other" (Moi 1985, 100). This moment represents the Oedipal crisis and is identified with the acquisition of language.

[20] See Mª José Ragué-Arias (1998a), who also comments on the productions *La Bernarda es calva* [Bernarda is Bald] (1994) and *Helénica, poemas para El Público* [Helénica, Poems for The Public] (1993), by the Metadonas and the Sorámbulas respectively.

[21] Some key plays representing this strand of theatre are Mark Ravenhill's *Shopping and Fucking* (1996), Rebecca Prichard's *Essex Girls* (1994), and Sarah Kane's *Blasted* (1995).

[22] O'Connor (1994, 158, 166) maintains that female writers on the other side of the Atlantic are not shy when it comes to declaring their support for the feminist cause and thus deal with contemporary women in a direct way in contrast with their Spanish counterparts, who tend to express a subtle disillusionment through historical, mythological, literary and film intertextualities, as well as parody, fairy tales and metatheatricality.

CHAPTER THREE

WRITING AS MILLENARY REDEMPTION IN *VOZES DO DESERTO* BY NÉLIDA PIÑON

PAULA JORDÃO

> "Good stories, [Hearne] suggests, have the flexibility 'to accommodate a shift in social values'." (Crew 2002, 83)

At the end of the first decade of the new millennium, when most communication is made on and through the internet, one might follow Hearne and ask if "good stories" still have the "flexibility to accommodate a shift in social values", particularly with regard to contemporary Brazilian reality and the position of women in this reality. Subsequently, one might wonder about the role Brazilian literature written by women has played and still plays in this shift. In other words, what possible changes have the last ten years brought to the position of women and in particular to women's literature in Brazil?

In a first attempt to obtain an answer, I would like to begin by referring to two texts that, written eight years apart, might help us get an idea on the subject. The former, "The Importance of Being Female", published in 2000 in *Brazzil* by the writer Nilza Amaral, leaves no doubt about the amount of work still to do in order to achieve equality between women and men (writers). In her text, Amaral begins by giving examples of both social and cultural discrimination against women throughout history,[1] and of women writers (such as Patrícia Galvão, Rachel de Queiroz, Clarice Lispector, Lygia Fagundes Telles, and Nélida Piñon, among others) who have fought for a path of their own in the social and literary world. Later on, she is quite clear that "There is a lot of research trying to explain how and why women write. But there is still a long way to go. Literary criticism has not recognised the right place of women in literature yet" (Amaral 2000).

Eight years later, in a review of some of the work of the writers Sonia Coutinho, Marina Colasanti, Adélia Prado, Lya Luft, and Nélida Piñon, the critic Luciana Namorato still recognises an urge to achieve social equality expressed in the subjects they approach. As she says:

> Characterised by both silence and verbal abundance, a fierce denial and an avid embrace of traditional female literary forms (fairy tales, prayers, diaries, letters), the literature written by women in twenty-first century Brazil oscillates between a celebratory and a pessimistic tone about issues such as sexuality and maternity, religion and mysticism, life in big cities, women's professional careers, education and financial independence, marriage and domestic life. (…) contemporary Brazilian women writers continue to push for a more egalitarian society in which the "feminine" can be rewritten on a daily basis. (Namorato 2008, 45)

With almost a decade separating their words, both Amaral and Namorato seem to be clear about the need for emancipation for women in Brazilian society,[2] regardless of the considerable efforts taken by female writers to change it.[3]

There is no doubt that Nélida Piñon is one of the writers who has played a crucial role in this change. She is one of the names included in the 1970s and 80s "boom" of Brazilian women writers, when "many Brazilian women poets and fiction writers expressed an ambiguity and discomfort concerning the female body and female identity that reflected well the reality lived by many middle-class women in Brazil at the time" (Ferreira-Pinto 2004, 161). The Brazilian writer has been faithful to her questioning of women's historical, social and cultural position throughout the years.

Piñon's novel *Vozes do Deserto* (2004) is a good example of this questioning. While revisiting the traditional and millenary tale *The Thousand and One Nights*, she rewrites it in order to give Scherezade, the female narrator of the traditional stories, a central place in the story, and consequently grant her autonomy and agency, rescuing her from a millenary cultural and social forgetfulness.

As I will demonstrate, *Vozes do Deserto* goes beyond the simple narration of traditional tales to offer the reader a revisionist version along gender lines of the canonical literary texts by which Piñon proposes the questioning of traditional social and cultural values regarding the position of women in Western culture. By establishing a metafictional dialogue from the perspective of the twenty-first century with the ninth-century *The Thousand and One Nights*, Piñon aims at the redemption of female subjectivity and identity from cultural oblivion and cultural erasure that have determined the image of women across the ages.

Empowering Perspective

One of the most well known and respected names of contemporary Brazilian literature, Nélida Piñon's work clearly transmits her social and cultural engagement with Brazilian reality and most particularly with the place women have in it. The first female president of the *Academia Brasileira de Letras* (The Brazilian Academy of Arts) for which she was elected in 1996 and 1997, she began her work with the publication in 1961 of her novel *Guia-Mapa de Gabriel Arcanjo* (*The Guidebook of Gabriel Arcanjo*) that reflects on Christian doctrine and its multiple interpretations. It is, however mainly from the 1970s onwards, that her work achieves full maturity with the publication respectively in 1972 and 1977 of the novels *A Casa da Paixão* (*The House of Passion*) for which she received the Mário de Andrade-prize and *A Força do Destino* (*The force of Destiny*).[4] In these novels, Piñon initiates a discourse in which she moves her attention to and preoccupation with the inner world of women and the place they occupy in daily reality. It is therefore not surprising that critics compare her to Brazilian women writers such as Clarice Lispector, Lya Luft, Helena Parente Cunha, and Márica Denser who have initiated what Helena Parente Cunha characterises as "a explosão da fala feminina" (the explosion of the feminine language) (Cunha 1999, 16).

In *Vozes do Deserto*, Nélida Piñon continues her "feminine language" by returning to *The Thousand and One Nights* with which she establishes her transgressive intertextual dialogue. The well known, traditional story tells about two brothers who are kings and whose respective wives are sentenced to death because they betrayed them with black slaves. Not entirely satisfied with this sentence, one of the brothers, King Shahriyar, decides to aggravate his punishment and extend it to all female inhabitants of his kingdom. Consequently, every night he chooses a virgin to sleep with, whom he sentences to death at dawn. When after some time almost all virgins in the kingdom have died, Shahrazad (as she is called in the original text), the Vizier's eldest daughter, decides to marry the king. Apparently suicidal and incomprehensible, her decision and sacrifice have but one aim: to stop the king's cruel killings. To achieve this she thinks of a stratagem. At the end of the night, she will beg the king to call her sister so that they can see each other for the last time. Before leaving, her sister will ask Shahrazad to tell one of her tales, a talent for which she is famous. With this, Shahrazad hopes to please the king and, consequently, postpone her death until, at least, the end of the tale. The stratagem works and Shahrazad continues telling her stories night after night for 1001 nights, until the king, who has fathered her three children, pardons her and allows her to live with him in peace thereafter.

In spite of being the cause and the pretext of the stories, the traditional Shahrazad occupies a very modest place both as narrator and as character in *The Thousand and One Nights* (Anon. 1961), since she remains dependent on the omniscient and dominant traditional narrator. Imprisoned in a *mîse en abyme* that deprives her of any possible agency as character, it is not her but her male heroes that play the most important roles in her stories, such as Sinbad and Ali Baba. Even her pardon at the end of the story does not bring much change to her situation of dependency. If, after all the years she is allowed to stay alive, this is only because of the caliph's benevolence and magnanimity.[5] Despite (or maybe because of) her existence as the caliph's wife, she remains limited and imprisoned in the most common narrative plot ending available to women under the patriarchal order: heterosexual marriage.[6]

A consequence of the "position of omniscience and authority" that narrators of traditional tales possess, Shahrazad's absence as narrator is a good example of the erasure gender undergoes in these tales (Jackson in Crew 2002, 78). It confronts us with behaviours, discourses, and cultural and social codes that transmit animosity towards female characters. This "position of omniscience and authority" that traditional narrators possess relegates women to inferior positions within the plot, causing them to lose their autonomy as subjects, and deprives them of part of their identity. A very brief survey of some of the most well known fairy tales shows us that heroines such as Sleeping Beauty, Snow White and others, are completely devoid of a voice of their own in the narration, dominated as they are by their plot. Furthermore, as characters, they equally fall prey to cultural codes and principles that reduce them to mere participants in their own events and mere justification for male heroism.

In *Vozes do deserto*, Nélida Piñon opts to give her main character a much more central place than the one given to her millenary consort in the traditional text. Even though we can also speak of an omniscient narrator in the Brazilian novel, his narrative authority is questioned and even deconstructed by the female protagonist's focalisation that gives her the presence and agency essential to the novel. Therefore, and even if Scherezade does not seem to have a real power as narrating subject, this apparent "lack" is neutralised by her dominating focalisation of events and characters by which she seduces us readers. In solidarity with Scherezade, we consequently take her side. We are aware of her courage when she faces the caliph's hegemonic power and of her possible death, and acknowledge her strong presence and agency, as the following quotation illustrates: "Scherezade não teme a morte. Não acredita que o poder do mundo, representado pelo Califa, a quem o pai serve, decrete por meio de sua morte o extermínio da sua imaginação" (Piñon 2007, 7). ["Scheherazade has no fear of death. She does not believe that worldly power, as represented by the Caliph, whom her father serves, decrees by her death the extinguishing of her imagination" (Piñon 2009, 3)]. As it occurs in the present tense and reveals Scherezade's perspective, this kind of narration therefore enables an evident closeness and identification between reader and protagonist that may apply what Andrea Wyile defines as an "immediate-engaging" narrative in which protagonists are the focalisers and the agents of their own narration (Wyile 1999, cited in Crew 2002, 78). As such, and even though *Vozes do deserto* is not narrated in the first person, Scherezade shares with Wyile's protagonists not only the dominant focalisation, but also the grammatical and narrative strategy the critic writes about: the use of "a timeframe that can be defined as continuous-present rather than time-past" [that] "enables readers to identify with the subjective thoughts and feelings of [the] characters" (ibid., 78-79). Finally, Scherezade's empowered focalisation that transmits her feelings, anxieties, and hopes, also transmits a female subjectivity, agency, and visibility that correspond to what Roberta Trites defines as the power of agency in feminist texts. As Trites says: "the protagonist is more aware of her own agency, more aware of her ability to assert her own personality and to enact her own decisions, at the end of the novel then she has been at the beginning" (Trites 1997, cited in Crew 2002, 79). Indeed, through this agency, Scherezade becomes what we could call a feminist bildungsroman protagonist, reaching out to and redeeming her traditional consort from inexistence and oblivion.

The power inherent in this female agency and transmitted through focalisation is not limited to Scherezade, but extends to the other female characters that share with her both the despair of their imprisonment and the hope of their freedom: her sister Dinazarda and the slave Jasmine. As to the former, and similar to what happens in the traditional text, Dinazarda's complicity with her sister constitutes one of the unquestionable facts of the story. However, in Pinõn's text, this complicity includes a quite new (and even controversial) aspect: the urge for independence that, as it unveils an agency unknown in the traditional text, depicts her as her sister's potential rival. We can see an example of this urge in her efforts to gain increasingly more power in the administration of the caliph's palace and consequently a higher hierarchical position.[7] Jasmine, in turn, completely inexistent in the traditional version, now plays a significant role as both autonomous subject and active actor in

Scherezade's liberation. At the service of the two sisters, Jasmine initially occupies a socially inferior position when compared to them. Yet, her position of inferiority or even subalternity quickly changes into one of (relative) equality since she shares with them the same situation of imprisonment. Furthermore, as she is the one able to go to the market in order to gather the narrative material Scherezade will use in her night repertoire to the caliph, Jasmine confirms not only her own agency as independent subject, but also her empowerment as actor in the plot, as she (indirectly) helps to delay Scherezade's death. Finally, since the market is equally the place where she fully realises her ethnic origins, Jasmine's realisation of her agency becomes also the realisation of her own ethnic self, as her focalisation in the following quotation clearly shows:

> As vozes do povo de Scherezade perseguem Jasmine. (...) por força da imaginação da princesa, volta a ouvir os brados das cabras, dos beduínos, nômades como ela. Vê-se de novo na tenda familiar, cujos detalhes recompõe na memória. (...) Mas, embora familiarizada com a vida palaciana, sobressaía-se na escrava o orgulho de haver pertencido no passado a uma realidade oposta àquela, cujas regras foram ditadas pelo sopro da escassez e da esperança. (Piñon 2007, 78-81)

> [The voices of Scheherazade's people pursue Jasmine. (...) through the force of the princess's imagination she once again hears the bleating of goats, the Bedouins, nomads like her. She sees herself back in the family tent, whose details she recomposes in memory. (…) But, although she is familiar with palace life, what stands out in the slave is pride at having belonged in the past to an opposite reality, whose rules were dictated by the breath of scarcity and hope. (Piñon 2009, 71-74)]

Through focalisation, Piñon lays bare another aspect of female subjectivity and agency that is totally absent in *The Thousand and One Nights*: female desire. Devoid of any sensuality or pleasure during the mechanical sexual exercise with the caliph, it is through her stories and characters that Scherezade transmits her passion and desire.[8] Yet, even though it is practically absent in *Vozes do deserto*'s protagonist, female desire is certainly present in Dinazarda and Jasmine. Witnesses of the compulsory sexual act between Scherezade and the caliph, it is as if they feel what the former cannot and will not allow herself to feel,[9] in a gesture of independence and even rebellion towards the caliph and his oppressive power. In their reflection of sensuality and lust, we can see the expression of a free and transgressive female desire that does not comply with any kind of patriarchal moral rules.

Finally, and perhaps in an unexpected way, it is not in Sherezade but in the caliph's adulterous wife, that female desire assumes a visible and defiant expression. Focalised by the caliph who repeatedly recalls the adulterous scene in a cruel but also paradoxically voluptuous masochism, his wife's sexual act appears as something grotesque and abnormal that seems to justify and inflame his deep hatred for everything that concerns female identity:

> Nestas horas, a sombra implacável da esposa, em flagrante desrespeito à imponência do trono, avança em sua direcção, degraus acima, lambe-o com o veneno da saliva, morde-o com uma boca que exibe dentes, língua. A apontar-lhe, com gesto voraz, a própria vulva, o lugar da crise e da traição, o depósito ígneo do seu sexo, do qual afloram lava, lama, secreções. Justo onde ela o açoitara, golpeando-o com a arma do desvairado desejo. Neste esconderijo, escuro e úmido, a Sultana experimentara gozos que o descomunal africano lhe trouxera como consigna da sua origem remota. (Piñon 2007, 148)
>
> [At such times, the implacable shade of his wife, in flagrant disrespect for the power of the throne, advances toward him, climbing the steps, licking him with the venom of her saliva, biting him with a mouth baring teeth and tongue. She points with a voracious gesture to her own vulva, the site of crisis and betrayal, the fiery depository of her sex, from which pour lava, mud, and secretions—exactly where she had lashed him, beating him with the weapon of delirious desire. In this dark and damp retreat, the Sultana had experienced orgasms that the outsized African had brought her from his remote origin. (Piñon 2009, 141)]

By describing the scene from the caliph's perspective and therefore exposing the hatred implicit in it, Piñon denounces the misogyny and the racism inherent in this perspective, as two aspects of the patriarchal dominant order that has served as cultural and ideological context to *The Thousand and One Nights* stories. Yet, eventually reconciled with his past of betrayed husband through Scherezade's words and tales, the caliph also turns into one of Piñon's male characters who reveal themselves receptive enough to learn with their female counter actors, as Naomi Hoki Moniz reminds us about *A Casa da Paixão* (Moniz 1984, cited in Dixon 2002, 205). With his despotic power exposed and denounced, he becomes merely a shadow of himself, the deconstructed replica of his traditional and misogynous consort, contributing to the undermining of *The Thousand and One Nights* misogynist ideology.

Genealogy

The stories recollected by Jasmine at the market and at the bazaar take Scherezade back to her childhood, when her nursemaid Fátima took her outside the palace to see and experience life outside her overprotected world, and to listen to stories that, though reflecting an unfamiliar and unexplored reality, contributed to shape her realisation of her identity. Through Jasmine's recollected stories, Scherezade (re)discovers not only her past (and present) but also the female anonymous authors whom she had never heard of but to whom she now owes her salvation:

> A arte que ela exercia à beira da cama deve parte da sua fabulação à vida do mercado de Bagdá e aos relatos concebidos nos serralhos dos palácios árabes, onde as favoritas registraram em palavras simbólicas, vedadas aos amos, suas frustrações. E que, ao se transmitirem de mãe a filha, estabeleceram parâmetros básicos entre suas sucessoras no harém do Califa. Muitas dessas histórias, tristes e repetitivas a despeito de se originarem de uma imolação individual, forneciam peso a um universo que, bem explorado, tornara Scherezade dona de ilimitado repertório. (Piñon 2007, 76)
>
> [The art that she exercises at the bedside owes part of its fiction to the life of the Baghdad marketplace and to the accounts conceived in the seraglios of Arab palaces, where the favourites recorded their frustrations in symbolic words, hidden from their masters—words that, transmitted from mother to daughter, established basic parameters among their successors in the caliph's harem. Many of these stories, sad and repetitive despite originating from an individual sacrifice, lent weight to a universe that, well exploited, had afforded Scheherazade an unlimited repertoire. (Piñon 2009, 69)]

To her, to narrate means, therefore, to share memory in the sense given by Sue Campbell, "how we learn to remember, how we come to reconceive our pasts in memory, how we come to form a sense of self, and one of the primary ways in which we come to know others and form relationships with them" (Campbell 2008, 42). Most particularly, it means to acknowledge and participate in the creation and reproduction of a feminine collective memory inherent in the transmission of those stories.

Scherezade's role in the creation and reproduction of this feminine collective memory and genealogy contrasts deeply with the erasure (the traditional) Shahrazad is object of, as narrator and character, in the cultural memory that comprises *The Thousand and One Nights*. This erasure or effacement might apply what Paul Connerton denominates a "repressive erasure", a kind of forgetting that "appears in its most brutal form, of course, in the history of totalitarian regime" (Connerton 2008, 60).[10] In the particular case of Shahrazad, this erasure takes place no less brutally, even though somehow more sophisticatedly. Throughout the years, the protagonist of *The Thousand and One Nights* has become the well known symbol of wit and shrewdness of the millenary (Arabic and) Western cultural legacy and order. Yet, these "qualities" are but the result of the mythmaking constructed by the same cultural patriarchal and misogynistic order that has moulded Shahrazad into the embodiment of universal submissiveness and has refused her any kind of autonomy.

In her intertextual dialogue with the traditional text by which she grants her protagonist a key role, allowing her to regain her agency, Nélida Piñon corrects, fills, and even revokes this repressive and erasing gap. Furthermore, by reusing texts that play a fundamental role in the Western culture and imaginary, she "attacks" the past from the present, to borrow Alexander Kluge's expression (2008, 67).[11] Through the intertextual reference to classic heroes and texts, like the Odyssey and the Iliad or the chronicles of King Arthur,[12] Piñon repossesses canonical texts of Western culture that she incorporates in Scherezade's stories, reducing them to "common" characters and "common" texts. By doing so, she proceeds to what Alicia Ostriker in her critical study of the work of American women poets in the 1970s and 1980s, calls "revisionist mythmaking". According to Ostriker:

> Whenever a poet employs a figure or story previously accepted and defined by a culture, the poet is using myth, and the potential is always present that the use will be revisionist: that is, the figure or tale will be appropriated for altered ends, the old vessel filled with new wine, initially satisfying the thirst of the individual poet but ultimately making cultural change possible. (1982, 72)

Finally, Piñon emphasises and salvages "that body of reusable texts, images, and rituals specific to each society in each epoch, whose 'cultivation' serves to stabilise and convey that society's self-image" (Assmann 1995, 132, cited in Kansteiner 2002, 182), that, implicit to collective memory, opens a new space for the cultural and social reaffirmation of the female subject embodied in Scherezade. As such, she manages (even if partially) to challenge and subvert the masculine authorial supremacy in the collective imaginary and replace it by the feminine alternative represented by the forgotten female characters in that imaginary ("Andrômeda e de Hécuba, mulheres golpeadas pela dor" (Piñon 2007, 129) ["Andromeda and Hecuba, women battered by pain"

(Piñon 2009, 120)] who regain by this a presence in that imaginary. *Vozes do deserto* becomes therefore the site where Piñon addresses collective memory as a changeable process, in the sense given by Ann Rigney: "a matter of...continuously performing, in process, involving both recollection and forgetting in the light of changing patterns of relevance and shifting social frameworks" (2008, 94).

Conclusion

In her essay "O eros da fala, o Mito da Criação e a Identidade do Feminino em *Vozes do Deserto* de Nélida Piñon" [The Eros of Language, the Myth of Creation, and Female Identity in Nélida Piñon's *Voices of the Desert*], Maria Alice Aguiar correctly emphasises the role discourse plays in the construction of female identity in *Vozes do deserto*. According to her, "Ao reavivar a voz de Scherazade—o mais notório símbolo da arte de envolver pelo ato de contar histórias—, a autora corrobora a afirmativa de que o discurso sobre a mulher constrói a mulher, inscreve o ser mulher no Tempo e no Espaço e valoriza a força da narrativa" (Aguiar 2005) [By reviving Scherazade's voice—the most notorious symbol of the art of engaging by words—the author corroborates the knowledge that discourse on women constructs women, and inscribes women in Time and Space, valuing the power of the narrative]. Following her, I would add that such inscription takes place through the transgression of social and cultural values within a millenary patriarchal order. By (re)inscribing women in *Vozes do Deserto* as active agents of their plot and of their destinies, Nélida Piñon redeems them from a misogynistic, silenced, and silencing past, granting them an empowered present through which they build up their presence in an exemplary future. Despite all that is yet to achieve in the new millennium with regard to women and their literary, social, cultural and sexual position, we can say that Nélida Piñon's *Vozes do Deserto* has undoubtedly settled (at least a part of) a millenary cultural debt. Good stories still "have the flexibility "to accommodate a shift in social values", which gives women hope for the second decade of the new millennium.

Works Cited

Aguiar, M A. (2005) "O Eros da fala, o Mito da Criação e a Identidade do Feminino em Vozes do Deserto de Nélida Piñon." Paper presented at the Congresso da Associação Internacional de Lusitanistas, Santiago de Compostela, Spain.

http://www.nelidapinon.com.br/panorama/inte/pan_resenas_erosdafala.php (accessed February 6, 2008).

Amaral, N. (2000) "The Importance of Being Female", *Brazzil*, October. http://www.brazzil.com/p25oct00.htm (accessed September 16, 2002).

Anon. (1961) *The Thousand and One Nights*. Translated and edited by N. J. Dawood. Edinburgh: Penguin.

Assmann, J. (1995) "Collective Memory and Cultural Identity", *New German Critique* 65, 125-133.

Campbell, S. (2008) "The Second Voice", *Memory Studies*, vol.1, 1, 41-48.

Connerton, P. (2008) "Seven Types of Forgetting", *Memory Studies*, vol.1, 1, 59-71.

Crew, H S. (2002) "Spinning New Tales from Traditional Texts: Donna Jo Napoli and the Rewriting of Fairy Tale", *Children's Literature in Education*, vol. 33, no.2, 77-95.

Cunha, H P., ed. (1999) *Desafiando o cânone: aspectos da literatura de autoria feminina na prosa e na poesia (anos 70/80)*. Rio de Janeiro: Tempo Brasileiro.

Dixon, P. (2002) "Género sexual e os paradigmas narrativos de Nélida Piñon", *Veredas* 5, 201-210.

DuPlessis, R B. (1985) "Endings and Contradictions" in *Writing Beyond the Ending*. Bloomington: Indiana University Press, 1-19.

Ferreira-Pinto, C. (2004) *Gender, Discourse, and Desire in Twentieth-Century Brazilian Women's Literature*. West Lafayette, IN: Purdue University Press.

Heilborn, M L. (2006) "Entre as tramas da sexualidade brasileira", *Revista Estudos Feministas*, vol.14, n.1, 43-59. http://www.scielo.br/pdf/ref/v14n1/a04v14n1.pdf.

Kansteiner, W. (2002) "Finding Meaning in Memory: A Methodological Critique of Collective Memory Studies", *History and Theory* 41, 179-197.

Mendes, J. R. (2006) "A população brasileira está condenada ao silêncio da própria alma". Interview with Nélida Piñon. *Balaio de Notícias*. July and August. http://www.sergipe.com.br/balaiodenoticias/entrevistaj91.htm (accessed February 6, 2008).

Moniz, N. H. (1984) "A casa da paixão: ética, estética e a condição feminina", *Revista Ibero-Americana* 126, 129-40.

Namorato, L. (2008) "Voices of the Feminine in Contemporary Brazilian Literature", *World Literature Today*, vol.82, issue 1, 43-45.

Ostriker, A. (1982) "The Thieves of Language: Women Poets and Revisionist Mythmaking", *Signs*, vol.8, no.1, 68-90.

Piñon, N. (2007) *Vozes do Deserto*. Lisboa: Bertrand Editora.

—. (2009) *Voices of the Desert*, translated from Brazilian Portuguese by Clifford E. Landers. New York: Alfred A. Knopf.

Rigney, A. (2008) "Divided pasts: A Premature Memorial and the Dynamics of Collective Remembrance", *Memory Studies*, vol.1, 1, 89-97.

Trites, R. S. (1997) *Waking Sleeping Beauty: Feminist Voices in Children's Novels*. Iowa City: University of Iowa Press.

Wyile, A. S. (1999) "Expanding the View of First-Person Narration", *Children's Literature in Education* 30, 185-202.

Notes

[1] Just to name a few examples: "The first legislation concerning the social role of women dates from 1827 assuring them only complementary study. Although men were [sic] allowed to go to school since 1840 women weren't given the same right before 1876. In the middle of the 19th century, women were still set apart from the cultural life even from their family members' lives. Their father decided about marriage and if they refused the chosen husbands they were sent to a convent to be nuns. (...) Visiting Brazil between April 1865 and July 1866, Swiss physician and naturalist Jean Louis Agassiz (1807-1873) wrote about women's education in Brazil: 'There is no woman that conjecturing about the subject is unaware of a life of oppression and restraint'" (Amaral 2000).

[2] We can find a good example of this urge for emancipation in Maria Luiza Heilborn's article "Entre as tramas da sexualidade brasileira. In the fabric of Brazilian sexuality" that demystifies the idea of Brazilian openness regarding sexuality and gender roles. (Heilborn 2006, 43-59)

[3] According to Cristina Ferreira-Pinto: "In the last decades of the twentieth century, female poets, fiction writers, and playwrights have produced the most important counterideological discourse in Brazilian literature, as they have strived to create an authentic language and fresh images suitable for the expression of new voices and a changing reality. … Brazilian women writers, either seen as a group or individually, have developed a feminist critique of the Brazilian "master narrative", particularly as it concerns the representation of the female body, sexuality, and desire "(Ferreira-Pinto 2004, 3).

[4] For more information see, among others, Mendes (2006).

[5] Such benevolence and magnanimity are clear in the following quotation from the epilogue: "Shahrazad ranged the little ones before the King and, again *kissing the ground before him*, said: 'Behold these three whom Allah has granted to us. For their sake *I implore you to spare my life*.' (…) The King embraced his three sons, and his eyes filled with tears as he answered: 'I swear by Allah, Shahrazad, that you were already pardoned before the coming of these children. I loved you

because I found you chaste and tender, wise and eloquent.' (…) When they [the great ones of the city] had all assembled in the great hall of the place, Shahriyar *proclaimed his decision to spare the life of his bride*." (Anon 1961, 239-240) (emphasis mine).

[6] This ending is not only typical of traditional tales. As Rachel Du Plessis reminds us in her chapter "Endings and Contradictions", this is also the case in the novels written in the eighteenth and nineteenth century. Imprisoned between marriage and death as the only possible endings for the stories they narrated and acted in, women were deprived of narrative agency and independence. This situation knew a (partial) transformation only in the twentieth century when protagonists were allowed an existence and destiny of their own that was not necessarily related to marriage (DuPlessis 1985, 1-19).

[7] The following quotations are a good example of this quasi rivalry: "Ou falasse da diligência com que Dinazarda, por iniciativa própria, introduzira significativas mudanças na rotina da corte. Algumas das melhoras visando a beneficiar os escravos. (...) Inconformada com o papel que desempenhava ao lado de Scherezade, Dinazarda estabelecera para si mesma escalas progressivas, com o intuito de realçar sua vocação de comando. Tanto que ao esbarrar à entrada dos jardins reais com algum cortesão, fazia aflorar na conversa questões delicadas, só para luzir o seu conhecimento" (Piñon 2007, 212-213) ["the diligence of Dinazarda, who of her own initiative had introduced significant changes into the routine of the court. Some of the improvements were designed to benefit the slaves. (...) Unresigned to the role she played at Scheherazade's side, Dinazarda had established for herself progressive steps, with the idea of accentuating her gift for command. So, when she would run into some courtier at the entrance to the royal gardens, she would cause delicate questions to surface, merely to demonstrate her knowledge" (Piñon 2009, 203-204)].

[8] We can see an example of this passion in the following quotation: "Mas Scherezade, fingindo obediência ao esposo, tinha ciência de não ser a cupidez, naquela circunstância, a melhor arma para vencê-lo. Sua fabulação verbal, plena de erotismo, consagrada à líbido dos seus personagens, parecia ser o suficiente para revitalizar o corpo gasto do Califa" (Piñon 2007, 216). ["But Scheherazade, feigning obedience to her husband, was certain that under the circumstances cupidity was not the best weapon to defeat him. Her storytelling, full of eroticism, dedicated to the libido of her characters, seemed sufficient to revitalise the Caliph's worn body" (Piñon 2009, 207)].

[9] See for instance: "Ainda que se retire da cena, na extremidade dos aposentos, Dinazarda participa dos folguedos amorosos, que lhe atiçam a fantasia. Ao seu lado, Jasmine, de infatigável diligência, inventa pretextos para permanecer naquelas dependências formadas por quartos unidos sob forma de arcos..." (Piñon 2007, 81). ["Even though she retires from the scene, into the far reaches of the chambers, Dinazarda participates in the amorous frolics that ignite her fantasy. At her side, Jasmine, indefatigably diligent, invents pretexts to remain in those quarters formed by rooms united by arches…" (Piñon 2009, 74)].

[10] In his essay, Connerton (2008) mentions that this repressive erasure does not always have to be negative. However, in the case of Shahrazad of *The Thousand*

and One Nights, it seems obvious that only the (negative) definition of the expression would apply here.

[11] With "attack of the present on the rest of the time", Kluge refers to the negative effects on the stability or identity of contemporary subjects because of the negative pressure of the "present of consumer capitalism" upon past and future (Kluge cited in Connerton 2008, 67). I am using Kluge's expression to focus on the importance of the use of the present as a way to revise the values of the past.

[12] This is, for instance, the case of chapter thirty. The following quotation illustrates this intertextuality: "Por força dessa atração, Scherezade mergulha na memória arcaica e nos arcanos de outras latitudes, revive enigmas históricos, como o reencontro de Príamo com Aquiles, após a morte de Heitor. E o reproduz com riqueza de detalhes, dando realce, por pura solidariedade feminina, aos lamentos de Andrômeda e de Hécuba, mulheres golpeadas pela dor" (Piñon 2007, 128-129). ["Under its attraction, Scheherazade plunges into the archaic memory and the arcana of other lands, relives historical mysteries like the encounter of Priam and Achilles after the death of Hector. And she reproduces it with richness of detail, from feminine solidarity emphasizing the laments of Andromeda and Hecuba, women battered by pain" (Piñon 2009, 120)].

CHAPTER FOUR

CONSTRUCTING A CATALAN FEMINISM IN THE NOUGHTIES OF THE 20TH CENTURY: THE LEGACY OF DOLORS MONSERDÀ

LAURA SOLER GONZÁLEZ

The late 19th and early 20th century was a time of change and progress in Catalonia, of political and economic growth, but above all of literary activity. After three long centuries, Catalonia was finally emerging from a period of literary, cultural and political decadence. From about 1500 to the mid-19th century, Catalonia had been the target of the central government, suffering a progressive loss of autonomy and a subsequent loss of independence in 1714, after its defeat in the War of the Spanish Succession. Catalan self-government ended and, with it, Catalan language and, consequently, Catalan literature, was put under severe threat. One of the salient factors of the literary decadence was the powerful influence of the Castilian literature of the Golden Age, which "interrupted the strong tradition of the medieval and pre-Renaissance Catalan literature" (Roca-Pons 1977, 47). However, "Catalonia was able to persist as a culturally distinct entity, albeit with its language absent from formal political institutions" (McRoberts 2001, 16). Catalonia did more than persist as, despite the loss of its political autonomy, it succeeded in undergoing a major economic recovery through the end of the 18th century. Thus, after centuries of adversity and oppression, the 19th century started as a time of economic regeneration and national awakening, which placed a great importance on the use of Catalan language and emphasised Catalonia's literary glory. It was considered a moment of cultural renaissance and rebirth of Catalan literature and culture. This revival movement, *La Renaixença*, had its starting point around 1833 with Bonaventura Carles Aribau's national poem "La Pàtria" and ran until the turn of the century.

Even though *La Renaixença* was considered a breakthrough in the reconstruction of a Catalan culture and identity, its foundations were based on the admiration of a distant past and an embellishment of the language. Towards the end of the century, intellectuals realised that a renewal of ideas was needed and Catalan culture and literature had to look to the future, opening up to modernity rather than mirroring a glorious past. As a result, in the wake of Catalonia's industrialisation, the turn of the 20th century saw the beginning of the modern period in Catalan literature. *Modernisme* started as an artistic, cultural and literary movement that embodied the values of the new century. It began in 1892 with the first Modernist parties in Sitges, near Barcelona, and it extended up to around 1911, when a new cultural movement, *Noucentisme*, overtook it. Catalan Modernism, equivalent to European *fin-de-siècle* movements, frequently presented contradictory currents: some authors were interested in naturalism, others in symbolism or parnassianism and others in sociological themes. According to Roca-Pons, "some writers showed characteristics that we consider modernist, but not one of the great figures of this period belong[ed] exclusively to one movement" (1977, 61). It was also during Modernism that Catalan institutions of culture were created to promote modernisation and to build a new society that would embrace the European trends of the time. The noughties of the 20th century (1900-1909) was thus a forward-looking time in Catalonia and a fertile period for literature.

Moreover, the noughties was a significant period for women and women writers in Catalonia, such as Dolors Monserdà, who saw an opportunity to develop their intellectual and artistic potential. As Anne Charlon (1991) rightly states, "Catalonia's specific circumstances and the history of Spain as a whole since the beginning of this century have marked Catalan women's writing with certain very particular traits" (13). Those traits refer to the female condition and the defence of language, which became two major subjects for women writers, who were doubly oppressed, for being female and for being Catalan. If the tone and subject matter of their works had many features in common with women's writing throughout the Western world, Catalonia's particular situation made Catalan women's writing distinctive:

> No és per atzar que sigui justament a Catalunya, on es va desenvolupar la indústria i amb ella la urbanització i el trasbals dels ritmes de vida, el lloc on la protesta femenina reprèn vigor i comença a expressar-se per boca de les novel·listes. El desenvolupament industrial sostingut pel treball femení posa a Catalunya en una situació a part, en relació amb la resta d'Espanya. (Charlon 1990, 16)

> [It is not a coincidence that it is precisely in Catalonia, where industry developed and with it urbanisation and the disruption of the rhythms of life, that female protest grows stronger and begins to be put into words by women novelists. The industrial development sustained by female workers places Catalonia in a special situation, in relation to the rest of Spain.][1]

The noughties provided a specific historical framework for the emergence and development of feminism in Catalonia, offering the social and political conditions for a fundamental link between the beginnings of feminism and the first novels written by women.

At the turn of the 20th century, economic progress, the development of industry, the growth of urban areas, and the power and wealth acquired by the newly emergent bourgeoisie were social factors that brought radical changes to the everyday life of women in Catalonia and caused the first feminist demands. These factors also triggered the first movements in favour of regional autonomy. Since the mid-19th century, with the *Renaixença*, a sense of Catalan national identity had already taken root in the texts of the intellectuals of the time, promoting an awareness of Catalonia's historical and cultural distinctiveness. This, coupled with industrial prosperity, favoured the rise of *Catalanism*e and promoted Catalonia's intellectual and cultural movements of *Modernisme* and *Noucentisme*. Yet it was not until the noughties of the 20th century that this Catalan national consciousness started to be entrenched in the female arena, when feminist awareness and national identity issues developed side by side. Moreover, the development of the women's movement in Catalonia became deeply connected to the Catalan nationalist cause, which shaped the orientation of the movement in a different way to the rest of Spain. Thus, "the mobilisation of women within the canons of nationalist discourse can give considerable insights into the gender construction of national identity and the development of gender identity and feminist consciousness" (Nash 1996, 48).

Considering Spain as a whole, the construction of feminism was a complex historical phenomenon that should not be regarded as a unitary movement, but one with different political, social, and cultural realities: one that would account for the profound regional differences within Spain. As Nash points out, "the uneven economic development in the different regions is crucial to the understanding of the sharp contrast in the social condition of women throughout Spain" (1996, 46). Catalonia was growing and was developing economically and culturally at a much faster pace than other regions, becoming more modern and open to Europe. With industrialisation, Catalan society changed rapidly and with it the position of women from all social backgrounds. Many women from lower classes were forced to work in factories and be confronted with new social issues, whereas many women from a more privileged background saw their traditional power (as mothers and wives) change in favour of a new lifestyle due to the rapidly acquired wealth of their husbands. This often affected the way they perceived themselves as women, questioning their place in society and raising issues never expressed before publicly. Thus, with the new century, a new female awareness was taking shape. Women at both ends of the social scale were discontented, either with the unfair working conditions or with the treatment they received in intellectual circles for being women. Their restlessness made them react to their situation, showing their concern either by participating in social struggles or by writing works that reflected the problematic of the moment and aimed to help in the fight for women's rights.

Even though the women's movement in Catalonia had been politically affiliated to the nationalist movement, the feminist agenda was not orientated to the demands for women's suffrage and political rights, as happened in England and the United States; this did not occur until the 1930s with the second wave of feminism and the introduction of the Second Republic. The weak parliamentary system set up during the 19th century Spanish Restoration and the transition from absolutism to a frail liberal state, in addition to the regional differences mentioned above, made Spain an unfavourable nation for the development of a political feminism. Thus, the demands of women were based on the achievement of rights in civil society, and their programmes were inspired by the social itinerary and collective expectations of Catalan women (Nash 1996). If the Catalan women's movement was closely connected to the fight for national and linguistic identity, this had in its early stages a very social and cultural dimension:

> De fet, tot i que la lluita catalanista serveix de base de tota l'obra de les novel·listes, no en constitueix pas el tema essencial, ni el més aparent. En canvi, la condició femenina, l'experiència femenina, els desigs de les dones i allò que elles refusen, són omnipresents en la literatura femenina catalana. Les novel·les i els contes escrits per les catalanes parlen essencialment de les dones, i les dones són, en la gran majoria, els personatges centrals. (Charlon 1990, 12)
>
> [In fact, although the Catalan struggle is the basis of all the works written by women novelists, it does not constitute the essential subject or even the most apparent. On the contrary, the female condition, the female experience, the desires of women and what they reject are ubiquitous in the Catalan literature written by women. The novels and stories written by

> Catalan female writers speak essentially about women, and women are, in most cases, the central characters.]

After years of silence, women finally made their way in a world constructed by men, trying to leave in their works their personal imprint as women. Yet this awakening of social feminism was above all about the difference rather than the equality between genders that we may find in feminist movements of other European countries.

It was in this particular context, at a time when literature was mainly written by men, that Dolors Monserdà emerged as a figure breaking through the Catalan literary scene. Monserdà belonged to the first generation of female writers, from the turn of the century to the 1930s, whose creativity showed the capacity of women and of the Catalan language. Born in the 19th century, in 1845, she developed her most influential works in the first decade of the 20th century. Monserdà became an example to other women of her generation, as she led the way to a new concept of *écriture* from a female perspective. For decades, the image of women in literature had been constructed through the lens of male writers. It was not until the turn of the century that women were first able to express their will to write openly about their own experiences.

Dolors Monserdà was an active participant in Catalan cultural life. She devoted her first years of literary activity to poetry, a genre in which it was more acceptable for women to write, but then took on other genres such as theatre, prose, and the novel. As a poet, she won several prizes in important literary contests and, in 1909, she became the first woman to be president of the *Jocs Florals* of Barcelona,[2] where Victor Català, an emerging literary figure of the Catalan scene, won the Fastenrath prize for the celebrated novel *Solitud* [Solitude]. Victor Català was the male pseudonym for Caterina Albert, who in 1898 had won a literary contest with her controversial monologue “La infanticida” [Infanticide]. The debate was mainly around the fact that such a piece of work was written by a woman. Afraid of the reactions that her future writings could cause when being associated with a female name, from that moment onwards, Caterina Albert, as other female writers had done before, decided to hide her identity behind a male pseudonym. This allowed her to create freely, for the independence of art and artist, without the eye of critics focusing on her gender and with the tranquillity of not having to censor her works (Charlon 1990, 20-21). By contrast, Dolors Monserdà’s choice was very different as she was determined to let the audience and the critics know that she was a woman and that she was writing for the improvement of society. She believed that, by taking the risk and showing her true identity, she was going to set an example for other women and succeed in her feminist commitment.

Monserdà's literary career followed a progressive path of professional and personal development. As Mas (2008) mentions in her study, in a letter of 30th of July 1906 to Josep M. Virgili, Monserdà confessed that writing had always been vocational for her: "M'he trobat, que la costum de fer corre la ploma, des de joveneta, me sia una mena de necessitat en el ponent de la vida" (xxix) [I have found that the habit of running the quill, which I have had since I was a young girl, becomes just now, at the end of my life, a kind of necessity]. Moreover, as Mas (2008) argues, Monserdà's need to write was not devoted to artistic purposes, but had a very specific aim: to teach and educate. Writing for the pleasure of writing was "una vel·leitat que no seria entesa ni permesa" (xxxi) [a caprice that was neither understood nor permitted]. Monserdà wanted to write openly, with the recognition of all, without hiding her name or her female condition. But as a woman, she needed a pretext to consolidate her status as a writer. Thus, she imposed upon herself a condition: that her works had to be of some use, that they had to have a message under ethical, moral and social values (Mas 2008, xxxi).

Consequently, Monserdà's literary ambition was, above all, to serve the female cause, as she clearly states in her *Estudi feminista* [*Feminist Study*] (1909), one of her most acclaimed feminist critical texts, where we find her ideological principles represented:

> Moltes voltes a descoberta i altres *per accidens* (així se pot veure en les novel·les que porto publicades), he fet el que avui s'anomena *feminisme*. És a dir, treballar pel millorament de la dona, per la defensa dels seus drets, per a protestar de les vexacions i injustícies de què se la fa objecte; i, en fi, pel perfeccionament de la seva missió a la família i a la societat. Escriure per la dona i que els meus escrits poguessin ser-li d'alguna utilitat moral i material, veus aquí els meus ideals literaris. (Monserdà 1909, 4)
>
> [Many times knowingly and others *by accident* (one can see it in the novels that I have published), I have made what today is called *feminism*. That is to say, to work for the improvement of woman, for the defence of her rights, to protest against the vexations and injustices to which she is subjected; and, finally, for the perfection of her mission in the family and society. To write for women in the hope that my writings could be of a moral and material utility, these are my literary ideals.]

Thus, she wrote about women and for women, with specific messages and models, aware that her texts acted as a vehicle of ideological transmission and social protest. From her position as a conservative and Catholic woman of the Catalan bourgeoisie, her aim was to help women of less privileged backgrounds, to fight for equality and better working conditions as well as to give moral examples that could be useful in their everyday life. It is interesting to note that she emphasised from the onset the word *feminisme* in italics to show the task she was willing to undertake. She is regarded by many as "the perfect symbol of the close link between the feminist struggle and literary activity" (Charlon 1991, 14), whereas others think that her feminism can actually be labelled as "antifeminism" (Sunyer 1997, 273) if we apply a more modern and progressive perspective. Through the analysis of Monserdà's personal and professional career, this article will assess what sort of feminism she performed and whether one can classify it as such. First, we will explore her contribution to different periodicals, her social task, as well as her feminist critical texts; we will then proceed to the study of one of her most celebrated novels, *La fabricanta* [The Female Manufacturer].

Dolors Monserdà took an active role in the public debate on the female condition, which became a central issue of discussion at social and political meetings of the time, especially strong during the noughties. The following words, pronounced in 1910 by Josep Pons, a delegate of Textile Art in Barcelona, at the constitutive meeting of the *Confederación Nacional del Trabajo*,[3] illustrate that the concern for the situation of women reached political circles and, therefore, some men also showed an understanding of the problem:

> Cuando la mujer acaba de derramar su sangre por espacio de doce horas para mantener los vicios de un explotador, llega a su casa y en lugar de descanso se encuentra con un Nuevo burgués compañero que con la mayor tranquilidad espera que haga los quehaceres domésticos. (Balcells 1974, 14, cited in Charlon 1990, 66)
>
> [When a woman has just shed her blood for twelve hours to maintain the vices of an exploiter, she arrives home and, instead of rest, she finds a New bourgeois partner who calmly expects her to do the housework.]

This shows the double shift, both in the public and private space, which female workers had to endure, being doubly exploited at home and in the factory (Nash 1988, 158). The society of the noughties was reluctant to accept women's access to paid labour as this was a sign of breaking with the established social gender roles and the division of the public and domestic spheres. Traditionally women and men were assigned different social functions: women were part of the domestic space, with their roles as mothers and wives, whereas men were part of the public sphere, being the breadwinners. Female labour was, therefore, considered a subversion of the fundamental order of the family and, particularly, was seen as a menace to the hierarchic power of the husband (Nash 1988, 154). With no legal or social support, women were forced to work long hours, with no recognition, low salaries, and no access to education or professional qualifications. Nonetheless, the presence of female workers increased in Catalonia and, in fact, as Nash (1988) points out, the contribution of female labour—harshly-treated, devalued and invisible—became, paradoxically, fundamental to the industrialisation of Catalonia and without it one cannot fully understand the economic development and the social evolution of the contemporary Catalonia (159).

In view of the unfair working conditions for women, Dolors Monserdà put all her efforts into making her task a social pedagogic mission, with a Catholic orientation and under the principles proposed by Pope Leon XIII's encyclical *Rerum Novarum*.[4] She was involved in the creation of organisations to help working women and to give support for the unionisation of female textile workers: in 1909 she founded *El Patronat per a l'Obrera de l'Agulla* [The Needleworkers' Board] in aid of seamstresses and served as president of *L'Associació Sindical d'Obreres* [The Association of Female Workers' Unions] and of *Lliga de Compradores* [Female Buyers' League]. Monserdà was also one of the first female journalists and feminist theorists in Catalonia. As a journalist, she published articles in different newspapers such as *La Renaixença* and *Premsa Catalana* [Catalan Press], under the guise of a Christian inspiration. Moreover, she wrote for several periodicals aimed at a female readership such as *La Llar* [Home] (1871), *Modas y Labors* [Fashion and Needlework] (1880), *El Figurín Artístico* [The Artistic Sketch] (1882) and *La Ilustración de la Mujer* [The Illustration of Women] (1883), and was an active contributor to two very important publications created during the noughties: *Or y Grana* [Golden and Maroon][5] (1906-1907) and *Feminal* (1907-1917), edited by Carme Karr.

The first publications for a female readership to appear in Catalonia were in Spanish; it was not until *La LLar* came along in 1871 that one can find the first such periodicals published in Catalan. *La Llar* was dedicated to the instruction of women, with theoretical articles about education and science, offering a different and less conventional perspective from that of the more commercial fashion publications. In 1880 Valentí Almirall, editor of *Diari Català*—the first newspaper in Catalan—commissioned Monserdà to create a supplement called *Modas y Labors,* whose main interest was to spread the Catalan language among women using the pretext of fashion. *Modas y Labors* became, after *La LLar*, the second periodical for a female readership written in Catalan and the first about fashion. In the inaugural issue, in the first lines addressed to "A nostras lectoras" ["Our female readers"], Monserdà showed her ambivalence towards fashion and consumerist themes and how she was "willing to utilise the seemingly frivolous medium of the fashion magazine as a vehicle for a nationalist project—in this case the promotion of Catalan" (Davis 2001, 50):

> La moda, eixa regina tan déspota, tan voluble, pero qual jóu acatem ab tan gran sumissió, quals decrets per obehirlos cerquém ab tan ardent interés, sera la missatjera, qu'en alas del desitj de propagar la llengua patria, s'obri pas per son interés y utilitat entre las damas catalanas, quants esforsos sian precisos pera portar notablement a cap la empresa.[6] (Monserdà 1880, 1, cited in Davis 2001, 49)
>
> [Fashion, that despotic queen, so fickle, but whose yoke we obey with great submission and whose decrees we follow with such ardent interest, will be the messenger that, with wings of desire to spread our nation's language, opens its way to the interest and utility of Catalan ladies, whatever efforts may be necessary to succeed in that enterprise.]

Monserdà also wrote articles in other fashion periodicals, *La Ilustración de la Mujer* and *El Figurín Artístico*, which were open to a wider female readership across Spain. In these, unlike the Catalan language project, the emphasis was on the social and educational endeavour of instructing women to be prepared for their everyday life at home and at work.

Moreover, the most important publications where Monserdà contributed were, without a doubt, *Or y Grana* and *Feminal*. The former still drew from the tradition of the *Renaixença* period, whereas the latter had a slightly more modern approach, closer to the principles of *Modernisme*.[7] *Or y Grana* was conceived as a platform for women to raise social issues and to write "with the conviction of women's importance to the education of citizens and the formation of a national consciousness" (Davis 2001, 49). Monserdà was invited to write the opening letter for the inaugural issue of *Or y Grana*, where she clearly underlined her principles and those of the publication:

> Deixeu que la dona, al educar els seus fills en l'amor de Deu y de la familia, hi ajunti'l de la patria, y no temau pel pervindre de Catalunya: aquells fills que en aquests tres amors nodrirán en el fons del seu esperit el noble sentiment del dever, el día de les elecciöns votarán homes que, com ells l'han complert en las urnas, el sápigan complir en el Parlament.

[Allow women, when educating their children in the love of God and the family, to add love of country, and do not be afraid for the future of Catalonia: those children who in these three loves will nurture the noble spirit of duty, on election day will vote for men who, like them, have done their duty at the ballot box and know how to carry it out in Parliament.]

Monserdà's words highlighted the importance of religion, family and education but, above all, the idea of pursing a national consciousness. Therefore, her message took a rather political turn and emphasised the significance of women in the process of achieving this national identity:

> La dona té especials condicions pera ésser verb impulsor en el fertile camp del sentiment. Estimar a Catalunya, y, buscant totas las deus que hi pugan contribuir, treballar pera que tothom l'estimi, fentla digna, forta y gran, heus aquí la tasca més apropiada á las sevas facultats; y aquesta tasca pot cumplirla en la llar, en las sevas relacións socials, y en el sagrat racés de les sevas oracións. (Monserdà 1906, 3-4)

> [Women have special conditions to be the verbal driving force in the fertile field of feeling. To love Catalonia and, looking for sources that can contribute to it, work to make it loved by everyone, to make it worthy, strong and great, here you have the task most suited to her faculties; and she can accomplish this task at home, in her social relationships and in the holy retreat of her prayers.]

As Davis (2001) argues, for Monserdà the domestic sphere was regarded as "the site of transmission of Catalan history and culture" because she saw "national values as ultimately being in the hands of women in their dual roles as mothers/teachers" (49). In Monserdà's writings, women were the nurturers of both family and country, the ones to teach future generations the Catalan values of the work ethic, cultural tradition, and language. In this regard, it is interesting to note that *Or y Grana* was subtitled "Setmanari autonomista per a las donas. Propulsor d'una lliga patriótica de damas" [Autonomous Weekly for Women, Promoter of a Patriotic League for Ladies], which clearly fits with Monserdà's intentions. Even though her ideology was still traditional and within the coordinates of "Home, Art, Country and God", she emphasised the need for the education of women, the fulfilment of their intellectual potential and a greater social agency. Both *Or y Grana* and *Feminal* were committed to the fight for female rights, especially the education of women and professionalisation of jobs done by women. Yet there were a few differences between them: unlike *Or y Grana*, *Feminal* was characterised by a major autonomy in relation to male guardianship, leaving aside the protective attitude of other periodicals for women and giving priority to a more informative agenda with a clear will to fight for the female cause (Cortada 2008, 213). *Feminal*, as a successor to *Or y Grana*, worked towards a major involvement of women in the literary and cultural life of modernist Catalan society. One of its aims was to inform readers about events taking place in Catalonia and Spain, but it also wanted to be open to European trends. Therefore, *Feminal* clearly became the unifying element of middle class Catalan women with intellectual and professional aspirations, as well as the voice of Catalan feminism of the beginning of the 20th century (Cortada 2008, 213).

Although Monserdà shared some of the ideas of *Feminal*, her feminism was more conservative, bourgeois and Christian, as demonstrated by the morality behind her feminist theoretical texts (Carbonell (1997, 19); Charlon (1990, 25); Tayadella (1986, 539)). During the noughties, she published *El feminisme a Catalunya* [Feminism in Catalonia] (1907), which explored the issue of women's syndicates; the aforementioned *Estudi feminista* (1909), which discussed the relation between women and politics, education and religion, issues that she had already introduced in her articles; and *Orientacions per a la dona catalana* [Guidance for the Catalan Woman] (1910), among others. Her social task, as well as her journalistic essays and novels, were part and parcel of her project to establish moral order and harmony in a society that she considered to be chaotic. She believed that economic progress, along with the industrialisation process, had positive aspects for Catalonia, but also some negative consequences for Catalan women of all backgrounds. Her texts above all, as she argued in her *Estudi feminista*, were written to help Catalan women: "per a enlairar-se, per a subvenir a la seva existència, per a cooperar al millorament de la dona obrera i la moralització de la societat" (Monserdà 1909, 81-82) [To take off, to provide for themselves, to cooperate in the improvement of the female worker and the moralisation of society].

Monserdà's novels encapsulated the moral, religious, and political principles predominant among her class and were a continuation of the ideological programme followed in her essays. According to Monserdà, novels were the most suitable genre to "dur a terme una mena d'apostolat moral sobre els seus contemporanis, amb la qual cosa la converteix en un instrument de divulgació ideològica" (Tayadella 1986, 540) [perform a sort of moral apostolate on her contemporaries, thereby becoming an instrument of social disclosure]. Monserdà was well aware of the power of writing to shape consciousness. Her novels were mainly addressed to a female readership and, by setting examples of moral behaviour, written to teach and educate women. Although the solutions she offered were nothing more than "good works" (Charlon 1991, 14), they were a first step towards an understanding of the condition of women for future generations. Monserdà became a chronicler of the city of Barcelona, of a specific time and a specific mentality, featuring settings and problems of the noughties. As Segura (1988) points out, Monserdà's novels are an extraordinary source of information about what women do and feel, and the spaces they occupy. They give valuable information about the colours and shape of dresses, with accurate descriptions of the garments of the women in the Barcelona of the last third of the 19th century and the beginning of the 20th. Moreover, they describe public spaces, streets and squares but, above all, they have "la gran virtut de traspassar les façanes i explicar-nos aquell món silenciat darrera les finestres i els balcons" (Segura 1988, 20) [the great virtue of getting beyond the surface, and telling us about that silenced world behind windows and balconies]. In depicting private spaces, Monserdà was able to denounce the relations of dominance that happened in that realm.

Monserdà represented the duality between public and private spaces of Barcelona's burgeoning textile industry, emphasising the changing role of women, moving from a domestic space to a workplace. Although she wrote during the modernist period, her novelistic style is not considered modern; it shows features of the Realist novel, with Romantic and Costumbrist touches. Alan Yates (1975) argues that the novel suffered in the early days of the 20th century the contradictions of the turn of the century; it was a moment of transition, of historical changes, of man's interior conflict, which produced a fragmentation of the genre and offered diverse provisional solutions. The novel went through a series of transformations that showed it was facing a period of artistic crisis, because it struggled to adapt to a new situation and a new sensibility. Novelists adopted hybrid solutions, which showed patterns and clichés of the 19th century novel as well as some other more modern features. Thus, *Costumisme* [Costumbrism] became a popular hybrid solution during Modernism, half-way between Realist and Romantic patterns, featuring details of a picturesque life, with stereotypical characters and often a nostalgic attitude towards a past on the verge of disappearing due to progress. In the prologue of *La fabricanta*, Monserdà clearly stated from the outset that her novels were going to follow this Customist pattern:

> Junt amb usos i costums que tant nos delectaren, no m'ha estat possible sostreure'm el desig d'ensajar en aquestes planes la reaparició de tipus i fets que la moderna constitució de la indústria i el modo d'ésser de la

> societat actual, fan quasi impossible que tornen a existir. (Monserdà 2008, 60)
>
> [Together with customs and habits that used to please us, I could not resist the wish to show in the following pages the reappearance of types and events that modern industry and present society make impossible to exist ever again.]

It is not then a coincidence that Monserdà gave her two most popular novels of the noughties the subtitle "*novel·la de costums*" [novel of customs], which indicates their sociological approach: *La família Asparó. Novel·la de costums dels nostres temps* [The Asparó Family. A Novel of Customs of Our Time] (1900) and *La Fabricanta. Novel·la de costums barcelonines 1860-1875* [The Female Manufacturer. A Novel of Customs of Barcelona] (1904).

According to Yates (1975), the label *novel·la de costums* seemed to confer modernity to the "antiquades obres" [old-fashioned works] of Dolors Monserdà (51). Yet Yates argues that this modernity was sporadic, "un 'modernisme' superficial" [a superficial 'modernism'], and it was rather a stereotypical realism that felt into a sort of "anodina estàtica" [a dull state] (29), which was most persistent due to its popularity. Moreover, Mas (2008) argues that the style of Monserdà's novels had to pay a high cost due to the moral message that Monserdà imposed on her writings for the sake of being allowed to write, as a woman, in a genre other than poetry. This filter was so strict that it made the ethical prevail over the aesthetic in her works. In doing so, Monserdà broke away from the modern tendencies of the moment and got into her own "sistema endogàmic de creació" [endogamic system of creation] (Mas 2008, xxxi). Therefore, Monserdà's novels were not modern in terms of style, but rather in terms of subject matter, written from a female perspective and to contribute to the development of a feminist consciousness.

Furthermore, Monserdà's novels were rooted in the ambivalent discourse of modernity (Carbonell 1997), in the context of the Catalan society of the turn of the century. On the one hand they showed the dramatic changes of modern society, in terms of economy, industry, art and fashion; and, on the other hand, they showed the contradictions and dualities that confronted modernity. As mentioned earlier when talking about the aesthetic crisis of the novel in Catalonia and elsewhere in Europe, traditional values and modern ideals clashed in a fast-changing society. In Monserdà's novels, a sense of moral balance and harmony prevailed over the values of modernity: "Lo mon camina, lo mon avansa, lo mon progresa... Mes, ¿La transformació del modo de ser íntim, moral, psicològich, ha sigut de tanta transcendència com lo material y extern?" (Monserdà 1900, prologue, cited in Carbonell 1997, 22) [The world walks, progresses... Yet the transformation of the inner, moral and psychological way of being, has it been of such transcendence as the material and external?]. Thus, Monserdà was concerned with the social transformations happening in Catalonia, more specifically in Barcelona where most of her novels were set, but at the same time she was aware of the consequences that these changes could entail, in terms of morality, religiosity and work ethic, as well as the ambiguous position of women in the face of modernity.

According to Carbonell (1997), in the narrative of Monserdà, women become the symbol of these transformations as well as "l'esperança moral davant els aspectes més nocius d'aquests canvis" [the moral hope in the face of the most harmful aspects of these changes] (22). The female image in Monserdà followed two major archetypes, which were in constant opposition and which, with some differences, remind us of the figures of "the angel in the house" and "the monster" that were popularised in Victorian England (Gilbert and Gubar 1979). In Monserdà these two archetypes tend to have characteristics of both Victorian figures and, therefore, they somehow overlap. *La fabricanta*, for example, is built up on the opposition of two female characters who follow these archetypal models. On the one hand, we have Florentina, a woman who falls into the traditional archetype, devoted and submissive, educated to please the husband, like "the angel in the house". The "angel" was passive and powerless, charming, graceful, beautiful, like Florentina: "d'esvelta figura i molt agraciada fesomia, era blanca i rossa" [with a slim figure and gracious features, she was pale and blonde] (Monserdà 2008, 66). But the "angel" was also "a Perfect Lady (...) strong in her inner purity and religiosity, queen in her own realm of the Home" (Showalter 1977, 14), qualities that Florentina seems to lack as she spends too much time worried about her own appearance and reading romance novels by the latest and most popular authors, such as "Fernández y González, Jorge Sand, Dumas, Sue, Víctor Hugo" (Monserdà 2008, 231).

A recurrent theme in Monserdà's novels is the negative influence that some fiction can have on women, as she believed it can foster an attitude of Bovarism[8] towards life, which would lead to an empty and superficial existence. Florentina does not realise what reality entails as she is guided by romantic ideals of love and marriage: "lo meu únic ideal per a casar-me és tenir un marit que estigui ben bojament enamorat de mi" (191) [My only ideal in getting married is to have a husband madly in love with me]. She is not at all presented as an ideal woman but rather as a sort of quixotic figure who lets her life unrealistically be heightened by her readings, experiencing the world through her imagination:

> La Florentina, que amb sa exaltada imaginació, comparà tot seguit la veritat i potència d'aquell amor que per anys havia subsistit callat i sens esperança d'ésser correspost, amb lo dels molts hèroes de novel·la que havia llegit; i, engrandint i poetitsant l'enamorament del seu cosí, a l'arribar a sa casa li faltà temps per a contar-ho a la seva mare amb tots los perfils i relleus que li suggerí el goig d'haver inspirat tan romàntica passió. (156)
>
> [Florentina, with her exalted imagination, compared the truth and power of that love that had survived silent for years without hope of being reciprocated, to that of many heroes of the novels that she had read; and, enlarging and poeticising the love of her cousin, once she arrived home she couldn't wait to tell her mother with all the possible details that the joy of having inspired such romantic passion had suggested.]

Towards the end of the novel, we learn that Florentina appears to be suffering from a nervous disorder, which is a consequence of her passion for fiction and her frustration at not having her romantic ideals fulfilled in the real world. It is interesting to note that this sort of female malady was typical of the Victorian angel's opposite figure, "the monster", or the so-called "madwoman" (Gilbert and Gubar 1979, Showalter 1985).

On the other hand, we have Antonieta, *la fabricanta* [the female manufacturer], a woman who is independent and intelligent, well-educated in humanities, science and arts. Unlike Florentina, Antonieta is balanced, fully aware of her actions and capable of running a family business and a household. Monserdà draws special attention to Antonieta's "qualitats morals" [moral qualities] (Monserdà 2008, 162), essential in order to be a good wife and mother and to educate children under Christian principles and family values of morality and respect. This sense of purity, reinforced also by the exemplary nature of her reading material [*El año cristiano* [The Christian Year], *El libro de las niñas* [The Book of Girls], *La revista popular* [The Popular Journal] and *Las madres católicas* [Catholic Mothers]), brings us back to the idea of the perfect lady, "the angel in the house" that the Victorians so much praised. Unlike "the angel", however, Antonieta is not pretty and charming: she is "morena, baixeta i prima, a no haver estat per sos bons ulls i hermós cabell, (...) se li hauria pogut donar el dictat de lletja" (66) [black haired, short and thin, and if it had not been for her good eyes and nice hair, (...) she would have been categorised as ugly], though she is "extremadament carinyosa i expansiva" (77) [extremely affectionate and expansive], and "sèria, reflexiva i amb sentiments finament delicats" (145) [serious, thoughtful and with fine delicate feelings]. Moreover, she has a most valuable quality, which "the angel" seems to lack: her dedication to non-domestic work. For Antonieta, work is one of the major pleasures in life and at some points her work ethic is even described in erotic terms:

> Amb els ulls brilliants, animat el rostre, alegre el cor (...) examinava les classes de teixits (...) i quan ses mans havien fruit prou estona amb el goig que li produïa el tacte de les peces, es ficava a l'escriptori. (247)
>
> [With shining eyes, joyful face, happy at heart (...) she was examining the types of textiles (...) and when her hands had had enough joy touching the pieces, she went to the desk.]

Davis (2001) states that Antonieta "has all the characteristics of the domestic angel which had become common in didactic fiction by the time Monserdà composed *La fabricanta*: piety, modesty and frugality" (52). Yet if it is true that she has some of these characteristics, she does not have them all, as she lacks the beauty and charm of the Victorian "angel" and she is not passive and submissive to her husband, but rather active and with an opinion of her own. Besides, she has other characteristics which, according to Monserdà, were essential for the improvement of the female condition and were a step towards modernity: education and a will to work. Therefore, the domesticity of the house is extended into the workplace and "the angel in the house" becomes what Davis (2001) calls "the angel at the desk". As Showalter (1977) points out, in relation to the Victorian context, "the first professional activities of Victorian women, as social reformers, nurses, governesses, and novelists, were either based in the home or were extensions of the feminine role as teacher, helper and mother of mankind" (14). Thus, at the beginning of industrialisation, before the factory system, there seemed to be no boundaries between work and home, as they both constituted the same body; husband and wife worked hand in hand for the family business, like Antonieta and her husband. But when small businesses grew and turned into factories, the production system changed as well as the social roles of owner and worker. The boundaries between work and home began to be established, setting up two different bodies with two distinguished spaces: the domestic and the workplace. These changes were bound to affect women from all different backgrounds: women from working classes were having to cross those fixed boundaries, leaving the private space to become part of the public one, mostly out of economic necessity; by contrast, women from more prosperous classes were compelled to stay at home, as is the case of Antonieta when her family becomes wealthy. When the business turns into a factory and with it they move up the social scale, she stops being an active worker, to become a *fabricanta* and, therefore, her new position obliges her to stay at home and be an "angel in the house" again.

The word *fabricanta* itself is a site for complex and fundamental issues for the novel. As the feminine form of *fabricant*, which comes from *fàbrica* [factory], it means not only producer or manufacturer of textiles in this case, but also the owner of a factory. The feminine form is not as commonly used as the masculine, and even less during that period of time when factories used to be ruled by men. Presumably, Monserdà plays with the meaning of *fabricanta*, to refer to both the wife of the owner of a factory and the owner herself. Thus, by using the word, Monserdà addresses all sorts of ironies regarding whether Antonieta is an active worker, the wife of the owner or the actual owner of the factory. Yet, throughout the novel, one comes to realise Antonieta's role goes beyond that of being married to the *fabricant*, as she has a very important function on the production system, first as a worker and then as a manager of the business's capital. The term, therefore, entails the change from the traditional manual system of production to the modern mechanical industry as well as the essential contribution of women in the process of industrialisation.

La fabricanta is a novel of opposites that exemplifies the dualities of modernity: we have two pictures of domesticity and two female characters with two different lifestyles, reading materials and economic systems. Modernity produces diverse reactions in each woman: whereas Florentina is influenced by fashion and new trends from Paris, Antonieta is measured and avoids falling into materialist temptation. On the one hand, Florentina is portrayed as a "female object", a victim of the new times, to the point that her consumerism brings misfortune to her husband, who due to speculation ends up losing his capital in the stock market. Monserdà condemns Florentina's Bovarism and "she mounts a ferocious attack on the woman as an object, the dreams of Prince Charming, the idea that the Love of her Life should be woman's reason for existence and should bring meaning to her life" (Charlon 1991, 12). She also praises Antonieta's wise choice of marriage, one cemented by a common work ethic and business concerns. On the other hand, Antonieta is the "ideal woman" who knows how to control capital, not falling into Florentina's consumerist habits and adopting the two faces of capitalism: production of goods and finance. Antonieta is "the epitome of the energetic, enterprising Catalan woman" (Nash 1996, 49), who exemplifies the role of women as crucial agents in the development of Catalan society. The secret of her success is based on two basic principles: working and saving. Throughout the novel, we see times changing and the effects of industrial progress on the two households: Florentina cannot face reality and her economic excesses end up in failure, whereas Antonieta's good labour and management brings her family prosperity. Although the endings seem different, a final common sense of disillusionment remains on both sides: Florentina's romantic expectations are unfulfilled and Antonieta's work ethic makes her rich but relegates her to stay in the home, as her newly achieved bourgeoisie position dictates. In the end resignation and acceptance of one's fate prevails:

> Lo jubilament, que el seu mateix bon criteri li deia que era tan lògic com just, li feia l'efecte d'una abdicació, ja que aquella passivitat la duia a una continua enyorança d'aquells anys de treball i de privacions de tota mena, però en los que la seva veu i el seu vot eren sempre imprescindibles. (246)
>
> [Retirement, which her good understanding told her was so logical and right, seemed to her an abdication, because that passivity led her to continually miss those years of work and privations of all kinds, when her opinion was always essential.]

Monserdà lived in a time of social, economic, and political upheaval, and in her essays and novels she analysed the consequences of these changes from a female perspective. Her originality lies in sexualising the conflict of modernity and turning it into a problem of the female gender (Carbonell 1997, 26). Likewise, Teresa Pàmies (1992) highlights the idea that the revolutionary aspect of *La fabricanta,* like most of Monserdà's novels, is placing women first, giving them a predominant role in the text, and not treating them as a decorative object blindly accepting the role that tradition imposed upon them (Pàmies 1992, 11, cited in Mas 2008, xxxviii)

Once having analysed Monserdà's professional and personal career, we return to the initial question of whether her "feminism" can be described as such and whether her writings can be categorised as "feminist". When Monserdà started her "feminist" activity in 1869, no one called it "feminism"; it was not until her critical texts *Feminisme a Catalunya* [Feminism in Catalonia] and *Estudi feminista* that the term was used for the first time in the Catalan context. However, it is clear from the study of her works that hers was a conservative, moderate and Catholic type of feminism, different from other feminisms present in Europe. She was aware of their existence and was worried that this "mal feminisme" [bad feminism] (Capmany 2000, 499), as she called it, would have a negative influence on the Catalan society. As Nash (1996) argues,

Monserdà "rejected the lay, foreign cultural basis of British and American feminism and redefined her version of feminism in consonance with Catalan cultural values and Catholic tradition" (48). She was closer to French feminism than to British suffragist feminism, as the former had a great influence from the Catholic Church and the social context in France was similar to that of Catalonia.

Moreover, Maria Aurèlia Capmany in her *El feminisme a Catalunya* (1973),[9] in trying to define the pre-history of feminism in Catalonia in relation to that in Europe, states that in a broader context there were two main types of feminism: conservative and revolutionary. Yet, according to Capmany, there was also a third type of feminism, a sort of cross between the previous two, that she describes in the following terms:

> Feminisme (...) obedient d'una política conservadora, aparentment liberal, decididament reaccionària, profundament antisindicalista que de la mateixa manera que procura exercir la seva influència en els medis obrers (...) descobreix en la dona un agent magnífic de propaganda i d'influència. (Capmany 2000, 496)
>
> [A feminism (...) obedient to a conservative politics, apparently liberal, but in fact decidedly reactionary, profoundly antisyndicalist, which, at the same time that it tries to exercise an influence on the working classes (...), finds in women the perfect agent of influence and political propaganda.]

According to Capmany (ibid.), this was the most suitable feminism for the Catalan society of the turn of the century, and the one Monserdà followed, as it met with a specific class, the Catalan bourgeoisie; with a favourable economic environment, industrial growth; a political group that could promote it, Catalanism; and with a gender that could believe in it, women. This type of feminism was both class- and gender-oriented, with a nationalist approach: it avoided interclass confrontation, and sought to provide education and cultural values to lower-class women. Yet how far can we go in claiming that this social Catalan feminism and more specifically that of Monserdà is a type of feminism? Can demands for women's social rights be termed as feminist intentions?

The debate on feminism has continued from the time Monserdà first introduced the term in Catalonia to the present day. For example, Caterina Albert, writing as Victor Català, draws a line between the notion of "feminisme" and "moviment femení", trying to separate what was happening in Catalonia from the rest of Europe, stating that Catalonia was more inclined to the latter as it was known for its normality, stability and measured approach (Català 1972, 1695, cited in Esteban and Mas 1993, 171). Albert appears to equate "feminisme" with the second type of feminism Capmany mentioned earlier, that happening elsewhere in Europe and with a suffragist demand. Therefore, she did not seem to consider the case of Catalonia as one of feminism but rather of the "women's movement". Yet Nash (1996) does not seem to separate "early Catalan feminism" from "women's movement", as she argues that it was precisely the women's movement which reformulated "other definitions of international feminism" and "openly proceeded to redefine its own version of feminism more in consonance with the ideological convictions of conservative Catalan nationalism and Catholic reform" (Nash 1996, 48). Nash, therefore, considers the Catalan case as one of a very specific and genuine feminism, which is closely related to the women's movement.

However, there are critics, such as Sunyer (1997), who argue that this social conservative feminism cannot be considered as such and women such as Monserdà should not have the label of "feminists". Sunyer believes Monserdà's task should not be regarded as exceptional, as her works promoted a very particular image of women "col·locada en unes tasques específiques i discriminadores per tal d'ofegar les idees i pràctiques autènticament feministes que apuntaven o es practicaven en les organitzacions revolucionaries" (Sunyer 1997, 273) [placed doing very specific and discriminating jobs in order to silence the authentic ideas and practices that were starting or were being practised in revolutionary organisations]. Therefore, Sunyer states that Monserdà should instead be called "antifeminist". While this could be partly true from a modern or more progressive point of view, it is a reductionist argument as, in the same way as Caterina Albert, it goes down to a very specific definition of feminism which links the feminist movement to the political and suffragist struggle. But as we have seen, this was not yet an option for early Catalan feminism, because of its specific historical and political context, and feminism in Catalonia had to wait still a few more years to get into a more revolutionary dimension to demand equality of political rights.

In contraposition with Sunyer (1997), Charlon (1990) states that to face the sexism of the Catalan literary world at the turn of the century and publish with a female name was itself "un acte militant" [a militant act] and those women who performed it were "feministes militants" [militant feminists] (20). If Sunyer's argument was reductionist, however, Charlon's seems too simplistic. As mentioned earlier, feminism was a complex phenomenon with many contradictions. It followed a non-linear development and should not be regarded in terms of preconceived notions of feminism. As Nash (1996) argues, "the history of feminism needs to identify and reconsider the many paths and strategies to women's emancipation" (52). Thus, when approaching feminism in Catalonia one has to bear in mind the many different strands and specificities that the definition of feminism can undertake and have a clear vision of the historical, political and social context in which it occurred.

Whether some call it conservative feminism, Catalan feminism, women's movement, militant feminism or antifeminism, one cannot deny the legacy of Monserdà's works and her contribution to the women's cause. In any of the cases, the feminine or feminist imprint is reflected in those labels critics assigned to Monserdà's work, which demonstrates her writings are considered "feminist" to a great or lesser degree. At a time when women were oppressed, she was brave enough to use her own name and social position to speak up and show what she thought, helping other women of lower social backgrounds. She was a path-breaking figure in the panorama of women writing at the beginning of the 20th century, influencing many female writers of her generation and creating a feminist awareness in the generations that followed. In the letters Caterina Albert exchanged with Dolors Monserdà from 1909 to 1919 and even in the inaugural speech for the *Jocs Florals* of 1917, Albert considered Monserdà "la cap de colla" [the head of the gang] (Esteban and Mas 1993, 189), "estímul i exemple vivent" [a stimulus and a living example] (Català 1972, 1696, cited in Esteban and Mas 1993, 173) and praised the importance of Monserdà's task and legacy to other feminists: "Sense vostés Catalunya no fora pas lo qu'es" (Esteban and Mas 1993, 182-183) [Without you Catalonia would not be what it is]. During her lifetime, Monserdà was appreciated by many of her contemporaries but not all paid her the attention she deserved and her work was sometimes underestimated, as Narcís Oller came to admit to Caterina Albert:

> Don Narcís (...) va dir-me que tenia remordiment de lo que havia fet i de les terrible injustícies que cometem els homes per lleugeresa, per inadvertència, per peresa, per lo que fos. Que havia llegit el darrer llibre que li havia dedicat Da. Dolors i estava absolutament d'acord amb mi; que aquella amiga valia molt més de lo que s'havia cregut ell sempre, de lo que es creia tothom. (Català 1972, 1818)
>
> [Don Narcís (...) told me he felt remorse for what he had done and the terrible injustice of men, out of flippancy, inadvertently, out of laziness or for whatever reason. He had read the latest book that Doña Dolors had signed for him and he absolutely agreed with me: that friend was worth much more than he had always thought, more than anyone believed.]

Monserdà's feminism is still not fully understood today and her texts are sometimes considered by some old-fashioned and of little literary value. There is a lot to be done in the study of her critical texts and novels to show Monserdà's real contribution to the creation and development of a feminist awareness in Catalonia and to confer on her the position that she deserves in the Catalan noughties of the 20th century: that of "la degana del feminisme català" [the doyenne of Catalan feminism] (Capmany 2000, 496; Nash 1996, 48), who succeeded in a world made by men, in the words of Virginia Woolf, in creating "a room of her own" where she could exercise her creative will.

Works Cited

Balcells, A. (1974) *Trabajo industrial y organización obrera en la Cataluña contemporánea 1900-1936.* Barcelona: Editorial Laia

Capmany, M. A. (2000) "El feminisme a Catalunya", in M. A. Capmany, *Obra Completa,* vol.7. Barcelona: Editorial Columna, 487-570

Carbonell, N. (1997) "Feminisme, modernitat i narrativa en Dolors Monserdà", *Lectora: Revista de dones i textualitat*, no. 3, 19-26

Català, V. (1972) *Obres completes.* Barcelona: Editorial Selecta

Charlon, A. (1990) *La condició de la dona en la narrativa femenina catalana (1900-1983).* Barcelona: Edicions 62

—. (1991) "An Overview of Women's Writing in Catalonia", *Catalan Writing*, no. 6, 13-17

Cortada, E. (2008) "Feminisme i educació a principis del segle XX", in *Pedagogia, Política i transformació social (1900-1920): l'educació en el context de la Fundació de l'Institut d'Estudis Catalans.* Barcelona: Societat d'Història de l'Educació dels Països de Llengua Catalana. Institut d'Estudis Catalans, 199-226

Davis, K (2001) "The Angel and the Desk: Reading, Work, and Domesticity in *La fabricanta*", *Catalan Review*, vol. XV, no. 2, 49-59

Esteban, S., Mas, M. C. (1993) "Caterina Albert-Dolors Monserdà: Deu anys de relació epistolar", in *Actes de les primeres jornades d'estudi sobre la vida i l'obra de Caterina Albert i Paradís "Víctor Català".* L'Escala: Publicacions de l'Abadia de Monserrat, 165-201

Gilbert, S. M. and Gubar, S. (1979) *The Madwoman in the Attic: the Woman Writer and the Nineteenth-century Literary Imagination.* London: Yale University Press

Mas, M. C. (2008) "Introducció a *La fabricanta*", in D. Monserdà, *La fabricanta: Novel·la de costums barcelonines (1860-1875).* Barcelona: Horsori Editorial

McRoberts, K. (2001) *Catalonia. Nation Building Without A State.* Toronto: Oxford University Press

Monserdà, D. (1880) "A nostras lectoras". *Modas y Labors* (February 15, 1880) I.

—. (1900) *La família Asparó. Novel·la de costums del nostre temps.* Barcelona: Imprempta de "La Renaixensa"

—. (1904) *La fabricanta: Novel·la de costums barcelonines (1860-1875).* Barcelona: Llibreria de Francesch Puig

—. (1906) "Carta Oberta a la redacció del semanari Or y Grana", *Or y Grana*, no. 1, 3-4

—. (1909) *Estudi feminista. Orientacions per a la dona catalana.* Barcelona: Lluís Gili Llibrer-Editor

—. (2008) *La fabricanta: Novel·la de costums barcelonines (1860-1875).* Barcelona: Horsori Editorial

Nash, M. (1988) "Treball, conflictivitat social i estratègies de resistència: la dona obrera a la Catalunya contemporània", in M. Nash (ed), *Més enllà del silenci: les dones a la història de Catalunya*. Barcelona: Generalitat de Catalunya

—. (1996) "Political Culture, Catalan Nationalism, and the Women's Movement in Early Twentieth-Century Spain", *Women's Studies International Forum,* vol. 19, nos. 1-2, 45-54

Pàmies, T. (1992) "Pròleg a tres veus" in *La fabricanta: Novel·la de costums barcelonines (1860-1875)*. Barcelona: Edicions de l'Eixample

Roca-Pons, J. (1977) *Introduction to Catalan Literature*. Indiana: Indiana University

Segura, I. (1988) "Unes experiències a recuperar", in I. Segura et al., *Literatura de dones: una visió del món*. Barcelona: La Sal, Edicions de les dones, 11-23

Showalter, E. (1977) *A Literature of their Own: British Women Novelists from Brontë to Lessing.* New Jersey: Princeton University Press

—. (1985) *The Female Malady. Women, Madness and English Culture 1830–1980*. New York: Pantheon Books

Sunyer, M (1997) "Feminisme a *L'Avenç*. 1893", in M. Arizeta and M. Palau (eds), *Paraula de Dona. Actes del Col·loqui Dones, Literatura i Mitjans de Comunicació*. Tarragona: Diputació de Tarragona, 273-278

Tayadella, A. (1986) "La novel·la realista: Dolors Monserdà", in M. de Riquer, A. Comas and J. Molas (eds), *Història de la Literatura Catalana*, vol. 7, Barcelona: Ariel

Terry, A. (1972) *A Literary History of Spain. Catalan Literature.* London: Ernest Benn Limited

Yates, A. (1975) *Una generació sense novel·la? La novel·la catalana entre 1900 i 1925*. Barcelona: Edicions 62

Notes

[1] All translations are by the author.

[2] The *Jocs Florals* was a poetry contest with floral prizes. They first took place during medieval times and were restablished during the *Renaixença* in 1859, as a way to promote Catalan language and literature.

[3] The *Confederación Nacional del Trabajo* (CNT) was a Spanish confederation of anarcho-syndicalist labour unions affiliated with the International Workers Association. The CNT was founded in Barcelona in 1910 and participated in the Spanish workers' movement, its efforts being focused on the principles of workers' self-management, federalism, and mutual aid.

[4] Issued on 15th of May 1891, *Rerum Novarum* was an open letter, passed to all Catholic bishops, which addressed the condition of the working classes. The encyclical, entitled "Rights and Duties of Capital and Labour", discussed the mutual duties between labour and obtaining capital, as well as the relationship between government and citizens. *Rerum Novarum* supported the rights of labour to form unions and affirmed the right to private property, rejecting communism and condemning unrestricted capitalism.

[5] *Or y Grana* [Golden and Maroon] refers to the colours of the Catalan flag, *la senyera*, which is red and yellow.

[6] The quotations from the periodicals cited herein do not observe standardised Catalan.

[7] We have to bear in mind that both movements were very close in time and they tended to overlap.

[8] Bovarism is a term derived from Flaubert's *Madame Bovary* (1857), denoting a tendency to escapist daydreaming in which the dreamer loses touch with everyday reality and obligations, imagining himself or herself to be a hero or heroine in a romance. When someone suffers from Bovarism, like Florentina, their fantasised world overlaps with the real world, making them feel frustrated when their romantic ideals are not fulfilled in everyday reality.

[9] Title taken from Monserdà's *Feminisme a Catalunya.*

CHAPTER FIVE

THE PRICE OF BENEFITS: CASH TRANSFERS IN ARGENTINA

SUSANNE MEACHEM

Argentina has experienced economic boom and bust cycles in approximately fifty-year intervals ever since independence from Spain. Each time, a new economic model was introduced and each time, policy makers were convinced that it was the one which finally would lead Argentina to sustained development (Green 1997, 11, 15).

International efforts to seriously tackle poverty and social exclusion in the new millennium have led the governments of over 40 countries worldwide to introduce conditional cash transfer programmes (CCTs) to reduce economic hardship in the poorest households. The Argentine government has brought conditional cash transfer programmes into force which target men and women in different ways. Those directed towards women foster traditional gender narratives and also discourage women from labour and community activism which basically translates into women's withdrawal from the public sphere. Instead of social inclusion, they effect an even more drastic marginalisation of poor women.

Looking back at the past ten years from a gender perspective, it can be said that women have borne the brunt of repeated economic crises, not only in terms of reduced financial resources but also with respect to their increased responsibilities within the family. This chapter looks at the nature and the consequences of these poverty alleviation programmes for women. It will be argued that despite their immediate relief of cash crises, they do not work in favour of women's emancipation, rather they reinforce women's traditional role in society as well as in the family.

At the beginning of the 1990s, the Argentine government enthusiastically implemented the neo-liberal model of economic growth. Praised by the IMF and the World Bank as one of their best clients, Argentina privatised industries, reformed tax structures and liberalised trade and capital flows. To start with, these reforms held the country's hyperinflation at bay but in the long run, the economic restructuring led to social, economic and political instability. A period of economic recession starting in 1998 and slow economic performance on a global scale in the years 2000-2001 further aggravated Argentina's situation until it culminated in the president's repudiation of the country's debt of over $130 billion in December 2001. It was the largest default in history.[1]

The government's response was a restrictive fiscal policy, the impact of which could be noted most rapidly in the closure of small and medium-sized businesses, which had counted a large proportion of women in their workforces. Furthermore, since the peso was artificially kept overvalued, many large corporations moved their factories abroad where wages were considerably lower in relation to the dollar. Again, their employees had been mostly women. The consequence was a slump with high levels of unemployment and increases in poverty. By June 2002 poverty in Argentina had risen to unprecedented levels: 51.4% of the population lived below the poverty line, set at $2 a day and 21.9% in abject poverty, below subsistence level (Lozano 2002, 1).

By 2007, a new social class had emerged: the "new poor". Approximately 10% of the population, or four million Argentines, could then be described as "new poor" in the sense that they were living below or very close to the poverty line, yet had not been historically poor (Curotto 2006, np). What has become clear from a recent study is that approximately 40% of Argentina's *nuevos pobres* [new poor] have regained jobs and consumption patterns equivalent to those that they enjoyed before the 2001 devaluation. Meanwhile, the rest look likely to face the prospect of remaining poor, despite the strong macroeconomic recovery that Argentina has benefited from subsequently. Soaring inflation since the devaluation has kept them in poverty because their salaries have not risen as quickly. This is especially relevant in keeping the new poor impoverished because they generally work in the service sector so tend not to be unionised (Ozarow 2007, 16). A large number of women who had worked in domestic service are particularly affected by this trend.[2]

At the end of the 1990s and the beginning of the new millennium, old and new problems in relation to unemployment had to be addressed. On the one hand, pressures in the labour market had been accumulating across Latin America but in Argentina particularly they reached a level of truly worrying proportions. Unemployment rates climbed into double figures and were still just under ten percent in 2009 (World Bank Database). This increase in unemployment affects male and female heads of households alike and pushes other family members to seek employment, often causing the unemployment of hitherto main bread winners. On the other hand, women have been experiencing greater pressures to enter paid work, often becoming the main provider for the family, within the context of generally high unemployment rates; they additionally have had to accept more unstable jobs, and lower pay.

Plan Jefes y Jefas de Hogar Desocupados

The strong macroeconomic recovery between 2004 and 2008 was short-lived due to the international banking crisis (the forecast for 2009 predicted a negative growth rate of -2.5%); the population living below the poverty line during the same period averages 34.7 percent. Argentina's Gini Index (distribution of family income) lies at 49, which places the country at number 27 of 134 countries (with Namibia at 1 and Sweden at 134). The poorest 10 percent of Argentines share just 1 percent of the country's assets while the richest 10 percent share 35 percent. In other words, the rich have become considerably wealthier during the first decade of the millennium while the poor have become even more deprived.

This presents the classical scenario with potential for popular protest. However, in order to stem the number of people descending into poverty and to avoid social unrest the government launched initiatives that pushed for the adoption of state policies to foster social inclusion by guaranteeing a minimum income to all citizens (Grugel & Riggirozzi 2007, 96). In January 2003, an arrangement was reached with the IMF for a $3 billion loan. Some of this money was subsequently used to implement the Conditional Cash Transfer programme *Plan Jefes y Jefas de Hogar Desocupados* [Plan for Unemployed Male and Female Heads of Household]. Based on the idea of social inclusion, the programme's objective is to provide unemployed heads of households with monthly cash payments. Regardless of sex, the beneficiary has to meet at least one of the following requirements: care for at least one child below the age of eighteen, a disabled child of any age, or a pregnant or incapacitated spouse. Conditional on twenty hours of work per week in productive, communal or educational activities, the recipient receives ARS150[3] per month with the objective of re-training and future re-insertion into formal employment (Ministry for Work, Employment, and Social Security 2002). In 2003, over two million beneficiaries participated in *Plan Jefes y Jefas*; however, with economic recovery, increased job creation and the availability of other social assistance programmes, the number of recipients decreased to just under one million in 2007 (Tabbush 2008, 6).

Based essentially on a Peronist cultural legacy, the idea behind *Plan Jefes* is that participation in the formal labour market constitutes the core element of social inclusion. One of Peronism's main achievements was the political, social, and economic integration of the working classes by including the worker as a crucial component in the construction of Argentine national identity. Perón's appeal to the working classes was due, to a large extent, on his ability to redefine the notion of citizenship within a broader, ultimately social context (James 1993, 16). The symbolic image of the worker was created within an environment of increased industrialisation and based on traditional notions of male-headed household structures and the conventional gendered division of labour. Equally as important was the insertion of the poor into national imagery. In order to assure their social integration a variety of welfare policies were implemented predominantly put into operation by the Eva Perón Foundation (Fraser & Navarro 2003, 114–133). These ideas of "dignity attached to work" and "social justice for all" became entrenched constituents of Argentine working-class culture.

Although Peronist ideology also strongly emphasised the dignity and the important contributions of women's work, they were mainly positioned as loyal supporters of Peronist men and their status as citizens hinged on their traditional roles as social and cultural reproducers of the nation (Molyneux 2000, 58). Both the Nestor Kirchner administration, beginning in 2003, and the presidency of his wife Cristina (2007-) seem to have been supporting this notion of a gendered division of the presentation of *argentinidad* and the designers of the publicity campaign advertising the *Plan Jefes* programme clearly applied these long-established gender images. The pamphlets mostly show pictures of men working in industrial settings. Where images of women are employed, they not only look masculine but also are shown carrying out "male" work. In fact, one of the pictures has to be examined very closely to see that it is actually a woman who is depicted (see Fig. 5-1).

Immediately notable however, is the high percentage of female beneficiaries within the programme: between 2002 and 2007, more than 65 percent were women; also worth noting is the high percentage of women without any formal qualifications (see Fig. 5-2).

At the same time, over 80 percent of participants in the programme are registered as upholding the requirement of twenty hours of work per week. A survey carried out by Tcherneva & Wray in 2005 provides a variety of data with regard to the success of *Plan Jefes* not so much in terms of the overall economic performance of the country as a whole but with regard to the personal improvement of the beneficiaries. So, for example, when asked if satisfied with the programme, over 70 percent replied affirmative; about the same number stated that they felt respected when signing up to the scheme (10–11). Most interesting, however, are the reasons given for the satisfaction, particularly that the opportunity to "do something" ranges far above the cash benefit (see Fig. 5-3). Looking at the type of work undertaken by participants in *Plan Jefes* reveals the gendered aspect of the programme. As can be observed, work in community projects attracts the largest number of beneficiaries (see Fig. 5-4); within this group, women form the majority of those participating in this type of work (Ministry of Work, 2004).

Fig. 5-1: Image of leaflet to promote *Plan Jefes y Jefas* showing a woman working in construction

Source: Ministry of Work, Employment and Social Security

Community projects include communal lunch rooms, educational services, health care and sanitation as well as care for children and the elderly. But it is not only the traditional female character of this sort of work that draws so many women into it; the fact that women with small children only have to work for four to six hours weekly[4] enables them to accommodate childcare and work conditionality at the same time (Pautassi 2004, 69). Even though this pattern continues a division of work according to traditional gender roles, participating women welcome the opportunity to take part in public activities and the interaction with people outside their domestic environment (Garzón de la Roza 2006, 83). This point is especially significant considering that 60 percent of female beneficiaries of *Plan Jefes* are single mothers who particularly welcome the chance to earn, look after their children and nurture social contacts simultaneously (Garzón de la Roza 2006, 84).

Fig. 5-2: Percentage of Beneficiaries according to Sex and Qualifications

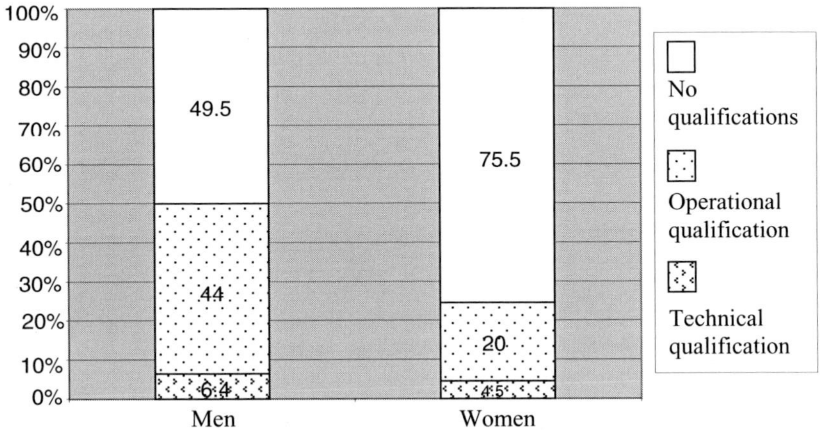

Source: Ministry of Work (2004, 54)

Consequently, the women expand their social horizon while amplifying their network of support. For the majority of women interviewed by Garzón, work in the community is an extension of their domestic chores since it involves childcare, care for the elderly, activities in communal kitchens and so on. However, these activities outside the home have enabled them to display a new sense of authority in front of their children and sometimes also their partners because even though the subsidy is very low, it guarantees women an income every month. This money provides them with a more solid position in the household, and in front of their partners. The women actually decide how to spend the subsidy, and in some cases they even administer the total family income (2006, 132).

Fig. 5-3: Reasons for Satisfaction with the Programme

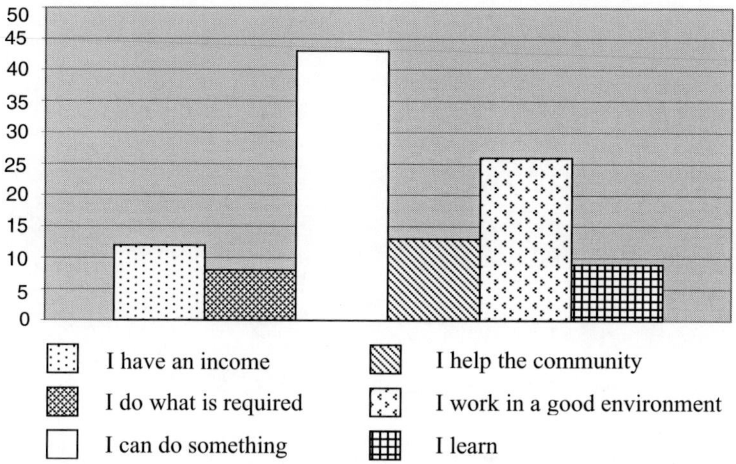

Source: Ministry of Work, Employment and Social Security, from data in Tcherneva & Wray (2005, 11)

Garzón also found that regarding women's self-perception, the experience of being a part of a collective survival project sponsored by the state has generated a personal re-valuing process. The interaction involved in their daily tasks puts them in contact with similar realities, providing them with new opportunities to reconstruct their own images and self-value (2006, 133-134). This is an important, positive effect that the women participating in *Plan Jefes* experience because it strongly contributes to self-recognition and identity formation of the individual women (and men). To identify oneself involves the existence of others whose opinions, expectations and appraisals in respect to the self one internalises (Taylor 1992, 27). These expectations of others are transformed into self-expectations (Gerth & Wright Mills 1964, 80). It could be argued therefore that the work conditionality within *Plan Jefes* is constructive for the development of self-recognition; a crucial element for achieving a sense of personal identity as Honneth points out (1995, 18-23). Seen in this light, the satisfaction with the *Plan Jefes* programme seems to be directly linked with the opportunity to work, to contribute to the well-being of the community, and, in turn, to experience a feeling of appreciation and independency.

Fig. 5-4: Distribution of *Jefes* Workers by Type of Activity %

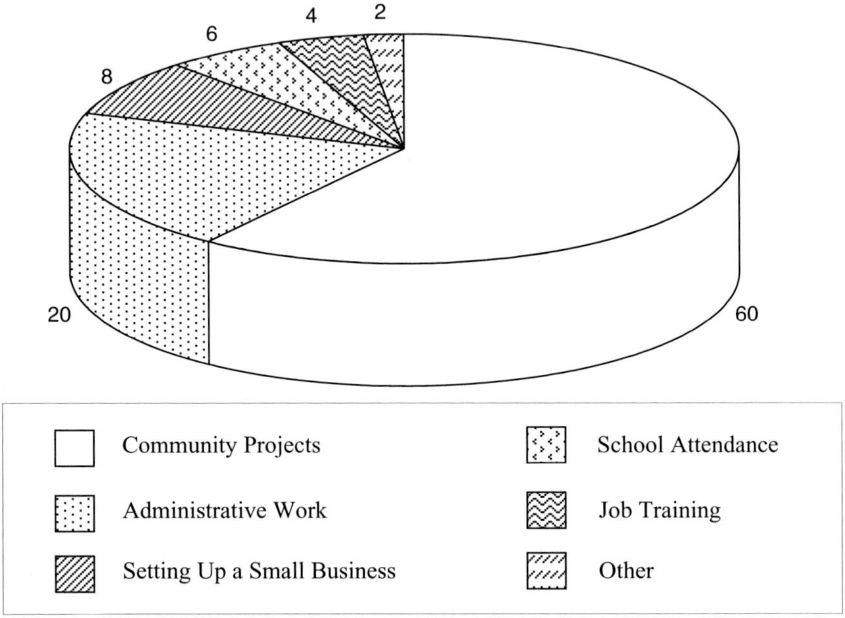

Source: Ministry of Work 2004, 53

However, unlike male heads of households, who use the programme as a temporary safety net and bridge between unemployment and re-insertion into the formal labour market, women tend to remain in the programme for much longer (Tabbush 2008, 10). They are less successful in finding permanent formal employment or in generating alternative income sources. This is due mainly to the fact that women continue to be responsible for the domestic work carried out by women of all ages within the family. It follows that women are much less likely to make the transition from the programme into the formal labour market than male participants because their workload constitutes an obstacle to their access to good quality jobs. Consequently, this non-paid work is a key factor for women's diminished career opportunities, in terms of the income they can expect, and the difficulties they have to face trying to harmonise productive and reproductive tasks (Pautassi 2004, 101-102). Furthermore, with greater economic restrictions and jobless or absent partners their emotionally supporting role within the household has become more difficult (Merlinsky 2008). Labour market crises not only affect the material conditions of households, the unemployment of either the male or female part of a couple often introduces changes in the roles they occupy in the organisation of the reproduction of the family group. To the extent to which these changes collide with traditional gender images, new conflicts emerge within the group (Merlinsky 2008).

Based on the premise that women as an oppressed social group ought to take the struggle for their emancipation into their own hands, feminism has demanded women's organisational, political and ideological autonomy as one of its most essential objectives (D'Atri 2007). In Argentina, women's struggle for independence and recognition in the public sphere goes back to the early nineteenth century and has been articulated through women's movements, feminist or otherwise, throughout constantly changing state formations until today (see for example Carlson 1988).

According to its gender equality policy, the Argentine government has recognised and included female-headed households into the range of beneficiaries. As the programme's title suggests, female concerns were incorporated in its design; however, between conception and implementation these considerations seem to have been lost in the labyrinth of bureaucracy. As Tabbush points out, experts not involved in these high-level discussions, as well as the media, showed genuine surprise at the high numbers of women enrolled in the programme and its progressive feminisation despite the male-targeted publicity campaign (2008, 9).[5] It can be observed that the return to formal employment has been much easier for men than it has been for women (Ministry of Work 2004, 68). Previous experience in construction and manufacturing industries allowed men to either find new jobs in these sectors, as promoted by government advertising, or to use their skills in order to locate informal sources of income, and therefore no longer need to partake in the programme (Pautassi 2004, 82-83).

It can be concluded that while *Jefes y Jefas* represents an improvement for women in terms of income it does not promote gender equality because it reinforces women's historic discrimination with the conditions imposed by the programme (Pautassi 2004, 103). Despite the claims of *Plan Jefes* to address men and women equally, it can be observed that gender perspectives have not been incorporated in the design simply because the programme does not account for women's different needs caused by their position within the family.

Programa Familias por la inclusión social

In 2004, the Argentine government decided to reformulate the cash transfer programmes, supposedly because of the recognition that poverty not only was rising but also because its nature was becoming increasingly heterogeneous, particularly amongst the participants in *Plan Jefes* (Resolution 3380/2009, Ministry of Social Development n.d.). Thus, in this resolution, the government distinguished between two differently problematic social situations which it sought to resolve with different policies:

1) "Las necesidades de las personas que tenían menores dificultades generales para encontrar un trabajo (por su situación familiar, cantidad de hijos que atender, formación, etc.)" [The needs of those persons who had minor general difficulties in finding work (because of their familial situation, number of children to look after, training, etc.)], i.e. men; and
2) "las de las familias en situación de mayor vulnerabilidad social (por número de hijos, niveles de deserción escolar, etc.) con menores posibilidades de acceder o sostenerse mediante el empleo" [(the needs) of families in situations of major social vulnerability (because of the high number of children, lack of education, etc.) with little possibility of finding employment or subsisting through it.] i.e. women.

According to this notion of having to distinguish between poor men and poor women, the alternative conditional cash transfer programme *Programa Familias por la Inclusión Social* [Programme for the Social Inclusion of Families] was created. Since its initial stages until the present, the number of its participants has almost tripled (see Fig. 5-5). *Familias* is partly funded by the Inter-American Development Bank and is directed towards poor women with one or more children. Even though its title suggests "the family" as beneficiary, subscription to the programme is the responsibility of the woman, who must be the mother, unless she does not live in the family home, is physically or mentally disabled, or there are any other evidenced reasons for her inability to register. Only in these cases are fathers allowed to sign up. Quite clearly, men are not meant to be *Programa Familias* recipients (Campos et al. 2007, 17).

The payments awarded range from a minimum of ARS155 per child or pregnant woman to ARS380 for six children or a maximum of ARS380 per family (Article nine of Resolution 3380/2009, Ministry of Social Development n.d.). Article five of the same document stipulates that the recipients of these funds must not participate in any other cash transfer programmes, unemployment benefits, or tax exempt pensions. Furthermore, they must not hold a job in formal employment and their income must not exceed the official minimum wage. However, the official minimum wage of ARS1500 only applies for people in formal employment since employers within the informal sectors do not usually feel obliged to pay the minimum. Approximately two million people are currently working in this sector, most of them women (see Chant and Pedwell 2008).

Fig. 5-5: Number of Participants in *Plan Familias*

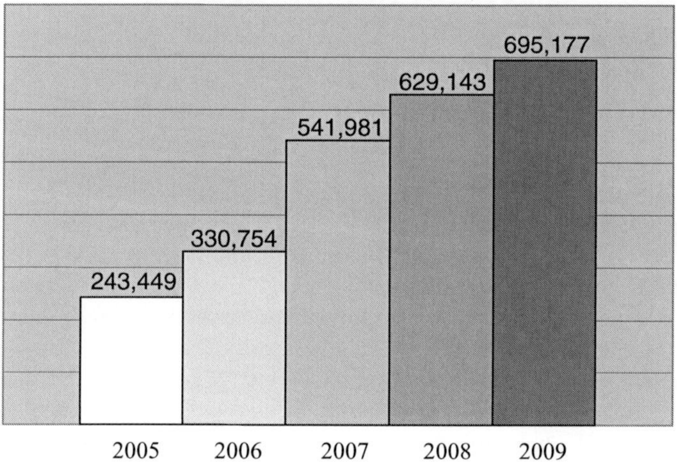

Source: Ministry of Social Development n.d.

As with *Plan Jefes*, the recipients of *Programa Familias* are required to meet certain demands; but unlike *Plan Jefes*, which is conditional on part-time work, the beneficiaries of *Familias* must demonstrate their commitment to healthcare and education within their families. Periodically and according to children's age, vaccination certificates have to be presented; every three months, the beneficiary has to provide evidence for their children's regular school attendance.[6] Without a doubt, this presents a step in the right direction for the wellbeing of children; for the women, however, the *Familias* programme drastically reduces women's chances to enter the formal labour market while at the same time leaving them short of funds. Even the maximum payment of ARS380 is nowhere near enough to survive, let alone with six or more children; additional income, however, is hard to come by. In any case, with a family of this size both formal and informal work seems hardly an option apart from the former's incompatibility with the programme. This lack of sufficient income either forces women to depend on a wage earning partner or on extended family to assist with childcare. It could be argued therefore, that the programme in its current form, rather than providing a way out of poverty, traps certain groups of women within it. As Molyneux notes, subsidies as low as this normalise poverty rather than seriously tackle it. Instead of presenting an effort to socially include the poorer sectors, further marginalisation and fragmentation occurs (2009, 63).

Admittedly, *Plan Jefes* has its negative features regarding women's return to formal work, not least because it mostly limits their occupations to traditional female tasks and does not solve the problem of women's double and triple workloads. However, the majority of recipients questioned welcome the combination of an opportunity to work and the safety net of the cash transfer. *Programa Familias*, on the other hand, once more relegates women to the domestic sphere and reinforces their image as an exclusively reproductive one, namely their maternal capacities.

There is no doubt that in the first decade of the new millennium Argentina has experienced dramatic social changes, unfortunately in a negative way. The number of poor and indigent people has risen drastically mostly due to the mismanagement of the country's wealth by subsequent governments. In this context of uneven development and social change the politicisation of gender, the family and the position of women become increasingly apparent. Because of their reproductive capacity, women have traditionally been seen as the transmitters of group values and traditions, and as agents of socialisation of the young. It has been woman as wife and mother—not woman as citizen, student, worker, and so forth—who is ideologically constructed in the discourses and programmes of social assistance and policy. Motherhood is an identity that can be negotiated and rearticulated within particular social and economic circumstances. It presents a contested identity where new images of motherhood emerge within particular discourses in a climate of social and economic change (Woodward 1997, 281-2). In this current economic crisis, it does not seem to be a coincidence therefore, that *Plan Familias* is directed specifically towards mothers. The government's emphasis on directing separate poverty-alleviating policies towards women is grounded on the idea that investing in women is one of the most efficient routes to ensuring all-round development benefits. It is well documented that targeting women specifically is a cost-effective way to stretch meagre resources (Molyneux 2006, 436).

Papanek observes that there is a paradox here that places women in a double bind: many societies make women the carriers of tradition or the centre of the family, insisting that, especially during periods of rapid social change, their actions and appearance should alter less quickly than that of men, or should not be seen to change at all. Demands for family stability and an unchanging role for women may be especially strong when the processes of change are perceived as threatening existing patterns of life (1994, 47). During a prolonged economic crisis like the Argentine one, long established cultural and social patterns may very well come to be perceived as being threatened in terms of changing roles within society, increased competition for jobs and greater workloads. It could be argued here that in order to maintain the traditional image of the male provider for the family and in agreement with Peronist ideology, the Argentine state is trying to remove women from the employment-seeking part of the population in order for men to occupy already limited job opportunities. It has to be remembered that historically, women have constituted a massive reserve army of labour in times of economic boom while being relegated back to the home during economic bust (Hollander 1977, 180). Repetition of this strategy is clearly visible with the implementation of *Plan Familias.* The double bind of greater exposure to social and personal change on the one hand and the responsibility for maintaining and reproducing group stability on the other seems to contribute to women's difficulties. Since fathers are hardly encouraged to ensure children's health and education the nation's future well-being appears to rest solely on women's shoulders while keeping the nation's poverty levels at bay seems to depend on the "quality" of mothers. The "good" ones who demonstrate a willingness to self-sacrifice are worthy of a handout.

Historically, working-class and women's movements have been a salient feature in Argentine politics since the nineteenth century. Additionally, the latter came to include motherhood movements, especially during the last military dictatorship. The strength of political motherhood[7] as an evolving social movement has been to introduce new human qualities into the public sphere and to define them as equally foundational in the legitimisation of the political community. However, even though women's role as mothers in relation to social change has been a frequently discussed issue in Argentina, women who organised in women's movements did not do so specifically *as* mothers.[8] Nevertheless, they joined political organisations as workers and employees, mainly in order to achieve higher pay and better working conditions. Having said that, even in this early participation in social movements, women took advantage of the state's emphasis on their roles as mothers precisely because existing policies, or the lack of them, made this role increasingly difficult. As Sara Ruddick has observed, "That maternal love, pleasure in reproductive powers, and a sense of maternal competence survive in a patriarchal society where women are routinely derogated, makes one wonder at the further possibilities for maternal happiness in decent societies" (1980, 344). Policies like *Familias* undoubtedly turn motherhood into a questionable choice of life since the inescapable poverty that comes with the programme prohibits experiencing the pleasure of being a mother in the sense that Ruddick also talks about in her article. With the introduction of social assistance programmes like *Familias*, this traditionally entrenched tendency of Argentine women to use their role as mothers in order to effect social change becomes severely shaken. One woman interviewed by Tabbush confirms this; she says: "I am waiting for their promise, social inclusion; I want that…However, for me, it is all a con, a way of keeping the poor quiet, still, so that they do not rebel against the state, so that they do not cause trouble…" (2007, 8).

One cannot escape this logic: by restricting women's activities to child-rearing in their homes, the chances for them to join a political movement are slim. Historically, women whose work is confined to the wife/mother role within the family have been very difficult to organise politically (Hollander 1977, 180). This difficulty arises from the fact that these women are isolated from other women who perform the same tasks.

Despite the state's claim to encourage women's return to formal work, it is covertly undermined. Talking about female work in the nineteenth century, Barranco has noted that deep down, nobody really liked women's pursuit of public activity; nobody really wanted them to leave their homes and go to work. There were not many sources that showed a great initiative by anybody to facilitate women's entry into the labour market (1997). It is quite obvious that not much has changed since then, not least because as Fiszbein et al. (2003) have noted, the government has failed to reverse certain structural changes in the labour market effected during the 1990s. Consequently, the "quality" of jobs has deteriorated significantly since the 2001 crisis. Particularly jobs in the service sector, that is, those mostly occupied by women, are non-unionised, low paid, and lack standard benefits associated with formal employment.

Nari notes that mothers have been a political object of the state which, beyond its specific goals, has allowed the political classes to impose or reinforce a female identity linked to motherhood. Furthermore, these questions became the subject of frequent public debate because they have been constructed as issues that are central to the future of society and the nation. Motherhood became politicised and on this public/political stage it has been re-introduced from different perspectives and for different reasons (2004, 150). The most significant politics of motherhood have focused on the implementation of new legislation and justifications for such actions abounded—from claiming rights that legitimately have been considered as pertaining to women to the notion that public health, particularly that of future citizens, is a duty of the state. In this sense, women have come to be perceived as the nation's reproductive asset. Their persons and bodies practically have ceased to belong to them; not they themselves but society decides over them (2004, 151).

Throughout Latin America, motherhood forms a core element in the construction of female imagery and women's devotion to the needs of other family members, particularly their children, is widely regarded as the most prominent maternal obligation. Programmes like *Familias* clearly seem to perpetuate this notion. It is only the children who are supposed to benefit from the cash transfer while the mothers are perceived as a mere tool to provide the state with a healthier and more educated population. In this sense, the state counts on the culturally entrenched image of the mother as a selfless being, particularly considering that women are central to the programme's functioning while the monthly payments are relatively low (Molyneux 2007, 35). In Nicaragua, as Bradshaw and Quirós Víquez have observed, supervisors of a similar cash transfer programme have deemed it a misuse of resources if adult family members consume any of the food purchased with programme money (2008, 835). Molyneux has argued that the programmes' targeting some needs over others even at household level reinforces social inequalities within the family itself and neglects the common-sense notion that children are more likely to be healthy and well educated if their mothers are too (2009, 64). What maternalist assistance programmes do reinforce, however, is the culturally constructed image of the altruistic, self-sacrificing mother. Exploring "The Construction of the Myth of Survival", González de la Rocha (2007, 47) finds that it has become a common notion amongst policy makers that the poor work harder, help each other, and eat less in order to make ends meet. It could be argued that, here, the myth of motherly altruism has been combined with the myth of the special survival skills of the poor in order to render the programme cost effective. At the same time, this practice has translated into a generalised bid to alleviate poverty almost exclusively *through* women which leads to the increasingly common situation where instead of development working *for* women, women end up working *for* development (Chant 2008, 183, Chant's italics). The construct of the "feminisation of poverty" has been instrumental in lending increased attention to gender within international discourses of poverty. However, a re-orientation of this concept seems necessary in order to appropriately reflect trends in gendered disadvantages of the poor and to highlight the growing responsibilities and obligations women bear in household survival. Even though, with respect to income, the difference in numbers between poor women and poor men is merely marginal in Argentina[9] it has to be pointed out that apart from lacking sufficient income, women suffer poverty in a more multifaceted way than men. So, for example, while many male programme participants feel free to keep the payments for themselves, women are traditionally expected to be much more selfless when it comes to using the money for the family (Chant 2008, 186).

It is not surprising that the Argentine government is trying to avert social upheaval at all costs. After all, social and political mobilisation of large sectors has shown the ability to topple two presidents in the last two decades: Alfonsín in 1989 and De la Rua in 2001 (see Cavarozzi 2004). Particularly the *Piquetero* movement,[10] emerging in the late 1990s, is interesting in the context of this paper. Unlike the social movements in the 1960s and 1970s who identified with particular political parties and social classes, the *Piqueteros* were characterised by a relative blurring of class frontiers, not in terms of a multiclass alliance but through ad hoc convergence and mutual reinforcement (Armony & Armony 2005, 36). Most protesters, regardless of social origin, used universalistic notions such as "citizen", "person", or even "human being", and they demanded to be "seen", to be "heard", and to be "recognised".

This relative class harmony is effectively undermined by the cash transfer programmes, particularly *Familias,* since they not only silence and isolate the recipients but they also make them appear as idle spenders at the cost of the tax-payer. After all, social movements have evolved within social sectors that have questioned the social order based on injustice, exclusion and inequality. They have flourished amongst individuals who recognise their condition to be typical of an entire group of people, thereby helping to establish the cultural conditions for resistance and revolt (Honneth 1995, 138). With the conditionality of the cash transfers the participants' traditional support networks which provided a space for communication with the like-minded in community projects or the workplace have become disrupted and the long established disposition of Argentines to voice their discontent in protest has diminished to the same extent as society has become more fragmented. The notions of social rights, dignity in work, and universal welfare traditionally associated with the concept of citizenship become increasingly separated. Instead of social inclusion, further marginalisation occurs. Even though the *Familias* programme does not preclude voluntary involvement in community projects as such, apart from the time issue, the satisfaction of carrying out paid work and the dignity associated with it are clearly absent if the programme participant becomes a mere recipient of hand-outs.

Thirty years ago, poverty was measured by the unsatisfied basic necessities of people in terms of adequate housing, access to infrastructure, education, and so forth. Poverty in terms of income was not that relevant. Now, as a consequence of the re-structuring programmes during the 1990s, poverty is defined solely by lack of income. However, as Feijoó (2003) points out, poverty is multidimensional. Families can lack sufficient income but still have access to public services, for example; they can be integrated or excluded; they can experience resilience to cope with restrictions or they can fall into passivity and despair. One major symptom of poverty is the feeling of disempowerment by those who suffer poverty. None of these facets of poverty can be measured in monetary terms. In this sense, "feminisation of poverty" occurs because it is not only women's share of poverty that has to be highlighted but also their burden of dealing with it which is arguably as burdensome and exploitative as suffering poverty. Instead of experiencing empowerment within the household through cash transfers, back-to-work initiatives and increased educational provisions, women often end up with more obligations as their fields of activity multiply (Chant 2008, 188, and Molyneux 2009, 51).

Conclusion

However well-intentioned cash transfer programmes like *Jefes* or *Familias* might be in terms of poverty alleviation, they do not present meaningful tools to further women's emancipation and personal development. It is simply not enough to incorporate a female element into the title of a social assistance programme and automatically claim that it works for both sexes in the same way. As a back-to-work initiative, *Plan Jefes y Jefas*, for example, has been much more successful for men than it has been for women; while it has been a mechanism for men to move onwards and upwards, women have experienced more difficulties in taking advantage of the programme's concept over and above the immediate financial benefit.

Plan Familias practically rules out women's participation in the formal labour market altogether. Designed exclusively for mothers, it fosters traditional gender narratives and imagery and, at the same time, places success or failure of social reproduction firmly on women's shoulders.

Familias effectively excuses men from taking part in childcare, emotionally and financially. Instead of empowering women in terms of financial independence and encouraging their capabilities to re-negotiate their position within the household and society in general, it traps them and their children in a state of "almost-poverty" at the outer margins of the social order.

The state, instead of re-distributing resources in order to create employment and improve social services for the poor, has unburdened itself from the responsibility to provide nationwide human development and has placed this task onto the shoulders of poor women; arguably for free, since it is not an explicit aim of the cash transfer programmes to meet the women's/mothers' needs on an equal level with that of their children. Moreover, for obtaining these few hundred pesos a month they have lost the fundamental markers of citizenship and *argentinidad*, established since the 1940s, like job opportunities, the ensuing dignity as a person, as well as universal welfare.

Women's participation in protests and movements for change has shown that they were mobilised not only as women but also as mothers, workers, citizens, and of course, as a combination of all of the above. Nevertheless, more often than not, they have been motivated by the wish to fulfil rather than subvert traditional gender roles. Women have demanded recognition, first and foremost, in their roles as wives and mothers; they have believed that these roles legitimise their sense of injustice and outrage, not only in the face of political oppression and the violation of human rights but also of economic policies and the lack of adequate labour laws, all of which have added to difficulties in carrying out this role.

Argentina's women's movements have historically been exceptional in their resilience and resourcefulness to make their voices heard. The motherhood movements have been particularly outstanding in challenging the state and its policies towards women. The large number of women participating in the cash transfer programmes could be the basis for a new activism that re-conceptualises the spaces of womanhood, motherhood and citizenship within financial crises management policies. In this sense, reflecting on these first ten years of the millennium, it seems that little progress has been made in providing modern, broadly acceptable approaches to alleviate poverty, particularly of women and children. Hopefully, the urgent need for appropriate strategies will be met in the near future.

Works Cited

Armony, A. C. & Armony, V. (2005) "Indictments, Myths, and Citizen Mobilization in Argentina: A Discourse Analysis", *Latin American Politics and Society*, vol. 47, no. 4, 27-54.

Barranco, D. (1997) *Presencia de la mujer en las luchas sociales Argentinas del principio de siglo*, Ministry for Interior Affairs. Available from: http://www.mininterior.gov.ar/agn/barrancos.pdf (accessed 17 January 2007).

Bradshaw, S. & Quirós Víquez, A. (2008) "Women Beneficiaries or Women Bearing the Cost? A Gendered Analysis of the *Red de Protección Social* in Nicaragua", *Development and Change,* vol. 39, no. 5, 823–844.

Buvinic, M. (2009) "Profile of Women in Latin America", Department for Gender and Development, World Bank. Available from: http://www.globewomen.org/summit/2009/Speeches/Web%20PDFs/Myra%20Buvinic-Eng.pdf (accessed 2 August 2010).

Cavarozzi, M. (2004) "Cómo una democracia de libro de texto desembocó en un régimen de partido único…es el peronismo, estúpido", *Política*, University of Chile, no. 42, 207-220.

Campos, L. E., Faur, E. & Pautassi, L. C. (2007) *Programa Familias por la inclusión social: Entre el discurso de derechos y la práctica asistencial.* Buenos Aires: Centro de Estudios Legales y Sociales (CELS).

Carlson, M. (1988) *¡Feminismo! The Women's Movement in Argentina from its Beginnings to Eva Perón*. Chicago, IL: Academy Chicago.

CEPALSTAT. Available from: http://websie.eclac.cl/sisgen/ConsultaIntegrada.asp (accessed 17 August 2010).

Chant, S. (2008) "'The Feminisation of Poverty' and the 'Feminisation' of Anti-Poverty Programmes: Room for Revision?", *Journal of Development Studies*, vol. 44, no. 2, 165-197.

Chant, S. & Pedwell, C. (2008) *Women, Gender and the Informal Economy: An Assessment of ILO Research and Suggested Ways Forward*, Discussion Paper, International Labour Office. Geneva: International Labour Organization. Available from: http://www.ilo.org/wcmsp5/groups/public/@dgreports/@dcomm/documents/publication/wcms_091228.pdf (accessed 12 August 2010).

Curotto, D. (2006) "El país crece con ganadores y perdedores – Argentina", *La Prensa Digital*, 17 April. Available from:

www.uca.edu.ar/uca/common/grupo32/files/06-04-17-romanza.doc (accessed 10 March 2010).

D'Atri, A. (2007) "Nuevas encrucijadas para el feminismo del siglo XXI". Available from: http://www.pyr.org.ar/spip.php?article12 (accessed 2 February 2010).

Feijoó, M. C. (2003) "La pobreza, según se mida", *Diario El Clarín*, 21 February. Available from: http://edant.clarin.com/diario/2003/02/21/o-02101.htm (accessed 9 August 2010).

Fiszbein, A., Giogvagnoli, P. I. & Adúriz, I. (2003) "The Argentine crisis and its impact on household welfare", *CEPAL Review* no. 79, 143-158.

Fraser, N. & Navarro, M. (2003) *Evita: The Real Lives of Eva Perón*. London: André Deutsch.

Garzón de la Roza, G. (2006) *Continued Struggle for Survival: How Plan Jefes y Jefas Affected Poor Women's Lives in Greater Buenos Aires, 2002-2005,* Master's Thesis, Washington DC, Georgetown University.

Gerth, H. & Wright Mills, C. (1964) *Character and Social Structure*. New York: Harbinger Books.

González de la Rocha, M. (2007) "The Construction of the Myth of Survival", *Development and Change*, vol. 38, no. 1, 45-66.

Green, D. (1997) *Faces of Latin America*. London: Latin American Bureau.

Grugel, J. & Riggirozi, M. P. (2007) "The Return of the State in Argentina", *International Affairs*, vol. 83, no. 1, 87-107.

Hollander, N. (1977) "Women Workers and the Class Struggle", *Latin American Perspectives*, vol. 4, nos. 1/2, 180–193.

Honneth, A. (1995) *The Struggle for Recognition: The Moral Grammar of Social Conflict.* Cambridge: Polity Press.

Instituto Nacional de Estadística y Censos de la República Argentina. "Valores mensuales de la Canasta Básica de Alimentos (CBA) y de la Canasta Básica Total (CBT) para el adulto equivalente en el aglomerado Gran Buenos Aires, desde septiembre 2000 en adelante", Ministry for Economy and Public Finances. Available from: http://www.indec.mecon.ar/nuevaweb/cuadros/74/sh-cba2.xls (accessed 15 June 2012).

James, D. (1993) *Resistance and Integration: Peronism and the Argentine Working Class, 1946-1976.* Cambridge: Cambridge University Press.

Lacunza, S. (2010) "The Gender Roots of Labour Inequality", IPS – Inter Press Service, 5 August. Available from: http://ipsnews.net/news.asp?idnews=52389 (accessed 16 August 2010).

Lozano, C. (2002) *Catástrofe social en Argentina: La situación a junio del 2002*. Buenos Aires: Instituto de Estudios y Formación de la Central de los Trabajadores Argentinos. Available from: http://168.96.200.17/ar/libros/argentina/iefcta/lozano2.rtf (accessed 9 February 2010).

Merlinsky, M. G. (2008) "Desocupación y crisis en las imágenes del género", XXII International Congress of the Latin American Studies Association, Miami, Florida. Available from: http://lasa.international.pitt.edu/Lasa2000/Merlinsky.PDF (accessed 10 April 2010).

Ministry of Social Development, Argentina. (n.d.) "Programa Familias por la Inclusión Social". Available from: http://www.desarrollosocial.gov.ar/Planes/PF/resena.asp (accessed 16 February 2010).

Ministry of Work, Employment, and Social Security, Argentina. (2002) Decreto No. 565/02 (Programa Jefes de Hogar). Available from: http://www.trabajo.gov.ar/programas/sociales/jefes/files/legislacion/decretos/decreto0565.pdf (accessed 9 February 2010).

—. (2004) "Segunda Evaluación del Programa Jefes del Hogar: Resultados de la encuesta a beneficiarios", Subsecretaría de Programación Técnica y Estudios Laborales. Available from: http://www.trabajo.gov.ar/downloads/biblioteca_estadisticas/toe1_04encuesta.pdf (accessed 8 August 2010).

Molyneux, M. (2000) "Twentieth Century State Formations in Latin America" in M. Molyneux & E. Dore (eds), *Hidden Histories of Gender and the State in Latin America*, Durham & London: Duke University Press, 33–84.

—. (2006) "Mothers at the Service of the New Poverty Agenda: Progresa/Oportunidades, Mexico's Conditional Transfer Programme", *Social Policy and Administration*, vol. 40, no. 4, 425-449.

—. (2007) *Change and Continuity in Social Protection in Latin America: Mothers at the Service of the State?*, United Nations Research Institute for Social Development. Available from: http://www.unrisd.org/unrisd/website/document.nsf/462fc27bd1fce00880256b4a0060d2af/bf80e0a84be41896c12573240033c541/$FILE/Molyneux-paper.pdf (accessed 9 February 2010).

—. (2009) "Conditional Cash Transfers: A 'Pathway to Women's Empowerment'?", Pathways Working Paper 5, Pathways of Women's Empowerment, IDS, Sussex. Available from: http://www.dfid.gov.uk/r4d/PDF/Outputs/WomenEmp/PathwaysWP5-website.pdf.

Nari, M. A. (2004) *Políticas de maternidad y maternalismo político.* Buenos Aires: Editorial Biblos.

Ozarow, D. (2007) *Argentina's Nuevos Pobres since the Corralito: From Despair to Adapting to Downward Mobility*, Thesis (MSc), Institute for the Study of the Americas, University of London.

Papanek, H. (1994) "The Ideal Woman and the Ideal Society: Control and Autonomy in the Construction of Identity", in V. M. Moghadam (ed.), *Identity Politics and Women: Cultural Reassertions and Feminisms in International Perspective*, Boulder, San Francisco, Oxford: Westview Press, 42–76.

Pautassi, L. C. (2004) "Beneficios y beneficiarias: análisis del programa Jefes y Jefas de Hogar Desocupados de Argentina", in M. E. Valenzuela (ed.), *Políticas de empleo para superar la pobreza*, Santiago de Chile: Oficina Internacional del Trabajo, 59-110. Available from: http://www.oitchile.cl/pdf/publicaciones/igu/igu019.pdf (accessed 13 April 2010).

Rock, D. (2002) "Racking Argentina", *New Left Review*, no. 17, 55-86.

Ruddick, S., (1980), "Maternal Thinking", *Feminist Studies*, vol. 6, no. 2, 342-367.

Schirmer, J. (1993) "The Seeking of Truth and the Gendering of Consciousness: The CoMadres of El Salvador and the CONAVIGUA widows of Guatemala", in Radcliffe, S. A. & Westwood, S. (eds), *"Viva": Women and Popular Protest in Latin America*, London & New York: Routledge, 30-64.

Sosa, C. I. & Molina, K. B. (2009) "Mujeres Piqueteras: Identidades desde la acción colectiva", Universidad Nacional de Catamarca. Available from: http://www.iigg.fsoc.uba.ar/jovenes_investigadores/4jornadasjovenes/EJES/Eje%201%20Identidades%20Alteridades/Ponencias/SOSA,%20Claudia%20y%20otros.pdf (accessed 9 August 2010).

Stephen, L. (2001) "Gender, Citizenship, and the Politics of Identity", in "Power, Policy and Neoliberalism", special issue, *Latin American Perspectives*, vol. 28, no. 6, 54-69.

Tabbush, C. (2008) *Contesting Gender Narratives in Development Policies: Women and Conditional Cash Transfers in Argentina*, Women in International Development Working Paper 292, East Lansing, MI: Women and International Development, Center for Gender in Global Context, Michigan State University.

Taylor, C. (1992) "The Politics of Recognition", in A. Gutmann (ed.), *Multiculturalism and "The Politics of Recognition"*, Princeton, NJ: Princeton University Press, 25–73.

Taylor, D. (1997) *Disappearing Acts: Spectacles of Gender and Nationalism in Argentina's "Dirty War"*. Durham, NC: Duke University Press.

Tcherneva, P. & Wray, L. R. (2005) "Gender and the Job Guarantee: The impact of Argentina's *Jefes* program on female heads of poor households", Working Paper 50, Kansas City, MO: Centre for Full Employment and Price Stability (C-FEPS), University of Missouri.

Vassallo, M. (2002) "Existir contra el aniquilamiento: Los piqueteros", *Le Monde diplomatique*, no. 38. Available from : http://www.insumisos.com/diplo/NODE/3211.HTM (accessed 10 August 2010).

Woodward, K., ed. (1997) *Identity and Difference*. London: Sage Publications.

World Bank Database. Entry for "Unemployment, total (% of total labor force)". Available from: http://data.worldbank.org/indicator/SL.UEM.TOTL.ZS?order=wbapi_data_value_2009+wbapi_data_value&sort=asc (accessed 18 August 2010).

Notes

[1] For a detailed analysis of the long-term social and political effects of Argentina's default and the most spectacular failure of neo-liberalism up until then see David Rock (2002).

[2] 18 percent of all female employment is concentrated in domestic services. Nine out of ten working mothers in Argentina are employed in private homes. Only about 45 percent of domestic workers are in formal employment and only 20 percent of these are also registered in the social security system leaving the rest without any health care or pension rights. The domestic sector is regulated in a way that grants domestic workers only half the labour rights that are legally enjoyed by all other workers (Lacunza 2010).

[3] According to the National Institute for Statistics, the "canasta básica alimentaria" [basic food basket] which measures the abject poverty line was ARS166.86 per person per month in February 2010. This amount is based on the calorie intake and nutritional content necessary to stay healthy. The "canasta básica total" [total basic basket] which measures the poverty line and includes non-food items was ARS366.12 at the same time (Instituto Nacional de Estadística, "Valores mensuales").

[4] In order to enable mothers of small children to balance childcare and their insertion into the labour market, their working hours are limited to four to six hours a week (Pautassi 2004, 69).

[5] Similarly, the Peruvian PAIT (*programa de apoyo de ingreso temporal* [Programme for Temporary Income Support]) created in the 1980s counted 85 percent female participation. Within the Chilean PEM (*programa de empleo mínimo* [Minimum Employment Programme]) in the 1970s, 73 percent were women (Buvinic 2009).
[6] For an extensive analysis and description of *Programa Familias* see Campos et al. 2007.
[7] This term was coined by Jennifer Schirmer in her article on "motherist" movements in El Salvador and Guatemala (1993).
[8] Not until the late 1970s, when the Madres de la Plaza de Mayo took up their protests, would such a strategy emerge. Diana Taylor argues in relation to the Madres that "the mothers movement did not begin when the individual mothers became acquainted in their search for their children; it originated when the women consciously decided to protest and agitate *as* mothers. That *as* marks the conceptual distance between the essentialist notion of motherhood attributed to the Madres and the self-conscious manipulation of the maternal role—understood as performative—that makes the movement the powerful and intensely dramatic spectacle that it is" (1997, 194, cited in Stephen 2001, 59).
[9] See CEPALSTAT, Estadísticas de género: Género y pobreza.
[10] A strong social movement by the unemployed of different sectors, the *piqueteros* gained increased support at the end of 2001 when the group turned into a collective activism of the unemployed, new poor and historically poor, that is to say, those who were most affected by the implementation of neo-liberal economic policies. Within these excluded sectors, women occupied a major role within the movement leading a variety of campaigns particularly those in relation to hunger alleviation initiatives and back-to-work programmes (Sosa & Molina 2009, 2). According to Vassallo (2002), 65 percent of *piqueteros* are women.

PART II

CULTURAL MEMORY IN THE NOUGHTIES

CHAPTER SIX

CATHARSIS AND CONFRONTATION: POST MILLENIAL MEMORY RESOLUTION IN CONTEMPORARY SPAIN

LORRAINE RYAN

The noughties can be characterised as the decade of memory in contemporary Spain, the decade which marks the reawakening of a latent Republican memory on both the social and political terrain. This new memory has extended the parameters of Spain's memory culture by acknowledging the urgent need to revisit and address the Franco era (1939-1975) as well as the Civil War (1936-1939). Buttressing these developments is "a new international morality", which promotes atonement as an indispensable component of memory politics (Streich 2002, 532). This has, in turn, fuelled the curiosity of the *la generación de los nietos* [the grandchildren's generation] in Spain towards the subject of the Civil War. However, although the noughties memory culture signals a new beginning in Spanish memory culture, residues of longstanding opposition to examining the past are still tangible.

In this essay, I argue that the aforementioned characteristics of the decade, such as the rise of a universal ethical mnemonic paradigm, the passing of the control of memory to the younger generation, and the dwindling of the biological memory of the Spanish Civil War, have all facilitated the incorporation of this memory into contemporary Spanish memory culture. Therefore, this decade has not just provided the backdrop for the unprecedented advances in Spanish memory culture, but has also been a crucial determining factor in the upsurge of memory: the noughties have, undoubtedly, provided the prerequisites for the recovery of a repressed memory, such as generational distance, and the empowerment of non-elites. This essay proposes, firstly, to analyse these factors, and then to assess the trajectory of memory during the noughties. For the purpose of brevity, this examination will be restricted to an analysis of the revisionist battles and the *Ley de memoria histórica* [Law of Historical Memory] (2007), and its aftermath. By focusing specifically on these aspects, I hope to ascertain the degree to which the post millennial memory culture has succeeded in eradicating the deeply rooted aversion to examining the past in Spain.

As a subject of scholarly inquiry, memory contains the implicit risk of evolving into a "catchall" term, to be bandied about in an imprecise manner, which effectively leads to only vague, polyvalent definitions. Thus, an establishment of the parameters of memory is necessary. Prior to embarking on my analysis of the noughties' memory culture, I will outline the theoretical underpinnings of my ensuing analysis of Spanish memory culture. During the Franco dictatorship, the memory of the Civil War constituted, in memory studies terminology, the usable past (Novick 2000, 6), a definitive version of events by which actors validate their claims to legitimacy and insert their current objectives within a venerable historical tradition. The usable past is eminently compatible with elites' quest for hegemony, and, consequently, may excise, vilify or marginalise the memory narratives of groups or events that are judged to be threatening to the dominant memory narrative. The usable past constitutes an integral facet of collective memory, as it heavily influences identity formation. The dominant order, consisting of politicians and the official cultural authorities, extrapolates certain "eternal truths" about their national character from the memory of this key event, which, in turn, causes the populace to subscribe to a particular self-perception (Novick 2000, 4). Collective memory constitutes an extremely efficient method of securing social unity, erecting as it does an implacable wall between "us" and "them", which leads to enhanced solidarity among the favoured, dominant group.

National memory is the abiding obsession of a Western society which has witnessed the demise of authentic memory due to the inviability of the nation-state as an interpretative framework, and the decline of the other institutions, such as the Church and parochial social mores, which had previously sustained genuine memory (Nora 1989, 10). Consequently, living memory has been substituted by a reverence for preservation; as individuals no longer actually construct memory, they seek to conserve trace-elements by symbolic *lieux de mémoire*, such as archives, anniversaries and monuments, which skilfully invest the past with present meaning (1989, 13). Concomitant with this over-abundance of memory is a frantic quest by ethnic minorities/repressed groups to recuperate their own memory, a trend which Nora attributes to the decline in the experiential aspect of memory (11). As he so aptly puts it: "the less collective the experience of memory is, the greater the need for individuals to bear the burden" (11). This individualisation of national memory structures has also led to a noticeable preoccupation with what Foucault terms counter-memory, that is, the memory of the repressed (1980, 53). The prominence of counter-memory has engendered a pluralistic history which has caused the general public to be more critical in relation to overarching epistemological concepts such as truth, knowledge and history itself, all of which were previously held to be infallible anchors of the nation state. Memory, in fact, has been adopted as a prized analytical mode, precisely because of the qualities for which it was once so devalued: namely, its mutability, its inclusiveness and its implicitly moral dimensions. The primordiality of ethical propriety has occasioned an unprecedented upheaval in national memory politics, as previous actions committed in the name of the nation—an objective which at the time conferred impunity—are now evaluated not on their original objective, but on a whole new set of ethical criteria.

This new ethical mnemonic paradigm is decidedly future-orientated, indeed even worryingly so, as in the words of Hayden White, "the present is a problem not because, it is becoming past before our eyes, but because it is being displaced by a future that presses down upon us like a tidal wave" (cited in Domansk 2008, 19). This onus on the future has meant that elites have dispensed with *realpolitik* which in the past dictated the primacy of economic realities over a trenchant examination of the past, as they are informed by the evidence which shows that "successful democracies have been built on forgetting, but this has shown up a generation later" (Garton Ash 1998, 41). Charles S. Maier even goes so far as to contend that collective responsibility for mass atrocities, a key component of *realpolitik,* is nothing more than a "wonderful tactic" (2003, 296). Certainly, *realpolitik* is shown to be reductionist, as it presupposes that the past within the political domain is only of value in its capacity as a political lever, and fails to appreciate the world of politics as a locus for the rectification of victims' grievances. In diametric opposition to this, the "politics of regret" (Coughlan and Olick 2003, 45) converts the political sphere into the primary agent of redress and the citizen, previously a powerless pawn in elite-led decisions, into a key player in memory politics. The "politics of regret" interprets forgiveness as an ability, not a pre-ordained right, which empowers the victim. In the words of Martha Minow:

> Forgiveness is a power to be held by the victimized, not a right to be claimed. The ability to dispense, but also withhold forgiveness is an ennobling capacity and part of the dignity to be reclaimed by those who

> survive the wrongdoing. To expect survivors to forgive is to heap yet another burden on them. (1997, 68)

The 1990s thus witnessed the institutionalisation of the "politics of regret" with Tony Blair apologising for the Irish potato famine and Jacques Chirac acknowledging the Vichy State's responsibility in the Vel d'Hiv roundup of 13,000 Jews. This universal ethical mnemonic paradigm was consolidated in the 2000 Stockholm Holocaust Forum which instated the Holocaust as an event with universal ramifications which effectively obliged countries to come to terms with their perpetration of human rights abuses. Therefore, the 1990s can be regarded as the precursor to the noughties' institutionalisation of atonement and redress for human rights violations.

These shifts in national memory cultures have had important ramifications for the study of memory. No longer do theorists circumscribe the limits of their study to the most prominent and much-articulated discourses, for silence can be laden with hidden and valuable significations, which can, in turn, illuminate the nature of power in society. Therefore, it is precisely where memory is most assailed that we must focus our attention. As Primo Levi so aptly puts it, "the absence of signals, is in its turn, a signal" (1989, 69). The ambits of the study of collective memory, Alon Confino argues, must be extended to incorporate explanations as to why certain versions of the past were accepted and others rejected (1997, 1398). Reiterating his stance, Barbara Zelizer contends that it is both the mechanics of "sharing, discussion, negotiation and often contestation" by which collective memory is constructed, and its significance for a wide range of issues that validate an inter-disciplinary approach to the study of memory (1995, 214). Evidently, memories which reveal the divergence between official memory and personal remembrances of an event are paramount to a more comprehensive understanding of memory, illustrating as they do the fact that collective memory is neither the exclusive preserve of individuals or communities. They also enable us to ascertain who possesses and experiences memory in a society, and how memory is perpetuated, questions which are vital to a more trenchant grasp of collective memory (Crane 1997, 1375). Silenced memories in our society can also be used to develop a more heterogeneous society by highlighting the victims of discrimination, and also remind us of the fact that forgetting is as much a constituent of an authentic, inclusive collective memory as remembrance. Therefore, when we critically analyse the dominant memory, "we should be asking ourselves by whom, where, in which context, against what?" (Davis and Starn 1989, 2). Worthy of reproduction are Susannah Radstone's comments on this theme:

> While undertaking an analysis of memory's specific articulations by particular discourses and institutions, we also need all the time to be asking whether there are inassimilable or incommensurable aspects to memory, and is so how can they be understood. In other words, we need to attend not only to the articulations of memory by the discourses and institutions of the public sphere, but also to the absences, gaps and slips produced by such articulations—absences that might beg questions concerning both memory's incommensurability or untranslatability and questions of power, politics and recognition. (2005, 148)

Clearly, the construction of narrative is crucial to collective memory, but it behoves the scholar to understand narrative in the broadest sense of the word, as encompassing repressed, silenced, minority narratives as well as the dominant one. The study of the interaction between collective and counter memory permits us to approximate to an iconoclastic counter-discourse, thereby undermining the dominant discourses, which subjugate concepts such as memory and power to their own needs. It also reconceives collective memory itself as a dynamic phenomenon in which the dominant and counter memory vie for much coveted space in the public's collective psyche. This necessarily involves reimagining collective memory as not a unitary, or indeed unifying, body of memories shared by all, but rather multiple subsections, which are widely diverse and frequently mutually exclusive. Thus, collective memory morphs into a capacious categorisation term that denotes a body of memories that facilitates the articulation, and from a scholarly perspective, the analysis of an ample gamut of memories by different groups in different geographical locations and at distinct temporal vantage points.

Having elaborated on the theoretical foundations of this essay, I will now proceed to analyse post-millennial Spanish memory culture, a task which requires a brief detailing of the Transitional memory culture. During the *Transición* [Transition], the memory of the Civil War was reconstrued as a collective tragedy. Such an interpretation, Victor Pérez Díaz (1993, 52) argues, has manifold consequences in both the political and moral terrain, as it necessitates an attenuation of the guilt and responsibility of both parties, which, in this case, would be made possible by the 1977 Law of Amnesty. Acclaimed as the pinnacle of the Transition, it had as its primary objectives the forgetting of the Civil War, and a bracketing of both sides in the same category, that of victim *cum* perpetrator. Acerbic and succinct, Theodor Adorno's comments capture the motivation behind this approach:

> It is no coincidence that the attitude that everything should be forgotten and forgiven, which would be proper to those who suffered injustice, is

practised by those party supporters who committed the injustice. In the house of the hangman, one should not speak of the noose. (1998, 94)

In the noughties, the extension of the parameters of Spanish national memory culture would undermine the "forgive and forget" mandate. While the 1990's marked the initiation of the transformation of Spanish national memory culture, the noughties witnessed the increased involvement in memory politics of *la generación de los nietos*. At the beginning of this decade, a survey found that political adhesion per se was no longer so inflammatory an issue in Spain as it had once been, and that the most virulent criticism tended to be reserved for the Franco regime (Barnes *et al* 2001, 29), a change which can be attributed to the incompatibility of Francoist tenets with the values of *la generación de los nietos*. Their second-generation remove from the events in question combined with their adhesion to European values conferred them with a healthy disregard for the myths of the Transition which had dismissed the past as irrelevant to Spain's progress. Manuel Rivas expresses the attitude of *la generación de los nietos*, which cleverly perceives inconsistencies in the right's supposed Europeanism and their inability to confront their own national past thus:

> ¿Por qué despierta tanta hostilidad la memoria histórica en la derecha española? Esa derecha que gira al centro que no quiere que ningún votante la vuelva a rechazar por miedo, que se pretende homologable con los gobernantes franceses y alemanes, que si asumen la memoria de la resistencia antifascista, ¿por qué hace una excepción con la dictadura franquista, una de las más crueles y prolongadas de la historia? (2008, 214)

> [Why does historical memory arouse such hostility in the Spanish right? Why does the same right which inclines towards the centre and who wants no voter to ever reject them again out of fear, which claims to be a counterpart of French and German governing elites who have confronted the memory of Antifascist resistance, make an exception of the Franco dictatorship, which was one of the longest and most cruel in history?]

The cosmopolitanism of these second generation proponents of Republican memory, combined with their repugnance of Francoist insularity and mediocrity, engenders a sense of entitlement to their own national memory, and a consequent belief in their own right to perturb exclusionary national memory structures, and to demand the inscription of their familial memory into them. In their view, Spain's democratic status is very much contingent on its ability to come to terms with the ramifications of its past, however antithetical to national interests that may be. Memory, or more specifically, the reclamation of their individual memory, is for them synonymous with democracy and Europeanisation, and their involvement in cultural and civic endeavours can be interpreted as a concerted effort to achieve inclusion, and also as an indicator of self-determination. This generation is conscious of the extant power of a significant sector of the population who are averse to the prospect of a cultural or legislative re-examination of the past. However, it is the interest and openness of their second generation counterparts which inspire them.[1] In a conversation with Imanol Uribe, Agustí Villaronga, the director of the critically acclaimed *Pa negre* [Black Bread] (2010), himself the son of a Civil War orphan, is sanguine about the future of memory in Spain:

> Imanol Uribe: Lo ves en la calle con el tema de la memoria histórica, la gente está muy dividida. Las dos Españas, otra vez. De entrada hay un público muy importante que está en contra de que eso se revise ni siquiera en el cine.
> Agustí Villaronga: Pero creo que le importa sobre todo a la gente mayor o a la clase política, que utiliza armas de todo tipo para atacarse. La gente joven ya no está en esas. (Brito 2011)
>
> [Imanol Uribe: You see in the street that people are very divided in regard to historical memory. The two Spains, again. From the outset, there is a significant sector of the public which is against any revision, even in the cinema.
> Agustí Villaronga: But I think that it only matters to older people or the political class, who use all types of weapons to attack. Young people are no longer interested in those things.]

Villaronga has astutely distinguished between the generations' perception of memory: for older people, it was a hegemonic tool that perpetuated partisan divisions, while younger people are repelled by such divisiveness, and eschew it in favour of an eminently ethical stance on memory's use in public life. Yet their impetus is also deeply personal as *la generación de los nietos* endeavour to decipher the missing parts of their beleaguered parents' lives, lacunae which have overshadowed their childhood and even moulded their personality. As Emilio Silva, the founder of the *Asociación para la Recuperación de la Memoria Histórica* [Association for the Recuperation of Historical Memory] explains:

> Hay un componente emocional muy fuerte: ser hijo de una persona a la que le han machacado la vida. Pues como me decía a mí una nieta, que me ha llamado por teléfono hace cinco años y que tiene su abuelo materno y otro hermano suyo en una fosa que no sabía donde estaba: "Es muy triste que me haya educado una madre que nunca ha sonreído." En el caso de los nietos, hay, por un lado, la ausencia del miedo: nosotros hemos crecido en

> una época donde nuestras ideas no determinaban nuestro futuro. Pero teníamos esa ausencia del miedo y una necesidad de explicar, por ejemplo, por qué esta sonrisa de esta mujer nunca estaba allí. (cited in Labanyi 2008, 145)
>
> [Being the son of a person whose life has been destroyed by others has a very strong emotional element. As a granddaughter, who rang me five years ago and whose maternal grandfather and one of his brothers were in an unknown mass grave, said to me: "It is very sad that I was brought up by a mother who never smiled." In the case of the grandchildren, there is, on one hand, the absence of fear: we have grown up in an era in which our ideas did not determine our future. But we had this absence of fear and this need to explain, for example, why that woman never smiled.]

Isaac Rosa echoes this sentiment, by affirming that only the knowledge of their parents' experiences in the Civil War will help young people explain "una infancia llena de imágenes falsas" [a childhood full of false images] (2007, 5). Judge Baltasar Garzón also recalls the hardship his parents, "los hijos de la generación de la guerra" [the sons and daughters of the war generation] as he refers to them, endured, and their consequent aversion to disturbing the status quo of Francoist Spain (Garzón 2005, 7). It was, however, the stories told within the family, that imbued him with the heightened ethical sensitivity characteristic of the second generation: "Son tantas las historias y las injusticias relatadas que, de alguna forma, quedaron grabadas en mi memoria infantil, y decidí hacer algo para que no volviera a repetirse" (2005, 13) ["So many stories and accounts of injustices remained inscribed in my childish memory, and I decided to do something in order that it would not happen again."] *La generación de los nietos*, therefore, are inflicted with postmemory, the inherited traumatic memory of their parents, which underlies their fragmented identity. Marianne Hirsch stresses that the resolution of postmemory does not have to be individual or familial, but is instead "more broadly available through cultural and public acts of remembrance, identification, and projection" (2008, 109), a fact which explains the generation's cultural and civic commitment to the recuperation of memory. Postmemory distorts the second generation's memory, and, consequently, they experience intense feelings of confusion and identificatory and temporal disorientation, afflictions which oblige them to embark on an investigation of their parents' past. Their level of empathy with their grandparents and parents' plight is exceptionally high. In their excellent case study of an exhumation in Fontanosas in Ciudad Real, Francisco Ferrandiz Martín and Julián López García found that two of the grandchildren interviewed, Juan Pablo García Gil de Álamo and Alberto Rivera Escribano, became involved with the campaign to exhume bodies in a mass grave in the town following their own investigations into the circumstances of their grandparents' death. Alberto Rivera Escribano's evocation of his grandparents' post-war experience is impressive for its depth of understanding of the issues involved:

> Lo cierto es que a estos siete inocentes les arrebataron sus vidas, y con ellas, todos los proyectos e ilusiones que transmitían al entorno familiar… con su ausencia fueron ellos, padres, esposas, hijos, hermanos, y demás familia cercana, los que tuvieron que soportar años de sufrimiento, de incertidumbre, de rabia contenida, de marginación, de discriminación social, y de desconfianza hacia sus propios conciudadanos. (Ferrándiz Martín and López García 2010, 240)
>
> [Certainly, they took away their lives from these seven innocent people, and with them, all the projects and illusions that the family environment transmitted… with their absence, it was them, parents, wives, sons, brothers and other closely-related family who had to endure years of suffering, uncertainty, contained anger, marginalisation, social discrimination and mistrust of their fellow citizens.]

Unlike their parents, these grandchildren did not regard national memory structures as threatening or even restrictive, but rather as entities which facilitated their postmemorial work; moreover, both displayed no reticence in accessing archives, and even persevering in order to obtain the oft elusive permission to enter military archives. National memory structures are thus individualised, reversing completely the dictatorship's imposition of a monolithic memory narrative in which the individual memory was totally subsumed. Furthermore, they demonstrate a concern with the generational reproduction of this recuperated memory, and are wholly determined that this individual memory will be transmitted to their children. In an interview, Carlos Iglesias, the director of *Ispanski*, a film which centres on the Republican children who were sent to Russia in the post-war period, affirms that his film-making is propelled by a conviction that his children should be aware of the existences of these injustices that form a hidden, but significant, part of Spanish history; he, in fact, declares that his greatest reward is watching the reactions of his teenage children as they watch his films (Villacastín 2011). For this generation, their duty is to rectify a biased memory narrative in order that their children will inherit and reproduce a purged, democratic memory culture. It would be reductionist, however, to dichotomise the individual and national memory structures as distinct entities for a reciprocity is clearly evident between the two: this generation's postmemorial work transcends the solely microsocial as they even perceive their work as vital to the urgently needed cauterisation of Spain's gaping memory wounds. Reflecting on his involvement in the aforementioned exhumation, Juan Pablo García Gil de Álamo states that

> Sí era una herida abierta, porque los familiares tenían esa herida, pero yo incluso creo que el pueblo tenía pendiente ese tema, porque ya era tiempo de cerrar página, o de cerrar un paréntesis que se abrió, cuando sucedieron los hechos. Mañana va a ser el momento idóneo de cerrar el paréntesis. (Ferrándiz Martín and López García 2010, 236)
>
> [Yes, it was an open wound, because the family members had that wound, but I even think that it was an unresolved issue for the village, because it was time to close the page, or to close a parenthesis which opened when the events happened. Tomorrow will be the ideal moment to close the parenthesis.]

By the same token, Iglesias's commitment to the generational reproduction of Republican memory can be interpreted as a desire to forge a future memory culture which will be devoid of the schismatic elements that characterised it in the past. This symbiosis of the national and individual memory structures augurs well for the future of Spanish memory for it corresponds to the contemporary view of a democratic collective memory as a repository of individual memories that encompass the national memory narrative.

Having examined the factors which enabled the rise of memory in the noughties, it is now opportune to attempt to examine the extent to which this novel memory culture succeeded in eradicating deeply embedded national memory myths. Certainly, this renewal of interest in Republican memory met with formidable opposition. It polarised the historical community with right-wing historians such as Pío Moa and Ángel David Martín Rubio "revising" key events of the Civil War. The historical conflict between revisionists and proponents of recuperation clearly demonstrates the shallowness of the Transitional memory paradigm, in which the memory of the Civil War had supposedly been neutralised, as twenty-five years later, it still retained enough political and social import to constitute a polemical site of contestation. Mary Douglas's remark that "the aim of revision is to get the distortions to match the mood of the present times" seems particularly apt in this case (1987, 69). Spanish revisionists rehashed the *aperturista*[2] rhetoric of the inevitability of the Civil War, by stressing the intolerable events which had preceded it, and of course, the reluctance of General Franco to stage such a *coup d'état*, as the following text so perfectly encapsulates:

> Franco se sumó a lo que inicialmente—y según el pensamiento del general Mola, su organizador—iba a ser una acción limitada para hacer posible la continuidad de la República. (...) Para desencadenar el Alzamiento tuvo que ocurrir un hecho tan increíble como que una patrulla de las Fuerzas de Orden Pública asesinase al jefe de la oposición, José Calvo Sotelo. (...) Nada, pues, de un golpe bonapartista (…). Era lo necesario para ganar la guerra y construir un nuevo Estado. No se trataba precisamente de una concesión, era cargar a Franco con una tremenda responsabilidad que nadie quería para sí. (Marchante Gil 2000, 285)
>
> [Franco joined what was initially to be, and according to its organiser, General Mola's ideas, a very limited action which would facilitate the Republic's continuity. In order for the Uprising to occur, a fact as incredible as the killing of José Calvo Sotelo by the Public Order Forces had to occur. Nothing, then, to do with a Bonapartiste coup d'état. It was necessary in order to win the war and build a new State. It was not a prize, rather it burdened Franco with a tremendous responsibility which nobody wanted.]

Traces of Franco as national saviour are all too readily apparent here, but how, one may ask, can the image of Franco as a benign dictator endure when confronted with incriminating statistics of repression? In keeping with the spirit of the revisionist movement, outright denial is eschewed in favour of an emphasis on the putatively crueller and unrestrained repression in the Republican zone. Martín Rubio posits that the much-vaunted control of Republican violence by the start of 1937 did not automatically bring an end to the repression, with massacres being perpetrated in Bilbao, Zaragoza and Jaén during that same year (1999, 52). Although he concedes that many Republicans were killed for petty motives such as personal vengeance, he proceeds to detail the sadism of a number of Republicans executed by the New State, thereby justifying the post-war repression (74). The impunity accorded to their equivalents on the Nationalist side is conceded, but neatly reduced to an inevitable consequence of civil war: in short, *vae victis*: "Lamentablemente, muchos de los crímenes registrados en la zona nacional quedaron impunes, como han seguido quedando impunes hasta hoy los cometidos por los vencedores de tantas guerras, algunas bien recientes" (Marchante Gil 2000, 291) [Unfortunately, many of the crimes registered in the Nationalist zone went unpunished, as have many committed by the winners of so many wars, some of them quite recent.] Neither is an acknowledgement of the full extent of the repression forthcoming. Martín Rubio prefers to emphasise the prompt bestowing of commutations (1999, 76), which research has established did not derive from any benevolent impulse on the part of the Regime, but from the urgent necessity to reduce the chronic over-crowding in the prisons (Vinyes 2002, 65). Similarly, facile dichotomisation prevails with key Republican figures being characterised as vain or megalomaniac, while the Nationalists are seemingly faultless (Moa 2004). But, what the revisionists really seek to achieve is to prevent the sacralisation, that is, the iconic status accorded to certain events such as the bombing of Guernica or the massacre in the Plaza de Toros in Badajoz in August 1936: "Vale, es cierto que en Badajoz, hubo cierta represión, quizás un poco más de lo debida, pero no hay que exagerar, esto pasó en otros lugares de ambas zonas y es cosa propia de la guerra." (Moa 2004, 151) [Okay, it is true that in Badajoz, there was a certain amount of repression, maybe a bit more than was necessary, but there is no need to exaggerate, this happened in other places in both camps and it is a typical part of war.] As crude and prejudiced as revisionism may be, it still poses a formidable threat to the emergence of a more inclusive history, as its very presence in the public domain normalises and sanctions it (Ridao 2007). Alarmingly, the success of the media savvy Moa seems to confirm the existence of an audience which consumes cultural production of the Civil War and Franco dictatorship in order to affirm their preconceptions and strengthen their ideological convictions, rather than explore the multifarious aspects of this historical period in all their complexity.

Despite the formidable pro-Francoist opposition with which they were confronted, in 2007 the efforts of the grandchildren eventually culminated in the passing of the Law of Historical Memory on 31 October. It stipulated the removal of shields, plaques and statues and other monuments of the Spanish Civil War that exalt the Nationalist side or that can be identified with the Franco Regime from public buildings, and also ratified the provision of funds for exhumations. Moreover, it created a council consisting of five members to investigate human rights grievances of either side of the Civil War with the power to make monetary restitution and to grant Spanish citizenship to the descendants of exiles. The Law also prohibited any political demonstrations in the *Valle de los Caídos* [Valley of the Fallen], the monumental basilica outside Madrid in which Franco is buried. It was acknowledged by victims' groups as a first step, but not a *definitive* law mainly because of the following shortcomings (Junquera 2007). Firstly, the law's condemnation of Francoist repression as "illegitimate" and "unjust", rather than "illegal", failed to satisfy victims' families. Secondly, the mandatory funding of exhumations by local government is followed by a codicil which makes the opposition of relations to exhumations a factor in the decision to proceed with the exhumation. Emilio Silva expressed the unfairness of this condition as follows: "El derecho de los que buscan a su familiar no puede quedar insatisfecho porque otros no quieran ejercerlo": [The right of those who search for their family member should not remain unfulfilled because others do not wish to exercise this right]. Thirdly, the refusal of many local government bodies to remove Francoist symbols has meant that the enactment of this clause is dependent upon goodwill, ideological affiliation and financial wherewithal, all of which are arbitrary criteria that may or may not be compatible with victims' demands. The Roman Catholic Church's obligation to remove Francoist symbols from churches also contains a codicil which protects the aforementioned symbols for artistic reasons. Fourthly, the failure to name the perpetrators of repression has been interpreted as an indicator of the government's pusillanimity, and the insubstantiality of the law itself.

The Law's support for an inclusive notion of victimhood, comprising both the clergy killed by the Republicans in the Civil War period and the Republican victims of Francoism, was considered by many to have been negated by the beatification on 28 October 2007, of 498 "martyrs" who died at the hands of the Republicans during the 1936-1937 period. This action was interpreted by many as a rebuttal on the part of the Vatican of Zapatero's liberal social policies, and a desire to promulgate a quasi-Crusade version of the Civil War. The public reaction to the Law was tempered with a certain sense of disillusionment due to several factors: it pointedly failed to satisfy Republican claims for trenchant judicial measures; moreover, it did not reconfigure their identity, as, under the Law, their identities remained the same, for their convictions were not legally rescinded, but rather condemned as "illegitimate". In short, moral censure did not invalidate their putatively criminal status. This effectively meant, as José Antonio Moreno Díaz bitterly pointed out, that his grandfather who was executed as a traitor who was disloyal to the *patria* legally remains "a traitor" (Moreno Díaz 2008).

The Law can most definitely not be interpreted as an unequivocal commitment to a more inclusive version of Spanish history, as Spanish politicians have either been overly cautious in articulating its objectives (socialist PSOE), or have deliberately misinterpreted these objectives (conservative PP). Not only did the PSOE clearly qualify its commitment to the recuperation of Republican memory, with María Fernández de la Vega classifying it as "un paso adelante" [a step forward] but Mariano Rajoy, leader of the PP, classified it as an enormous error, claiming that the majority of Spaniards did not want to talk about the Civil War (Encarnación 2007, 46). He, thereby, ignored the Law's social import, that is, its capacity to reincorporate Republican memory into Spanish contemporary society, and chose to position it within the Transitional mnemonic framework thus associating any discussion of the past with wilful trouble seeking. Indeed, Jorge Fernández Díez, a spokesman for the PP, branded the Law "sectarian", and paralleled it with the creation of the schismatic atmosphere of the Civil War (Encarnación 2007, 47). In the light of such polarised reactions, the Law was potentially divisive, an accusation which in fact echoed the Transitional manipulation of memory that had converted the past into a taboo. Newspapers such as ABC perceived a deliberate attempt "de distraer la nación" [to distract the nation] from more pressing problems, while the Roman Catholic Church contended that history was unchangeable (Encarnación 2007, 47). The Archbishop of Seville declared that the future was of the utmost priority, and that revisiting the past was a futile exercise, comments which again recalled the Transitional future-orientated memory policies (Cajiao 2008, 12).

But, perhaps, the most disappointing aspect of the Law was its aftermath: the failure to implement the Law's clauses. Both the Association for the Recuperation of Memory and Amnesty International have lamented the fact that the Law's implementation, for the most part, has become the responsibility of private citizens' groups. Thus it was not unexpected that soon after the passing of the Law, 1,200 families of the Republican disappeared—estimated to be 50,000—entreated Judge Baltasar Garzón to take action to bring Francoist executioners to justice and to facilitate the carrying out of exhumations (Nolan 2008). The indictment of the Francoist executioners proved problematic as up to forty of them are now dead. Garzón, however, did proceed in October 2008 to request details of executions and victims' documents from local councils and churches. His planned indictment of Francoism soon assumed Herculean proportions, incorporating as it did the investigation of *los niños perdidos del franquismo* [the lost children of Francoism], children forcibly taken away from their families, the opening of the grave of the poet Federico García Lorca and the excavation of the *Valle de los Caídos*. All these plans were abandoned, however, when the *Audiencia Nacional* issued an injunction on 7 November 2008, blocking exhumations that had been ordered by Garzón. On 8 June 2009, the first exhumation ordered by Garzón would be carried out in Zamora. 60 are still pending and local councils have yet to provide a date for opening these graves. Highly significant is the fact that campaigners referred to Garzón's initiative as "the first application of the Law of Historical Memory", an affirmation which underscores government inertia, as his action was taken a year after the approval of the proposed

Law, and even more importantly, was not the result of a governmental order (Nolan, 2008). It is disturbing to note that most of the noticeable achievements of the last few years have been the work of private individuals or associations. For example, it was due to the 20 year crusade of one man, Antonio Hantañon, that the names of 850 people buried in a mass grave were uncovered, while the Association for the Recuperation of Historical Memory blocked the Valencian City Council's plans to build over mass graves (González 2009, 180).

The disappointment of the proponents of the recuperation of memory has been compounded by the failure to implement change in the public sphere. In the period 1996-2009, the history syllabus has not been revised in order to promote a more inclusive memory culture, a direct consequence of which is that many people have a negative attitude towards the recuperation of historical memory. In the words of Julián Casanova:

> Mucha gente que respeta la democracia, que vota, que no tiene ninguna duda de que el democrático es el mejor sistema que existe, cuando se la dice que durante el franquismo se cometieron crímenes políticos lo siguen negando, piensan "ya están otra vez, estos pesados". Este, sin duda, es el mayor poso del franquismo que queda en la sociedad española actual y, en buena parte, se produce por un déficit de enseñanza de historia. Desde los años 70 con la Ley Villar Palasí hasta la entrada en vigor de la Logse en los colegios no se tocó la historia del siglo XX español. (Martín 2009, 6)
>
> [When you say to many people who respect democracy, who vote, who have no doubt that democracy is the best system ever, that political crimes were committed during the Francoist dictatorship, they continue denying it, they think "there they go again, those bores". This, undoubtedly, is the greatest remnant of Francoism in current Spanish society, and, in large measure, it was created by the lack of the teaching of history. From the 1970s with the Villar Palasí Law until the implementation of the Logse in secondary schools, twentieth-century Spanish history remained untouched.]

Redress for the Republicans is not the only issue at stake here: a balanced view of history is essential from an explicitly pedagogical point of view, as history teaches us how to deal with both the present and the future. Waldron proposes that history is vital to our moral development as it provides us with templates on how to deal with social problems; therefore, our comprehension of the past is a reflection of our adherence to certain moral principles such as the inclusion of marginalised groups in society (1992, 24). The absence, therefore, of an inclusive history in the public sphere, is a serious shortcoming. Even more disturbing is the fact that as Spain is a country with low readership levels, with only 39% describing themselves as readers, the majority are bereft of coherent historical information in order to formulate their opinions and judgments of the Civil War (Cajiao 2008, 12).

The transformation of the Spanish landscape was another expectation which has only partially been fulfilled. The dismantling of Francoist statues has been a slow and laborious process, with the *Ayuntamiento de Santander* [Santander Townhall] only dismantling its statue of Franco four years after receiving an official order to do so. Moreover, the fate of the *Valle de los Caídos* remains undecided and the government has been remarkably reticent to convert it into a museum (Keeley, 2008). Many councils also complain of the failure of the Zapatero government to finance the removal of the statues. As the Law did not stipulate any sanction for failing to comply with this particular clause, the degree of compliance demonstrated by local councils depends on multiple factors such as political affiliation, possible public opposition, and local politicians' views on the urgency of its implementation in comparison to other pressing matters. Seville has no intention of changing the name of the Carrero Blanco street, while the mayoress of Valencia, Rita Barberá (PP), has categorically stated her opposition to the Law (Cué and Díez, 2007).

The Law, therefore, can be judged to be successful insofar as it has succeeded in raising consciousness about the Republican experience during the Civil War and the Dictatorship. It has, however, blatantly failed to deliver on many of its main promises, such as the provision of finance to families searching for their disappeared, and the removal of all Francoist symbols. The Law was undermined from the outset by the PSOE's refusal to annul the Francoist sentences and to take definitive action regarding the future of the *Valle de los Caídos*. The failure to widen the parameters of the history syllabus is also a cause for disquiet, as it ensures that ignorance and prejudices regarding Spanish history will prevail in the future. Republican identity is being consolidated more in the cultural sphere than in the public arena, as films, novels, history books and documentaries all combine to address existing biases against the Republicans by depicting the hardship they suffered in the post-war years. The current plethora of television series centring on the 1931-1975 period, such as *14 de abril: La República* [14th of April: The Republic] (2011), an increasingly politicised *Cuéntame como pasó* [Tell Me How it Happened] (2001), and *Amar en tiempos revueltos* [Love in Difficult Times] (2005) is a far cry from the 1996 refusal of TVE, the state broadcaster, to show a documentary focusing on the 1963 executions of the anarchists Granados and Delgado (Ryan 2009, 127). In *Dietario Voluble* [Inconstant Diary],

Enrique Vila Matas criticises contemporary production for its lack of subtlety and attention to the development of character, and laments the fact that Spain has not produced anything on par with the Oscar-winning German production *The Lives of Others* (Florian Henckel von Donnersmarck, 2005) (2008, 117). His comments are well founded, as, undoubtedly, the cultural memory boom, while rendering a previously taboo memory tangible and accessible, has succumbed to the facile trap of Manichaeism, with exemplary Republicans and contemptible Falangists proliferating. The Catalan writer, Jordi Sierra i Fabra's popular Inspector Mascarell series recounts the tribulations of a beleaguered, honourable policeman who confronts nearly insuperable obstacles to solve crimes committed by the greedy, depraved and malevolent Falangist Barcelonese bourgeoisie. Similarly, Manuel Rivas' *El lápiz del carpintero* [The Carpenter's Pencil] contrasts the hugely accomplished and magnetic Doctor Da Barca against the mediocre and psychopathic police officer, Hector. This tendency to binary oppositions lessens the credibility of the characters, and it may be surmised that it could also reduce its appeal for the more discerning reader or spectator.

Perversely, the political manipulation of memory for electoral purposes has reinforced the commitment of second generation writers such as Almudena Grandes, as she has lambasted the State interest in the opening of graves as a cynical electoral ploy (Marzo, 2009). She has reserved her greatest condemnation for the Law of Historical Memory, as she considers that its failure to overturn the convictions renders it somewhat pointless: "Si no se van a anular los procesos, no sé de que estamos hablando" (Grandes 2009) [If they are not going to annul the verdicts, I do not know what we are talking about']. Alfons Cervera is similarly scathing on the subject of the government's lack of action and considers his writing as an important means of counteracting this political inertia while making his own personal contribution to the memory debate (Ryan 2007). It is clear that the second generation's cultural commitment is being stimulated by the half-hearted political action, for it seems that the cultural arena has become one of the few public fora which can reclaim justice without the seemingly mandatory allegiance to the Transitional rhetoric. Grandes highlights the incompatibility of adherence to Transitional memory myths with her own inclination to write about the defeated of the Spanish Civil War:

> La transición española en realidad no fue ninguna transición porque no se discutió ni se debatió. Se llegó a la elegante conclusión de que lo más elegante y moderno era pasar página y eso impidió que se contaran otras historias que son las que a mí me interesan. (Anabitarte 2002, 3)

> [Frankly, the Spanish transition was not a transition because it was not argued and debated. The elegant conclusion was reached that the most elegant and modern thing to do was to turn the page and this prevented the telling of other stories, which are the ones that interest me.]

Unfortunately, one cannot be too optimistic about the impact of the efforts of these writers as it will only reach a culturally engaged audience, which, as I previously mentioned, is a minority audience. Implicit in the government's political inaction is a disjuncture between public and private Republican memory, as the public memory adopts a policy of containment, designed to mollify public demand by "cosmetic reform", while private associations and individuals actually implement measures, often not only without substantial funding but also in the face of active opposition from town councils.

The PSOE's appeasement of public demand results in the introduction of apparently decisive measures which lack power due to their non-obligatory nature. Therefore, victims' groups are dependent upon the ideological adhesion of the politicians who control town councils and their attendant willingness or reluctance to finance exhumations. This failure to implement the measures contained in the Law does not point to cynical political inactivity; rather, it is a reflection of the extant power of the Transitional memory paradigm, which emphasises the future to the detriment of a past that it dismisses as best forgotten. The PSOE's marked reluctance to forge a coherent commitment to Republican memory, of which they are the democratic inheritor, denotes a subscription to a conceptualisation of collective memory as a potentially subversive element, menacing the much-vaunted democratic stability. Having not fully dispensed with the idea of memory for the victims as a magnanimous concession, rather than a fundamental human right, PSOE politicians frame the issue in terms of optional measures and vague discourse. Furthermore, this negative perception of collective memory effectively means that elites fail to capitalise on the openness of *la generación de los nietos*, whose contemporary view of collective memory as negotiable, individual and inclusive, makes them ideal potential political actors with whom to edify a modern Spanish collective memory. State level discourse remains ambiguous, apparently enacting measures to memorialise the Republican experience, while simultaneously shirking on the economic, cultural and political ramifications of a fully inclusive memory culture. To cite just one example, the removal of Francoist monuments has not been accompanied by the construction of monuments to the Republican dead, acknowledging the institutionalised repression to which they were subject during the dictatorship. Therefore, on a purely practical level, the descendants of victims have little or no actual physical space in which to perform the mourning and superation of their repressed memories that are consequently circumscribed to the limits of the private sphere. It can only be concluded that while measures decreed by PSOE politicians may symbolise recognition and partial commitment to Republican redress, the reality is that the victims have to be satisfied with placatory measures which are insufficient to remedy their grievances. A fundamental conceptual problem needs to be addressed, that is, the PSOE's viewing of the resolution of the lacunae in Spain's memory culture as a non-compulsory issue, which is at odds with proponents of the recuperation of Republican memory's perception of it as a matter of the utmost importance for Spanish identity, credibility as a democratic, European nation, and its future.

As the above discussion illustrates, the rise of memory during the noughties has by no means been a chance occurrence. It was, in fact, the noughties which brought together the prerequisites which enabled the transition from a static to a mature memory culture, mirroring the experience of other European nations. The coming of age of the deeply committed second generation and the flourishing of a universal ethical memory paradigm engendered an environment in which Spain could confront its past. To paraphrase the words of Walter Benjamin (1968 (1940): 268), the noughties have seized hold of memory as it flashes up not in a moment of danger as he said, but in a period of stagnation, and converted it into a priority. Its prioritisation, however, has not culminated in sufficiently cogent measures. It remains to be seen whether this decade will succeed in diluting deeply ingrained mnemonic myths which hinder this redress.

Works Cited

Adorno, T. (1998) "The Meaning of Working Through the Past" in T. Adorno (ed.), *Critical Models: Interventions and Catchwords*, New York: Colombia University Press, 89-103.

Anabitarte, A. (2002) "Almudena Grandes: Lloro muchísimo escribiendo." *Babab,* vol. 15 (September). Available from: http://www.babab.com/no15/almudena_grandes.htm. [Accessed 2 December 2004]

Barnes, S.H., P. McDonough and A. López Pina (2001) *The Cultural Dynamics of Democratization in Spain* London: Cornell University Press.

Benjamin, W, (1968 (1940)) "Theses on the Philosophy of History" in H. Arendt (ed.), *Illuminations*: *Essays* and *Reflections*, New York: Harcourt, Brace and World, 255-268.

Brito, S. (2011), "Basta del brochazo gordo y de los buenos y los malos", *El Público*. Available from: http://www.publico.es/culturas/359882/basta-del-brochazo-gordo-y-de-los-buenos-y-malos [Accessed 14 February 2011].

Cajiao, E.C. (2008) "La Recepción de la Ley de la Memoria Histórica en España", *Analisis Politico* vol. 21, no. 63, 1-15.

Confino, A. (1997) "Collective Memory and Cultural History: Problems of Method", *The American Historical Review* 102: 1386-1403.

Coughlin, B. and J. K. Olick (2003) "The Politics of Regret: Analytical Frames" in John Torpey (ed.), *Politics and the Past: On Repairing Historical Injustices*. Lanham: Rowman and Littlefield Publishers, 37-62.

Crane, S.A. (1997), "Writing the Individual Back into Collective Memory", *The American Historical Review* 102: 1372-1385.

Cué, C.E. and A. Díez (2007) "La ley de Memoria Histórica obligará a los ayuntamientos de retirar los símbolos franquistas." *El País*, 10 July. Available from: http://www.elpais.com/articulo.espana/ley/Memoria/Historica/obligara/ayuntamientos/retirar/simbolos/franquistas/elpepuesp/20071 [Accessed 8 June 2008].

Davis, N.Z. and R. Starn (1989), "Introduction", *Representations* 26: 1-6.

Domanska, E. (2008.) "A Conversation with Hayden White", *Rethinking History*, vol. 12, 3-21.

Douglas, M. (1987) *How Institutions Think*. London: Routledge and Kegan Paul.

Encarnacion, O. G. (2007) "Pinochet's Revenge: Spain Revisits its Civil War", *World Policy Journal*, vol 24, no. 4, 40-56.

Farell, T. (2002) . "Memory, Imagination and War", *History: the Journal of the Historical Association*, vol. 87, no. 285, 61-74.

Ferrándiz Martín, F. and J. L. García (2010). *Fontanosas, 1941-2006: Memoria de carne y hueso*. Ciudad Real: Diputación de Ciudad Real.

Foucault, M. (1980) *Language, Counter-memory, Practice*. New York: Ithaca.

Garton Ash, T. (1998) "The Truth about Dictatorships", *New York Review of Books*, 19 February, 35-41.

Garzón, B. (2005) *Un mundo sin miedo*. Barcelona: Plaza Janés.

González, J.M (2009) "Spanish Literature and the Recovery of Historical Memory", *European Review* vol. 17, no. 1, 177-185.

Grandes, A. (2009) "Memoria y Libertad." Available from: http://www.elpais.com/elpaismedia/ultimahora/media/200905/18/sociedad/20090518elpepusoc_2_Pes_PDF.pdf [Accessed 10 October 2009].

Hirsch, M. (1997) *Family Frames: Photography, Narrative and Postmemory*. Massachusetts: Harvard University Press.

—. (2008) "The Generation of Postmemory", *Poetics Today* vol. 29, no. 1, 103-128.

Humblebaek, C. J. (2005) "Remembering the Dictatorship: Commemorative Activity in the Spanish Press on the Anniversaries of the Civil War and of the Death of Franco" in K. Zeimer and J.W. Borejsza (eds.), *Totalitarian and Authoritarian Regimes in Europe: Legacies and Lessons from the Twentieth Century*. Oxford: Berghahn Books, 490-516.

Junquera, Natalia (2007) "Las asociaciones esperan que la ley de memoria histórica no sea definitiva", *El País*. Available at: http://www.elpais.com/articulo/españa/asociaciones/esperan/Ley/Memoria/sea/definitiva [Accessed 5 November 2007].

Keeley, G. (2008) "Old Divisions Revive as Spain Removes Last Remaining Statue of Franco." Available at: http://www.timesonline.co.uk/tol/news/world/europe/article5365827.ece?print=yes&r [Accessed 5 September 2008).

Labanyi, J. (2008) "Entrevista con Emilio Silva", *Journal of Spanish Cultural Studies* vol. 9, no. 2, 143-155.

Levi, Primo (1989) *The Drowned and the Saved*. London: Abacus.

Maier, C. S. (2003) "Overcoming the Past? Narrative and Negotiation, Remembering the Reparation. Issues at the Interface of History and the Law", in J. Torpey (ed.), *Politics and the Past: On Repairing Historical Injustices*. Boston: Rowman and Littlefield, 277-295.

Marchante Gil, A. (2000) "Franco en la historia", *Razón Española* 104, 281-317.

Martin, A (2009) "No querer hablar de la memoria histórica es el mayor pozo del franquismo", *Tribuna Complutense*, 14 April, 6.

Martín Rubio, A.D. (1999) *Salvar la memoria: una reflexión sobre las victímas de la Guerra Civil*. Badajoz: Fondo de Estudios Sociales.

Marzo, I. (2009) "Almudena Grandes ESCRITORA: Los padres de la transición tienen que entender que 30 años después ya no valga." Available at: http:www.diariocordoba.com/noticias/imprimir.asp?pkid=478053. [Accessed 15 December 2009].

Minow, M. (1997) *Between Vengeance and Forgiveness: Facing History after Genocide and Mass Violence*. Boston: Beacon Press.

Moa, P. (2004) *Los mitos de la guerra civil.* Madrid: La esfera de los libros.

Moradiellos, E. (2003) "Ni gesta heroica, ni locura trágica: nuevas perspectivas históricas sobre la guerra civil", *Ayer* no. 50, 11-41.

Moral, F. (2001) *Veinticinco años después: la memoria de los españoles del franquismo y de la transición a la democracia.* Madrid: Centro de Investigaciones Sociológicas.

Moreno Díaz, J.A. (2008) "Perspectivas sobre la Ley de Memoria Histórica", *Entelequia. Revista Interdisciplinar.* Monográfico, no. 7. Available from: http://www.eumed.net/entelequia/es.art.php?a=07a14. [Accessed 19 September 2009].

Nolan, R. (2008) "Judge Looking into Fate of Franco's Victims", Der *Spiegel* Online. Available at: http://www.spiegel.de/international/europe/0,1518, druck-576051OO.html [Accessed 5 December 2008].

Nora, P. (1989) "Between Memory and History: *Les Lieux de Mémoire*", *Representations* 26, 7-25.

Novick, P. (2000) *The Holocaust and Collective Memory: the American Experience.* New York: Bloomsbury.

Pérez-Díaz, V. (1993) *The Return of Civil Society: The Emergence of Democratic Spain.* Massachusetts: Harvard University Press.

Radstone, S. (2005), "Reconceiving Binaries: The Limits of Memory", *History Workshop Journal* 59: 124-150.

Ridao, José María (2007) "El revisionismo ataca", *El País*, 18 October. Available at: http://www.elpais.com/articulo/espana/revisionismo/ataca/elpporesp/20060718elpepinac-31/Tes/ [Accessed 15 September 2008].

Rivas, M. (2008) *A cuerpo abierto.* Madrid: Editorial Alfaguara.

Rosa, I. (2007) *Otra maldita novela sobre la guerra civil.* Barcelona: Seix Barral.

Ryan, L. (2007) Entrevista con Alfons Cervera, Universidad de Valencia. 3 February.

—. (2009) "For Whom the Dominant Memory Tolls: The Suppression and Re-Emergence of Republican Memory in Contemporary Spanish society" in L.Rorato and A. Saunders (eds.), In: *The Essence and the Margin: National Identities and Collective Memories in Contemporary European Memory Culture.* Rodopi. Amsterdam, p. 119-135.

Sánchez-Biosca, V. and R. R. Tranche (2000) *NO-DO: El tiempo y la memoria.* Madrid: Editorial Complutense.

Streich, G. W. (2002) "Is There a Right to Forget? Historical Injustices, Race, Memory, and Identity", *New Political Science* 24, 525-543.

Vila-Matas, E. (2008) *Dietario Voluble*. Barcelona: Anagrama.

Villacastín, R. (2011). "Carlos Iglesias: Hace 20 años me habría planteado irme a Hollywood". *Diez Minutos*, April 5, 24-28.

Vinyes, R. (2002) *Irredentas: las presas políticas y sus hijos en las cárceles de Franco*. Madrid: Temas de Hoy.

Waldron, J. (1992) "Superseding Historic Injustice", *Ethics* vol. 103, no. 1, 4-28.

Zelizer, B. (1995) "Reading the Past against the Grain: the Shape of Memory Studies", *Critical Studies in Mass Communication* 12: 214-240.

Notes

[1] "La generacion de los nietos" does not solely refer to the second generation who have not experienced the Spanish Civil War, as that demographic group constitutes a diverse entity, composed of grandchildren who are, variously, indifferent, hostile, slightly interested, and passionately committed to the recuperation of historical memory. *La generacion de los nietos* are the second generation proponents of the recuperation of Republican memory. Their counterparts, the consumers of cultural production concerning this period, can be said to experience what Marianne Hirsch terms "affiliative postmemory" (2008, 112), in effect, a subscription to the tenets of the postmemory and an empathy with its proponents, while not actively being engaged in its recovery.

[2] During the *aperturista* [opening] period, 1957-1970, the Franco Regime discarded its hyperbolic depiction of the Civil War as a battle between good and evil, in favour of an exculpatory rhetoric which concentrated on embellishing the progress of the post-war years. Although the inevitability of the Civil War still remained integral to this discourse, it pointedly desisted from inveighing against the Republican enemy. The Franco Regime's achievements rather than its origins became the source of its legitimacy, a fact which was reflected in the Regime's propaganda, with attempts being made to hypostatise the elements which would qualify it as "un estado de derecho" [a state governed by the rule of law]. The making of a documentary, *El camino de la paz* [The path of peace], heralded this new era, unfettered as it was by aggressiveness towards the Republicans. Significantly, the war is described as destructive, but not explicitly linked with the Regime, instead standing as a separate element in the triad: war, peace and legitimacy. One can also perceive a hitherto inconceivable largesse, which amounts to a type of equalisation of the two sides in the Civil War, in the following speech made by Franco in the Valle de los Caídos [Valley of the Fallen]: "No es un monumento a los vencedores, lo es más bien a los que cayeron en la guerra y así asegura para las generaciones futuras su simbolismo" (Sánchez Biosca and Tranche 2000, 435) [It is not a monument honouring the victors, rather it honours those who died in the war and in so doing, it ensures its symbolism for future generations]. A subduing of the bellicose nature of commemorative events

was also apparent during this period: the Victory Parade on 1 April started to be celebrated in late May, and from 1966 onwards, it was no longer deemed worthy of a national holiday (Humblebaek 2005, 491). Likewise, its name changed to Desfile de la Paz [Peace Parade] in 1964, in consonance with the image of the Civil War as a harbinger of national harmony. The cultural arena reflected this change in the memory narrative, with Isaac Montero's 1964 novel *Una cuestión privada* [A Private Question] depicting the troubled conscience of a Nationalist officer who shot a Republican soldier during the Civil War, while the novels of Juan Marsé, *Encerrados con un solo juguete* [Imprisoned with Only One Toy] and *Esta cara de la luna* [This Side of the Moon], delineated the trials and tribulations of post-war life for the Republicans.

CHAPTER SEVEN

SUBJECTIVE PASTS AND THE IMAGINATIVE POWER OF THE IMAGE IN *BUCAREST*, *LA MEMÒRIA PERDUDA* AND *NEDAR*

ABIGAIL LOXHAM

The first decade of the new millennium has seen Spain pass the controversial *ley de la recuperación de memoria histórica* [law for the recovery of historic memory]. Unsurprisingly, this has led to a cultural re-examination not only of the silenced stories of those the victors wanted to erase from their version of history but, and significant here, also probing assessments into the function of memory and its role in the culture of a country newly anxious to admit the polyphony of histories previously ignored.

The Catalan directors whose films I examine here have embraced the possibilities that this new millennium offers for aesthetic freedom. Their contribution to the debate that surrounds recent legislative change is to acknowledge a highly complex relationship between personal history and a collective past. This frequently takes the form of cinematic recuperation and piecing together, given that this past often exists only in traces and fragments. In this context the significance of their status as Catalan cultural products lies in their engagement with events particular to Catalonia and its past, and the complex process of recuperation that new legislation is enabling in this nation. More than this, and pertinent to this study, is the emergence from Catalonia in a new millennium of a contemplative, reflexive cinematic mode, which lends itself to this particular examination of representational strategies, as it simultaneously interrogates its own status as aesthetic product.[1] The problematic nature of nomenclature in this instance (definitions of "historical memory" and the perennial and thorny conceptualisation of the "nation" in the Catalan context) is addressed in more sophisticated terms by other studies. Of concern in this case is the specific cinematic, documentary response to the past and its representation. To label these works as Catalan is not to elide the problematic association of such facility of categorisation; rather, I choose to mark the Catalan identity of these works because it is a significant facet of their identity, one that has suffered the silencing with which they both grapple and which benefits from the more inclusive approach that these directors adopt. They mark their own national provenance in their dominant use of Catalan but they are concerned with subverting definite categories of identity and this, I believe, extends to any simplistic labels of national identity as it does to over-facile interpretations of the structure of memory.

The examples of new cinematic production that I use to explore the alternative formulations of history and memory in Spain in this new millennium are the documentaries *Nedar* (Carla Subirana, 2008) and *Bucarest, la memòria perduda* (Albert Solé, 2006). I would argue that what these films have in common is an approach to the moving image and its cinematic qualities which proves to be a peculiarly noughties concern: the complex relationship between memory and history. In this case they focus on family memories and their concomitant impact on the inherited identity of the filmmakers themselves. Through close examination of their formal and narrative properties I locate an emerging noughties aesthetic which is specifically concerned with the contradictory potential of cinema, as an ephemeral art form, to represent the material and tangible nature of memory. This emphasis on materiality is evidenced through an insistence on the trace with its multifarious interpretations, a trace which in its materiality might resist the noughties trend towards the virtual and impermanent.

The term trace in this context can be understood as a residue or marker of presence (although, as with the cinematic art itself, it is frequently a presence which points to, or frames, an absence). Jo Labanyi understands Spain's Derridean ghosts as "the traces of those who were not allowed to leave a trace" (2002, 1). She configures Spain's past as a "ghost story" because of those elements that have been left out and forced to remain invisible. In these moving-image texts the traces are sought out and used to piece together the lost narratives of these silenced voices, made invisible by history. These traces take the form of fragmented and dispersed memories and personal recollections, objects that transmit these memories and rescued documents. These traces are then rendered doubly present as they become a new cinematic trace. In its specificity to documentary Walhberg extends this definition to the experience of memory in a reading of trace that informs the documentaries under scrutiny: "The trace opens up to time experience and recollection; it designates the transcendental impact of an image-memory, the aporia of memory and imagination" (2008, xiv).

Cinematic construction as a means of unifying and making visible these traces is thus both the formal project and the thematic concern of these works. They share an insistence on the materiality of subjective experience, and, in this respect, these directors find their place in a tradition of embodied cinema that enables the intersubjective responses embedded in this evocation and imagination of history. They embark upon a dialogue with the past that negotiates images and objects—traces—and requires recourse to lived experience, in a remembered, or imaginatively projected, past lived through a cinematic present. Both directors privilege the ambiguity of different realms of cultural knowledge and, specifically, the multi-layered temporality that necessarily invokes the difficulty of concrete representations of history and memory.

It is in this peripheral location that Carla Subirana and Albert Solé find themselves at the beginning of a new millennium. Their focus of attention is on the intricate nexus of experience, imagination, memory and history. The concern here is not to clarify and delimit these as discrete categories but rather to mobilise the connections between them and the gaps inherent in their interpretation. Obfuscation and opacity would seem to lie at the core of the official versions of history that the law tries to redress. The texts highlight these attempts to obscure through omission by inserting themselves at the point of confluence between the official and the remembered, what is included and what is left out, deftly moving between past and present and the imagined temporal planes in between. Resina points out the necessity of exclusion in the assembly of a coherent transmission of the past: "Current debates on historical amnesia are not so much about the loss of the past as about the politics of memory. The dispute is really over which fragments of the past are being refloated and which are allowed to sink" (2000, 86). Reviving these fragments of the past in a new century (and millennium) is complicated by the anxiety that surrounds those lost pieces. The new millennium is typified by our virtual connection to reality; a plethora of screens (mobiles, computers, television) through which experience is mediated and the past is represented. I would contest that the emphasis in these works on material traces attends to an anxiety of lost materiality which equates to lost or silenced histories, and a corresponding anxiety concerning the status of the medium itself, as it moves from celluloid to digital. They both mobilise the virtual to evoke the material through the imaginative capacity of film. The noughties have seen a revival of documentary practice which is concerned with precisely this "politics of memory" and in which *Nedar* and *Bucarest* take their place. History is called into question by the cinematic image, which is based on our capacity for imagination and a subjective and imaginative relationship to that moving image, and by extension the past that it depicts.

In their interrogation of the construction of the image and by inference the image's role in the (re)construction of the past these productions concentrate on layers of the past which are revealed through a combination of the virtual space of film and the material spaces and objects it records. Of course, when these layers are made visible they call attention to what is in-between (spatially and temporally), to that which has covered over the marks of what went before. In this sense, imagination must fill the gaps. This imaginative response is not a fantastical one but one which stems from the confluence of experience and our embodied responses to that experience or as Kathleen Lennon suggests in her philosophical reading of this type of embodied imagination:

> The world, the experiences of which constitute our subjectivity, is an imaginary world and (…) the embodiment which constitutes our mode of being in that world is an imaginary embodiment. Here the notion of imaginary existence is not, as in many theories of the imagination, to be contrasted with the real, but rather to be taken as the condition for there being a real for us. (2004, 107)

This approach acknowledges the importance of experience as constitutive in the formation of memory, and the way in which films make meaning, exploits what is within the image and what is outside of it, the absences that frame it. Merleau-Ponty explains this affective power of the image as it is required to function in the process of imagination (stemming etymologically and practically from the image): "time and space extend beyond the visible present, and at the same time they are *behind* it, in depth, in hiding" (Merleau-Ponty & Lefort 1968, 113). These directors seek to uncover what it is that lies behind official discourse and in doing so they create the formal and narrative ellipses that Merleau-Ponty explains as temporal and spatial sites of possibility.

In *Bucarest* truth and authenticity are immediately under scrutiny: when Albert Solé (son of the late Catalan socialist politician and one of the founders of the constitution, Jordi Solé Tura) discovered, as a child living in Romania, that he had not been born there he began to feel exiled from an authentic sense of self. As he discovers his parents' actual exile and films his father's developing internal exile it is through this creation that an emerging narrative constitutes not a definitive version of personal history but rather a means to analyse it, a new way of looking through and into the past and a new version of understanding that past which encompasses its contradictions and imperfections as sites of possibility and becoming.

Nedar traces another personal history, this time that of the director's mother and grandmother, as Subirana takes on the role of detective in the search for her grandfather's identity. Political reality is inescapable as the political dissidence with which her grandfather was involved inevitably pervades her engagement with his past; the collective unrelentingly intrudes on the personal. Solé's film similarly links the personal to the political collective, this time more explicitly, as he recalls his father's political exile and later returns to Spain through his childhood memories and those of his mother (his father's estranged first wife). The collection of personal testimony and the directors' insistence on the travelling camera, that travels into the past with them, points to a possibility of shared inhabitation of the past via this reconstruction. None of these memories are to be accepted as unproblematic as one of Subirana's grandfather's compatriots underlines with his emphatic, "*No entiendo nada. No sé nada de nada*" [I don't understand anything. I don't know anything about anything].

The importance of the revelatory capacity of the image is evidenced as Subirana and Solé both open their films with screen shots of sonograms and MRI scans respectively, thus conflating and problematising the capacity of technology to record the materiality of the body and at the same time to provide us with images that are not accessible to the human eye but must always be mediated and made possible by virtue of technological imaging. Subirana emphasises the sound of the womb accompanied by an extreme close-up of the image, not immediately recognisable as a foetus *in-utero*, emphasising the affective capacity of the image as it appeals to our imaginative capacity, and metonymically encapsulating the project of the piece as a whole. This type of close-up highlights the haptic qualities of the image and relates to the creative attempts to hold onto history that I examine in due course. This safe, secure pre-memorial uterine space is reflected by the water of the swimming pool in which we see the director swimming alone, at various moments throughout the piece. These lone swimming sections interrupt the main narrative by providing a space for the director to speak directly to the viewer, thinking aloud the problems of retracing her family's difficult past and reconstructing a history which her grandmother kept from her mother and from her.

Here the material traces move us through an imagined and reconstructed past as the significance of trace as a verb and its various definitions encapsulate the process at work through the recording and assembly of these images. The OED offers the following useful definition of the verb "To follow the footprints or traces of; *esp.* to track by the footprints; also with the traces as object". This physical tracing is a feature of both films as on many occasions as we watch hands sorting through objects, feeling their texture and putting them into a new order (cinematic montage made visible through filmed objects). We are aware of the process of tracing as an artistic device, a reworking with the aim of bringing an image, a recalled and reconstructed image in this case, into sharper relief. Further recourse to the dictionary makes explicit the link with the past, and an understanding of it in the present, as an alternative definition offers "To follow the course, development, or history of". Thus the material traces become a means of transmission of memory, from past to present and then present to past as they offer a way into the personal and collective histories under investigation here.

The use of medical images in this process is doubly significant as both directors trace the personal journeys of their parents into Alzheimer's and dementia. The MRI transparencies of the brain, and the advancing of the disease through it, provide a material representation of fading memory and the light and dark shaded areas of these cerebral sites represent the traces of these memories. These degenerative illnesses encapsulate the fragility of memory. The capacity of technology to offer a virtual rendering of the material and to preserve the spatial encoding of this foray into the past evokes the parallel function of cinema here. Spain's attitude to its recent past is frequently configured as amnesiac in nature: the *pacto-de-olvido* [pact of forgetting] was assumed to provide the required stability for a successful transition to democracy. The recourse to memory loss as a trope for these new films—coinciding with Spain's recovery of the past through the *ley de recuperación de la memoria histórica*—configure amnesia as unstable but draw out its productive relationship to memory. We see the fragmentation of personal memory in its relationship to collective history and bear witness to its crumbling, as these films follow the decline of Subirana's mother and Solé's father. The reconstruction, which begins as a result of this fading memory, relies on a combination of the personal memories of these directors combined with archival research of documents and images, which legitimise their story, giving them something tangible from which to create these stories. Marlin Wahlberg examines the use of such material in documentary and explains its value as trace in the creation of these narratives:

> Similar to the historian the documentary filmmaker uses material vestiges of the past to recreate and narrate the historical event. The implied ambivalence of the trace as passage and mark is related to the

> historiographic incentive of this documentary quest and the culture of recollection and forgetting that belongs to the image as archive. (2008, 101)

These "vestiges of the past" have several functions. They provide a material link to the past and, as the camera records them, they open up the possibility for a new type of interaction with the cinematic image, underlining its participation in material history. The cinematic image enables a dynamic relationship with these products of the past as they enter into a new relationship with the testimonies of the characters presented therein. They epitomise the dialogue between past and present that is the concern of these documentary filmic essays and they articulate the contrasting stasis of this variety of documented history against the dynamic possibility of its subjective recollection through a succession of cinematic images. The dynamism that film can lend to static objects is something I will return to later but for now the material trace (these archival objects) are presented as a millennial concern as we become "possessive spectators" in Mulvey's interpretation (2006, 170). This corresponds to an anxiety in Spain which involves a desire to take hold of a collective history, literally to prevent it slipping out of their grasp. Rather than committing violence against the narrative as Mulvey asserts in her reading, a new variety of narration emerges which utilises stasis—lingering shots of photographs or Solé's camera that points to the absences in the now uninhabited erstwhile headquarters of the dissident pirate radio station La Pirenaica—to create productive new spaces of meaning.

This is a mode of representation which presents a meditation on the possibility of permanence in the face of overwhelming transience rendered all the more profound by the dwindling use of film stock and the changing nature of cinema in the noughties. Both cineastes use these thematic and formal concerns to depict the same sense of time passing and time passed, that cinema not only evokes but also embodies. Mulvey's conception of the possessive spectator emerges because of her examination of DVD and the way in which our power to stop the image utilises this stillness for a prolonged contemplation that creates new meanings. If these pauses are constitutive parts of the image then these gaps are created for us and become the spaces in which the imaginative faculties are able to work. These pauses are pre-empted by these directors as prolonged contemplation of places, people and objects in the examples cited above. Early in *Nedar*, as Subirana's grandmother makes her first trip to the site of the monuments to those who fell during the Civil War, the director pauses the image as time freezes in a contemplation of the elderly woman's face and the director's voiceover begins before a cut to a shot of her once more in the swimming pool, voice and body separated by this technology and mirroring an equivalent temporal and emotional separation from the past. The director swims out of the frame at the end of this shot, leaving the camera to linger on the disturbed surface of the water, reminding us of what was there but is now gone. This returns us to the trace, a remnant of what has been present, of which the stone monuments are a further iteration; meaning resides in these traces and residues because of the way in which they are framed. As Jenny Chamarette argues, taking her cues from Merleau-Ponty and Derrida, "This trace is the residue of something whose nature can only be accessed by the manner in which its absence is framed but which co-informs the nature of whatever frames it" (2007, 39). Meaning resides in the films because of the way in which they frame and access these traces.

Framed absences that create a presence are metonymic of the cinematic art itself, and in these films the material objects point to the erased pasts that Subirana and Solé look to give voice to. As Subirana and her mother search for their grandfather/father they revisit the same memorial that her grandmother frequented earlier in the piece. When they find his name on one of the stone pillars engraved with the names of war casualties they both dwell on its tactility, touching the grooves that the recorded letters leave in the stone, as though it is through this touch that the person and the past will become real. This trace is a ghostly absence, made present through the stone memorial and by the camera that records it. In another scene Subirana visits the archives in her search for records of her grandfather; as she tracks along rows and rows of folders containing—one assumes—the documents of numerous personal histories, the ageing paper and the fading information it contains are recorded and brought to life through this inclusion within the profilmic image.

The passing of time and the immortalisation of events on screen provoke questions of authenticity which plague documentary representation, and point-of-view: whose history is this and by whom is it represented? This question is addressed to some extent by the self-reflexive practice of Subirana and her inclusion of a variety of formal techniques which mark breaks between the more serious investigative strands of her piece and the *noir* style episodes which interrupt these musings. More interesting perhaps than the narrative creativity is the effect that these have on the rhythm of the piece in relation to an investigation of possessive spectatorship and the imaginative mode of engagement with the cinematic image that is enabled by this type of filmmaking. The juxtapositions here are temporal ones as the time of history, referenced through the imagined historical excerpts, is placed side-by-side with the time of the image, both the time of its creation and then the time of its re-viewing. Subirana and Solé pursue an approach that privileges this creative manipulation of images described by Wahlberg:

> Although there are many documentary strategies to represent historical experience, the autobiographical mode of contemporary film and video produces the most compelling results. Examples where the personal desire and imagination of the filmmaker meet with social activism and a will to grasp the historical moment incorporate aspects of film and subjectivity within a field that has traditionally been associated with the veracity of photographic representation and the persuasiveness of rhetoric discourse. (2008, 9)

Time is not embalmed within the image but the image forms and informs a new temporality which breathes new life into the past so that it may be re-examined and re-viewed through the framing of traces in these productions. Thus, returning to Labanyi's trope of cultural hauntings, there is a spectral presence in these Spanish cultural products of the noughties. These creations constitute a ghostly presence in two ways; being made visual through the imaginative capacities of the spectator and the creative techniques of the filmmaker and, like those spectres explored by Labanyi, as the effaced and forgotten characters of the past.

It is through an affective relationship with these filmed material and historical objects, figured as traces, that a new subjective engagement with memory and history emerges. As I have already demonstrated, the dynamic potential of cinema is its gift to the objects that it contemplates.

Of concern to Subirana and Solé is the significance of these recorded objects in relation to memory and history, and their cinematic depiction in these instances. An experiential understanding of our engagement with these texts points to a specifically embodied understanding of this encounter between image and viewing subject, one in which we search for meaning through an imagination informed by our own embodied experience of the world. This is reflected and expanded upon by the use of objects as material traces of the past in these films, as they evoke a particular variety of interaction and an understanding of their function in relation to memory. Laura Marks in her excellent work in this area equates the fetishisation of objects with a similar attitude to the documentary image:

> All documentary images are fetishes, insofar as they are indexes of the event documented. However, they do not transparently reflect it, but opaquely encode it. When documentary is accused, as it often is, of fetishising the people and events it represents, this is because it maintains

> the fetish in a state of fixity. But the fetish object may be coaxed to unfold into memory. (2000, 125)

Like the objects they record, these documentaries become mobile fetishes, or as Marks labels them, "travelling objects" by virtue of the connections that they forge with memory and their role in the intersubjective transmission of these memories. The positive ramifications for this type of documentary emanate from the way in which it can also function as connective tissue; it blurs the subject/object binary that is the assumed framework of interpretation in the cinematic space. In dissolving this division *Nedar* and *Bucarest* point to a similar potential blurring between the personal and collective nature of historical recollection and the material role that moving images might play in an investigation of the lost elements of both.

Solé demonstrates anxiety for this lost material memory as the documents he films alongside black and white photographs of his family's past in exile and on their return to Spain function as *aides memoires* in some particularly poignant scenes with his father. They look through documents with his father's second wife and attempt to prompt these rapidly fading memories, as though holding the material evidence of his stay in prison will prove successful in slowing the inevitable decline by unfolding and transmitting the encoded history that Marks argues they may contain. The cinematic image becomes the means by which we can appropriate the material reminders of our collective past, an experience pertinent for a family whose past has been so deeply imbricated in the political situation of a country and at times lived so publicly within that country. It is as though by putting the documents together he can create the past for this family that had been excluded, as Labanyi posits, from the official discourse of its time. The director does not eschew the tendency to mendacity that the medium can entail, nor does he offer the cinematic version of this past as a reconstituted ideal. The documents which provide access to this past are filmed in layers, as a family photograph from his childhood is overlaid by documents (rendered semi-transparent by the method of filming) typed in French and replete with crossings-out and alterations, making visible the obfuscations that have been a barrier to this nation's understanding of the past. The film's slippery subjectivity is highlighted in this use of photographs as both Subirana and Solé construct from the outside stories in which they both also play an integral part. They present several versions of self, the children in photographs, the son or daughter in the family history and the authors of their respective works. This constitutes a further blurring between the subject and object of cinema that mobilises its potential for a variety of intersubjective perspectives which are also brought to bear in their own relationship with the objects of the film. Isabelle McNeill's apposite exploration of these themes in the context of recent French cinematic production leads her to the following conclusion about the documentary maker's interstitial relationship with their work:

> Like the objects they film, the filmmakers themselves are in a liminal position between private and public, between the private self that exists beyond the frame and the public persona of the screen "I" that we hear or see. At the same time, their personae are partly constructed by the objects that captivate their filming gaze, their (fantasised) subjectivity conjured by the museal accumulation of memory objects and of the personal associations they weave between them in the operation of montage and commentary. (2010, 82)

It is in this "operation of montage and commentary" that these films seek, and find, their cinematic contribution to an experience of times passed. I initiated this investigation through an interest in the omissions and obfuscations that are necessarily constituent of the cinematic representation of a fading past and, through the autobiographical slant of both works, this reveals itself as a process of examining the self from both inside and outside the frame. The particular success of *Bucarest* and *Nedar* lies in their ability to exploit the content of the frame in order to evoke the subjective, emotional and imaginative content of the process of memory and present it as a cinematic, dynamic and mobile process. Less important than the accurate retelling of history is the democratic process that its investigation can give rise to.

Meaning is seen to reside precisely in the affective responses to filmed objects and evocative spaces created in film's liminal spaces. Inserting still images within the moving picture, either in the form of extended contemplation of a filmed object, or a photograph (with its indexical link to the moving image itself) causes a significant rupture and creates a space for a new type of contemplation and imaginative response. These are the spaces that had previously been covered over or omitted from official versions. The traces of a material past are embraced by the visual and the virtual in a confluence of past and present, memory and history, the personal and the collective in such a way that new subjectivities and subjective versions of the past emerge from these creative documentary offerings.

Works Cited

Chamarette, J. (2007) "Flesh, Folds and Texturality: Thinking Visual Ellipsis via Merleau-Ponty, Hélène Cixous and Robert Frank", *Paragraph*, vol. 30, no. 2, 34-49.

Labanyi, J., ed. (2002) *Constructing Identity in Contemporary Spain: Theoretical Debates and Cultural Practice*. Oxford: Oxford University Press.

Lennon, K. (2004) "Imaginary Bodies and Worlds", *Inquiry*, vol. 47, no. 2, 107-22.

Marks, L. (2000) *The Skin of the Film: Intercultural Cinema, Embodiment and the Senses*. Durham and London: Duke University Press.

McNeill, I. (2010) *Memory and the Moving Image: French Film in the Digital Era*. Edinburgh: Edinburgh University Press.

Merleau-Ponty, M., and Lefort, C. (1968) *The Visible and the Invisible*. Evanston: Northwestern University Press.

Mulvey, L. (2006) *Death 24x a Second: Stillness and the Moving Image*. London: Reaktion Books.

Resina, J.R. (2000) "Short of Memory: the Reclamation of the Past Since the Spanish Transition to Democracy" in J.R. Resina (ed.), *Disremembering the Dictatorship: The Politics of Memory in the Spanish Transition to Democracy*. Amsterdam: Rodopi, 87-125.

Wahlberg, M. (2008) *Documentary Time: Film and Phenomenology*. Minneapolis: University of Minnesota Press.

Notes

[1] This style of documentary seems to be part of a noticeable trend with directors such as José Luis Guerín, Mercedes Álvarez, Isaki Lacuesta, Esteve Riambau and Joaquim Jordà (by no means an exhaustive list) attracting attention for their innovative approach to the depiction of real events.

CHAPTER EIGHT

LA FORJA DEL PRODIGIO: PEPITO ARRIOLA

ALISON SINCLAIR

> Me pregunto: ¿quién es responsable de la historia de Pepito Arriola? ¿El destino? ¿La siniestra trayectoria del pasado siglo XX? ¿Quién se acordará de él? Fue la leyenda viva más importante de la música española. Nadie subió tan rápido y tan alto, y nadie tampoco desapareció en la bruma del olvido con la facilidad que le sumió a él. (Morán 2004, 28)
>
> [I ask myself, who is responsible for the history of Pepito Arriola? Destiny? The sinister path of the twentieth century? Who will remember him? He was the most important living legend of Spanish music. No-one else rose so swiftly and so high, nor did anyone else disappear so rapidly into the mists of oblivion as the way in which he was so easily absorbed.]

The eclipsing of the memory of sexual reformer Hildegart Rodriguez by Aurora, her mother and her murderess (Sinclair 2007, 147-51), has in its turn eclipsed a further narrative, that of the life and outstanding talents of Pepito Arriola (1895-1954), Aurora's nephew. From the account Aurora gives (see Cal 1991, 28; Rendueles 1989, 24) Aurora was able to "practise" childcare and education on him, in advance of her conception of her eugenic child, Hildegart. Arriola would indeed become a child prodigy pianist, recognised by the Spanish Royal Family and performer in public from his earliest years. His story, strikingly elusive in its detail, can be read not so much or so simply as a life in itself, but variously as an account of cultural enthusiasms and fashions (prodigies, spiritualism, extremes of mind and body) that can be observed in Spain in the 1900s, and more widely in Europe. In the 1900s, the remnants of nineteenth-century malaise persisted in Spain, to some degree arguably heightened by the disaster of 1898. The sense of menace of decadence triggered, among other things, a fascination with extreme cases, and extreme phenomena (including mysticism, the paranormal, and other ways of achieving exalted states) that might serve as solutions. But the exaltation of such extreme cases was by no means simple. What we can observe in the case of Arriola is also to do with the power of ownership (itself linked to the uncertainties of the age). It is an example of cultural and psychological appropriation, both in its own time, and in relation to the nationalisms of the 2000s. This paper concentrates on the little that is known of Arriola's early years, with a focus on the jockeying for position that can be observed in claims for "owning" and "nurturing" his talents.

I come to the story of Pepito Arriola as a second displacement in cultural memory. In both cases it is Hildegart's mother that is the major pivot in this relegation to oblivion. Until recent years the life and activities of Hildegart Rodríguez had been lost to view. A notable silence during the Franco regime of writings on her was lifted slightly in 1977 when two of her major works, *El problema sexual tratado por una mujer española* [The Sexual Problem as Observed by a Spanish Woman] and *La rebeldía sexual de la juventud* [Sexual Rebellion and the Young] were republished, the same year in which the film, *Mi hija Hildegart* [My Daughter Hildegart] by Fernando Fernán Gómez appeared. While the first two works allowed Hildegart's own words to come to a more modern audience, the film placed its emphasis on Hildegart's mother as much as on Hildegart itself. The displacement of Hildegart by Aurora would be characteristic of later writings on Hildegart (Cal 1991; Rendueles 1989). It is clear that the figure of the mad mother who murdered her daughter in 1933 and became an icon of extreme behaviour and attitude at her trial not only eclipsed the tragedy of the loss of the daughter, but also marked the relegation to effective silence of the activities of eugenics and sexual reform with which Hildegart had made her mark in public life (Sinclair 2007, 147-161). Even more so, this tragic event arguably contributed to the eclipsing of the prodigy who had preceded Hildegart.

Pepito Arriola, born on 14 December 1895, was the illegitimate child of Josefina Rodríguez Carballeira (born 1873), daughter and oldest child of Francisco Rodríguez Arriola and Aurora Andrea Carballeira López.[1] Josefina was twenty-two at the time of his birth (see Cal 1991, 20-28). Her sister Aurora, who would become Hildegart's mother, was born in 1879, hence six years younger, and a third sibling, Francisco, born in 1884, was later to be considered a wastrel by Aurora (the telegrammatic form of the clinical notes reproduced by Rendueles [1989, 19-20] emphasises the dismissive attitude of Aurora to her brother). Two further children died in infancy, and are recorded briefly in the clinical notes: Francisca, who died aged six (Aurora was unable to remember the cause of death when interviewed by the psychiatrists at Ciempozuelos) and Dolores, who died a few days after her birth, because of a congenital heart defect (Rendueles 1989, 19). It is striking that the dramatic death of the infant Dolores appears to have passed into "family memory" (conceivably because of the element of congenital inadequacy), whereas the other death is mislaid, at least by Aurora, in terms of her faulty or dismissive recollection of her.

Cal notes that as soon as Pepito was born accounts began to differ about what happened (Cal 1991, 28). The two competing strands were that offered by Aurora, according to which she looked after Pepito until the age of about three and a half, and the account that Josefina would provide to the press when Pepito became known as a prodigy. In general, press accounts of Pepito tend to follow Josefina's line. My intention is to look at the dynamic of this competitive memory, and to include other appropriations, both of the time, and of more recent date.

The differing stories of the two sisters, in particular their claim to Pepito that is relayed in their accounts, reflects in part a rupture between them but it is one that is not so absolute as has been thought. The departure to Madrid in 1899 after Josefa had unequivocally taken control of Pepito is one key date. Matters of finance and family management would seem a clear further motive for some discord. At their mother's death in 1905, Cal reports that "poco después de repartir la familia la herencia de la madre, el padre de Aurora hizo testamento a favor de ella" [shortly after the family had shared out the inheritance of the mother, Aurora's father made his will in favour of her] (Cal 1991, 23). It is not clear, however, that this disposition in 1905 was responsible for a complete rupture, despite Josefa's departure first to Madrid, then to Germany, with Pepito. It was presumably the will seen by the notary Cándido Conde Fernández on 27 March 1913 in Ferrol that made the difference. In this the father was to make Aurora executrix of the will, and ensured the lion's share for her, and her descendants (Dopico Vale and Mera Castro 2003, 9a). The date of this will makes less likely the existence of a real rupture earlier than Cal suggests. Ocampo also rightly draws attention to the ongoing presence of Aurora in the background, particularly in October 1911 when Pepito visited Ferrol, as reported in *El Correo Gallego* 16 October 1911. Aurora, furthermore, would be the family member designated to unveil a commemorative plaque to Pepito (Ocampo 2003, 54, 59).

Josefa's Story

As Pepito's mother, Josefa was without doubt also the manager of his publicity, as well as his performance. This included not just the promotion of her son to potentially interested patrons, but also the projection of an image of protective maternal love. Indeed, in relation to his performances in London in 1906, an announcement in the *Times* on 13 October of that year declared: "To avoid any mental or physical strain his parents only allow him to make an occasional appearance in public to encourage him in his work." By this stage, Pepito was, however, some seven years into his public life, and the intensity of exposure had already been considerable.

In general, the picture that Josefa offered of her child, and her role in nurturing him as a prodigy, emphasises naturalness, almost an artlessness of attitude, a maternal devotion of response to a child who surprised her in his infancy with a little divined musical gift. This is what comes through in the majority of the press coverage in Galicia in the years of Pepito's infancy, and it would seem plausible to see Josefa as the prime mediatrix for this information.

There is, in these local press accounts, no signal of family strife, of the illegitimacy of Pepito's birth, or of any strains or pressures surrounding his upbringing. This is at odds with all that will emerge subsequently (mainly but not exclusively as the result of the murder of Hildegart by her mother Aurora). Yet in Josefa's account of the early years there are odd details that suggest something curiously reminiscent of her sister's attitude to the upbringing of a child. El Caballero Audaz reports on his interview with the Arriola family, quoting Josefa:

> Verán ustedes. Vivíamos nosotros en Ferrol—ya saben ustedes que Pepito es de Galicia—. Al cumplir año y medio le quité el ama y le puse niñera. Pero al nene esta sustitución no le agradaba; echaba de menos el pecho, no quería estar con la niñera y, claro, a falta del ama, prefería estar conmigo. Yo, que sentía y siento una gran pasión por la música, me pasaba horas enteras tocando el piano, y el niño, sentadito a mi lado, se extasiaba oyéndome. (Dopico Vale and Mera Castro 2003a, 8)
>
> [Let me tell you. We lived in Ferrol—you know that Pepito comes from Galicia— . When he was one and a half I took his wetnurse from him and gave him a nanny. But the child did not like this substitution; he missed the breast, he did not want to be with the nanny, and of course, not having the wetnurse, he preferred to be with me. Having felt then, as I do now, tremendous passion for music, I used to spend hours on end playing the piano, and the child, sitting at my side, was in ecstasies listening to me.]

This quotation is from a statement made with reference to the prologue to the biography of Pepito by Justo Zamora. A striking feature about the biography is its date: 1900—more than a little early to consider a life ready for recording, but also perhaps an advance sign of how Pepito was recognised (or treated) as a being who might be packaged and presented to the world. In the quotation we can see furthermore Josefa's level of determination, in her decision to move Pepito from a wetnurse to a nanny that was apparently not in tune (or in time) with his own wishes. We can also see a detail open to more than one interpretation. In her activity of endless playing of the piano, which she puts as the frame for her child's ecstatic pleasure (he is presented as an accomplished picture by the diminutive "sentadito"), is arguably also an involuntary glimpse of a narcissistic woman who intervenes thoughtlessly in the affairs of others, and then by chance gives pleasure to her child (there is no conscious turning towards him in this extract).

Josefa was clearly the instigator of Pepito's life of performance, first to patrons, and then to a public. In an interview in 1918 with María Luisa Castellanos for *Asturias* of La Habana, Pepito would say that his first concert was 28 March 1906. It would appear that by this point, and at the age of twenty-three, his recollections of infant performances had faded from view, or that he only thought about his performing career seriously beginning when he was ten. There is a revealing comment, however, on Pepito's early years of being on show, an experience that still overshadowed his emergence as a person of talent:

> Él ya no era el niño prodigio que había sido, había perdido la parte de animal de feria que da la precocidad a todos esos niños que saltan a los medios de comunicación, pero quedaban los rescoldos y, por tanto, cierto interés de la prensa hacia su persona, seguramente más por el niño que había sido que por el joven con talento que era. (Castellanos 1918)
>
> [He was no longer the infant prodigy he had been, he had lost that aspect of the circus animal which makes for precocity in all those children who hit the headlines, but there were still some traces of it, and thus, there was still some interest in him from the press, no doubt more because of the child that he had been than because of the talented young man that he was.]

A flurry of activity ensued from Josefa's "discovery" of Pepito's musical talent. They left for Madrid on 2 November 1899 (Dopico Vale and Mera Castro 2003b, 16), giving a first concert on 4 November 1899 (Cal 1991, 28). The next day he was invited by the queen María Cristina to perform in the Palace. Three days later he performed before the *infanta* Isabel, and later before Alfonso XIII (Ocampo 2003, 50). A performance in the Ateneo took place in March 1901 (Ocampo 2003, 53). Before this, however, he had been taken to perform before the Congrès de Psychologie on 6 October 1900 (Richet 1900).

It seems evident that Josefa, Pepito's mother, had a clear perception not only that it mattered to get patrons (appearing before royalty ensured the funding of Pepito's studies in Germany), but also that it was important to have "scientific recognition" of her son's qualities. Hence not only this appearance before the 1900 Congrès de Psychologie (Richet 1900), but also one in 1903 at the Psychological Institute of Leipzig, which resulted in a telegram dated 12 February 1903 and sent by her to *La Voz de Galicia*. Here is further evidence of her conviction that one had to go to the top to get recognition (Pepito handed the telegram on his prodigy status to Kaiser Wilhelm) but also the source of certification from the institute, where they affirmed that "consideran a Pepito Arriola como un prodigioso fenómeno de organización para la música" [they see Pepito Arriola as a prodigious phenomenon of organisation for music] (Cal 1991, 30).

A Prodigy Abroad

Accounts of Arriola's life attest to his developed professional activity in the giving of concerts, particularly in his early years. Early performances with the Berlin Philharmonic would be followed by visits to the USA, and to Cuba in 1910 (see Dopico Vale and Mera Castro 17). Two examples are looked at here: his appearances in London in 1906 and 1909, and his visits to Buenos Aires 1912-14 and 1920. Both can be seen as a public "production" of the child genius.

Arriola visited London in 1906 and again in 1909. The 1906 visit was the occasion for strong publicity emphasising his "prodigy" nature. Thus the *Times* of 13 October 1906 carried a collection of five small adverts leading up to his appearance in the Albert Hall, outlining briefly his life and nature as a phenomenon. The first of these emphasises not only his infant prodigy status, but also places him in the context of attracting the attention of professionals, not in music, but in psychology:

> Born Dec. 14, 1896, at Ferrol, Spain. Developed such remarkable talent for the piano that he was taken to Paris at the age of three years and presented before the Psychological Congress as a phenomenon. At six years of age he was sent to Germany to study under a grant from the King of Spain.

A second announcement added:

> After studying at Leipsic and Berlin, made his first appearance under the special protection of the Emperor and Empress of Germany. Has been

> frequently invited to play at the German Court and possesses several magnificent gifts from the Imperial family.

By 1909, aged twelve, he was back. Promoted by the agent Daniel Mayer, and described as "the sensational young Spanish pianist" (*Times* 1 June 1909, 6) "the marvellous young Spanish pianist discovered by Arthur Nikisch" (*Times* 3 June 1909, 10) he was given repeated puffs before the concert itself on 10 June 1909, the only one of several performers to have such specialist treatment.

The day before the concert itself, in the *Times* of 9 June 1909 (10), there was a return to the detailed treatment given on his first appearance in London in 1906, with quotations from that year from various British newspapers. A quotation was given from the *Daily Telegraph* of 15 October 1906 which put Arriola firmly in the category of extreme phenomena. The elevation of tone here is suggestive of some of the mystic attributes associated with some of the circles where such phenomena were explored and celebrated, and not—given that these examples are from the English press—restricted to Spain

> In the last five and twenty years there have been numberless piano playing prodigies, but none of them could compare in the richness of the divine gift of touch with that of this latest wonder-child. Here we are face to face with something of so remarkable a nature and so inexplicable as to be numbered among the current wonders of the world.

The *Daily Graphic*, meanwhile, also of 15 October 1906 and cited in this same number of the *Times*, referred to him as "this dark-haired little imp in his blue velveteen suit and big lace collar". The audience's response was written up with verve: "Pepito's success was overwhelming and he was recalled to the platform again and again, being at last compelled to appease the insatiable audience with an encore". In advance of a further 1909 concert at the Albert Hall, Arriola would be referred to in the *Times* on 25 September 1909, (10), as "The Modern Mozart". There were also two visits to Buenos Aires, July 1912 to the autumn of 1914, and 1920. They were given remarkably prominent coverage by *Nosotros*, the cultural journal of Buenos Aires, first published in 1907.

By 1912 Arriola was fifteen, and yet his youth was emphasised from the start, not least by the photograph that appeared in *Nosotros* in July 1912. Seated at the piano on an adjustable three-legged piano stool, Arriola's demeanour of quiet concentration is striking. But this is hardly more striking than his attire of a loosely fitting short jacket and trousers that end at the knee with a brief frill, in a type of Little Lord Fauntleroy breeches. It is a move on from the blue velveteen suit, but even with different fashions in mind, was still remarkably exotic, as if he were to be enclosed in a sort of cultural time-capsule. His new costume, coupled with a hairstyle that is a shortened form of a pageboy cut, communicated not just youth, but greater youth than his actual years, and with some sense of uncertainty of gender. He is clearly presented as a phenomenon, his photograph ("Célebre pianista de quince años" [A celebrated fifteen-year-old pianist]) preceding his actual appearance at the Teatro de la Ópera.

The story Arriola tells for the journalist of *Nosotros* in this number is familiar in that it is fundamentally a shortened account of that given in James Francis Cooke's *Great Pianists on Piano Playing* (1913):

> Me gustaba tanto la música y me divertía de tal manera recorriendo el teclado y sacando bonitos sonidos, que el piano fue en realidad mi primero y mi mejor juguete. Me encantaba oír tocar a mi madre, y contínuamente le pedía que ejecutara algo, para que yo pudiera repetir las mismas piezas después de ella. (A. A. B, 1912, 242)[2]
>
> [I so much enjoyed music and loved running my hands over the keyboard and drawing beautiful sounds from it, that the piano was in truth my first and best plaything. I loved listening to my mother play, and was forever asking her to play something, so that I could repeat the same pieces after her.]

The interview with Cooke (1913) in fact raises the possibility of a type of ventriloquism of the sort that would be speculated about by Mrs Gillett-Gatty in relation to Hildegart and Aurora, her mother, in her comment in a letter to Havelock Ellis on 1 July 1933, just after Hildegart's murder, that:

> I wonder if you now realise, not that Hildegart was a Trilby to Doña Aurora's Svengali, but that until Hildegart was got hold of by the Federalist Party, she was a perfectly intelligent human Dictaphone, into which her mother spoke & Hildegart subsequently wrote, or uttered the message. (Sinclair 2007, 128)

Ventriloquism, or the adoption of the presentation by others, would also be a feature of Hildegart's initial presentation of herself to Ellis as a "eugenic child" in her letter to him of 2 December 1931 (see Sinclair 2007, 133-4). In the case of Arriola's version of himself given to Cooke, a similar style of recitation of the view arguably presented by others can be seen:

> So much that was of interest to me was continually occurring while I was a child that it all seems like a kind of haze to me. I cannot remember when I

> first commenced to play, for my mother tells me that I wanted to reach out for the keyboard before I was out of her arms. I have also learned that when I was about two and one-half years of age, I could quite readily play after my mother anything that the size of my hand would permit me to play.
>
> I loved music so dearly, and it was such fun to run over the keyboard and make the pretty sounds, that the piano was really my first and best toy. I loved to hear my mother play, and continually begged her to play for me so that I could play the same pieces after her. I knew nothing of musical notation and played entirely by ear, which seemed to me the most natural way to play. At that time, word was sent to the King of Spain that I showed talent, and he became interested in me, and I played before him. (Cooke 1913, 41)

What we can see from the "production" of Arriola, not restricted to his immediate family (albeit to be repeated in uncanny fashion in the "production" of Hildegart by her mother and others) is how general a phenomenon of the time it was. Arguably an inheritance of the nineteenth-century interest in the display of eccentricities and monstrosities, it now comes into the world of commerce and politics, as well as the world of education. It speaks of the possibilities that can be hoped for, longed for, in times of strife and despondency, while placing examples before the public of standard-bearers of exceptional development.

Aurora's Story

Speaking from her incarceration (firstly in prison, and then in a mental hospital) there is a competing appropriation of Pepito by Aurora. This is in the account of her life and circumstances given to the psychiatrists in Ciempozuelos. In the fourth entry of the clinical note, dated 3 November 1936, some three years after her murder of Hildegart, Aurora is cut and dried in her classification of the diverse members of her family. Peremptory, summary, negative, noting memorably of her own mother that "Tenía más sexo que seso" [She had more sex than brain] (Rendueles 1989, 17), Aurora labels her sister equally memorably, but also simplistically: "Muy mala hermana. Rencillosa, liosa, "Mala madre y mala esposa"" [A very bad sister. Quarrelsome, confusing. "A bad wife and mother"]. She was seen as a breaker-up of other couples, and homosexual (Rendueles 1989, 18). It is possible that some of the telegrammatic style results simply from the fact that this discourse has been subjected to note-taking, and is not woven into a smooth discourse. It is also possible that in the course of taking the family history, those conducting the interview were seeking the classifications and labels that Aurora offered.

Even with these *caveats*, it is notable that Aurora passes immediately from this negative portrait of her sister not to the birth itself, nor to how it was received in the family, but to her own subsequent role. Thus it is noted that "La paciente se dedicó a la educación artística del hijo de su hermana" [the patient dedicated herself to the artistic education of her sister's son], making the further claim that she was his "directora espiritual" [spiritual director], both claims striking given that he was still an infant when he passed to his mother's care. As the notes pass into what seems closer to a verbatim record, the seamlessness, the ambition and the fixity of the self-image that Aurora had in relation to him is notable, not least that she is recalling at a distance of some thirty-seven years:

> Hice de él algo de lo que después he hecho con mi hija, fue lo primero que yo he formado, que he dirigido, entonces tenía yo 14 años. Le cantaba, tocaba el piano enfrente de él para formarlo. "Cuando apenas tenía un año, ya tarareaba las canciones conmigo, fue prodigio musical, porque yo, cuando era un muñeco, cuando todavía sólo era un muñeco, lo empecé a formar". "*Sentía cómo mi alma iba al niño y cómo se modelaba el alma de éste*". (Rendueles 1989, 19, emphasis as in original)
>
> [I did with him what I later did with my daughter, he was the first one that I had formed, had directed, and I was 14 at the time. I used to sing to him, play the piano to him to educate him. "When he was only one, he used to hum songs with me, he was a musical prodigy because I, when he was no more than a doll, began to shape him." *"I felt that my soul went out to the child and that it was modelling his soul"*.]

With the optimism of hindsight, emphasising (or misrecollecting voluntarily or involuntarily), Aurora in this makes herself two years younger than she actually was at the time.

The version of these events offered by the psychiatrists José Sacristán and Miguel Prados y Such appointed as expert witnesses for the trial of Aurora moves this account into a smooth discourse (either because they perceived it as such, or because they wanted to present a version that would be more acceptable for the legal destination of the document) here inserting or recording what is omitted from the clinical notes, that is, a sense of reaction on the part of Aurora to her sister's illegitimate child. It is as though Pepito is to be made more legitimate in the family romance by virtue of recording a reaction of shock by Aurora to his illegitimate status:

> Al llegar a los doce años, la procesada sufre una fuerte impresión. Su hermana mayor trae a la casa paterna el fruto de sus amores ilegítimos. Pasados los primeros momentos de disgusto, provocados por este incidente doloroso y ante la indiferencia de la madre por el hijo, la procesada pone todo su interés y entusiasmo al servicio del recién nacido. A partir de este instante lo toma como cosa propia y se dedica a él por entero. El cuidado y las atenciones que el niño requiere son sus ocupaciones favoritas. (Rendueles 1989, 201)
>
> [When she reached the age of twelve, the accused suffered a major shock. Her older sister brought the fruit of her illegitimate love affair back to the family home. After an initial reaction of annoyance provoked by this painful incident and given the mother's indifference towards her infant, the accused directed all her interest and enthusiasm to looking after the newborn. From this point she took him over as her own thing and dedicated herself to him entirely. Her favourite pastime was looking after and attending to the child.]

In this account Aurora is virtually normalised, endowed with normal human reactions, although it would appear that her age has been reduced by her in her account to the psychiatrists so that she appeared to be twelve and not sixteen at the time of Arriola's birth. Her activity is conceivably made age-appropriate with that of a twelve year-old with the reference to her taking Pepito as "cosa propia" [her own thing]; this is less unsettling than is her reference to him as a "muñeco" [doll] when she began to shape him. It is also made plain in Aurora's direct account, as conveyed in the clinical notes, that she considered she had used Pepito as a dry run for her task of shaping Hildegart into a genius or prodigy who could work for peace (see Rendueles 1989, 19, cited above).

The "Scientific" Story: Are Prodigies Born or Made?

The existence of prodigies, whether in the arts, or mathematics, or performing skills, inevitably raises the question of whether their occurrence is an example of random felicity, or whether there are factors to which it can be attributed. Prodigies, it should be emphasised, are not geniuses, although there is a temptation to bundle together these two sources of extreme achievement.

An article by Ruthsatz and Detterman (2003) considered the data that might explain the rare phenomenon of musical prodigies, and their case-study, that of a six year old, has interesting details that have a bearing on Arriola's case, particularly in their observation that memory plays a key role in the production of those perceived as geniuses. Their definition of prodigies is that they are "children under ten years of age who perform culturally relevant tasks at a level that is rare even among highly trained professional adults in their field". They refer to two famous examples, both discussed by Géza Révész, Mozart and Erwin Nyiregyhazi, who "were reported as having an early onset of musical ability coupled with an extraordinary memory for musical pieces" (2003, 510). The accounts of Aurora and Josefa compete about which of them fostered Arriola's early talents, both during Arriola's early years and flourishing as a prodigy, and in the re-visitation of Arriola's case that would take place in the twenty-first century. Ocampo (2003, 48, 50) firmly places Josefa as the early influence, whereas Dopico Vale and Mera Castro (2003, 9, 16) equally firmly signal Aurora in this position. In both instances, however, we find the idea that Arriola at the age of two and a half or three heard music played by either Josefa or Aurora and then went on to reproduce it spontaneously. A lengthier account comes from Aurora's conversation with Eduardo de Guzmán, reprinted by Martínez López (2003, 63-4). Guzmán was the interlocutor chosen by Aurora for her version of her life, and visited her in prison between her arrest and the trial in 1934. The novel that ensued, co-authored with Ezekiel Endériz includes this account of the "discovery" by her of Arriola's talent:

> Yo, como todas las muchachas de la época, tocaba el piano. Creo que no lo hacía del todo mal. En cualquier caso, llegué a tener una afición desmedida a la música. Cuando tocaba, sentaba a Pepito a mi lado. A veces, en broma, cogiéndole las manos le hacía aporrear las teclas. Así transcurrieron muchos meses. Cada día, el niño seguía con mayor interés y atención lo que yo hacía; se le veía extraordinariamente conmovido por la música. Hasta que una tarde, inesperadamente, ocurrió lo extraordinario...
> (...)
> Acababa yo de tocar una jota. De repente, Pepito apoyó sus manecitas en el teclado y empezó a tocar. Yo escuchaba asombrada, abstraída, sin acabar de comprender lo que estaba sucediendo ante mis ojos. El niño repetía, superándolo, cuanto yo había hecho. Eran los mismos compases, idénticos acordes, pero arrancando al piano tonalidades nuevas, dando a la música una sonoridad tan extraordinaria y sorprendente que no parecía arrancada del viejo piano familiar. (Guzmán and Endériz 1933, 47)

> [Like all young girls of the time, I played the piano. I think I did so not at all badly. In any case, I came to have an excessive love of music. When I played, I used to sit Pepito at my side. Sometimes, as a game, I used to take his hands and get him to hammer away at the keys. Many months passed in this way. Each day, the child followed what I did with increased interest and attention; you could see he was exceptionally moved by music. Until one afternoon, out of the blue, something extraordinary happened…

> (…)
> I had just played a *jota*. Suddenly, Pepito put his little hands on the keyboard and began to play. I listened, amazed, engrossed, unable to understand what was happening before my eyes. The boy was repeating, with mastery, all that I had done. He was playing with the same beat, the same chords, but managing to extract new tonality from the piano, giving the music such an unusual and surprising tone that it seemed not to have been produced from the old family piano.]

The account offered by Josefa, and conveyed by Richet (1900, 433) suggests a less intense relationship, while still indicating aural memory as the prime factor in Arriola's early playing:

> L'enfant avait à peu près 2 ans et demi lorsque je découvris pour la première fois, et par hasard, ses aptitudes musicales. A cette époque, un musicien de mes amis m'adressa une sienne composition musicale, et je me mis à la jouer au piano assez fréquemment; il est probable que l'enfant y faisait attention; mais je ne m'en aperçus pas. Or, un matin, j'entends jouer dans une chambre voisine ce même air musical, mais avec tant d'autorité et de justesse, que je voulus savoir qui se permettait de jouer ainsi du piano chez moi.
> J'entrai dans le salon, et je vis mon petit garçon qui était seul et qui jouait cet air. Il était assis sur un siège élevé, où il s'était mis tout seul, et, en me voyant, il se mit à rire et me dit: *Coco, mama*. Je crus qu'il y avait là un miracle véritable.

> [The child was about two and a half when for the first time and by chance, I discovered his musical aptitude. At this time, a friend of mine who was a musician had dedicated one of his compositions to me, and I used to play it fairly often on the piano; probably the child paid attention to this; but I did not notice. Then, one morning, I heard the same musical melody being played in an adjoining room, but with such accuracy and authority that I wanted to know who it was who was taking the liberty of playing the piano like that in my home.
> I went into the living room and saw my little boy there, on his own, and playing that melody. He was sitting on a raised seat, where he had climbed up on his own, and when he saw me, he began to laugh and said, *Boo, mummy*. I thought that a real miracle had happened.]

The initial reception of Arriola by the public arena was when he was less than three years old, and presented to a series of groups to be understood, recognised, and—eventually—promoted. One of the most significant events was his performance before the Congrès de Psychologie on 6 October 1900. This was written up by Charles Richet (who would win the Nobel Prize in Physiology or Medicine for his work on anaphylaxis) in the section "Psychologie" of the *Revue Scientifique* (of which he was a director), as a "Note sur un cas remarquable de précocité musicale" [A Note about a Case of Remarkable Musical Precocity], notable for its careful scientific observance, consistent with Richet's status as positivist (see Gordon 2008, 151). This piece was subsequently attacked by E. W. Scripture in 1908 in a number of the *Journal of the American Society for Psychical Research* where Scripture alleged that a series of eminent scientists, including Sir William Crookes, Sir Oliver Lodge, Lombroso, W. Barrett and Camille Flammarion had been victims of hoaxes.[3] The response by Richet came the same month, in a journal that now declared his intellectual context, the *Annales des Sciences Psychiques*, in an article whose title also indicated a shift in focus, "Des limites de l'incrédulité" [The Limits of Unbelief], with a photograph of Arriola at the age of three and a half, when he had appeared before the Congrès de Psychologie. Scripture had asserted that Richet had been taken in by Arriola's mother. This assertion (somewhat unfortunate in the choice of example, given the later musical career and success of Arriola) while apparently couched in generous attitude, was dismissive of what he saw as Richet's emotional attitude which blinded him to the trickery. As Richet quotes Scripture, whose reference is to a professor of physiology in a world-famed University:

> No kinder, simpler, more charming man ever lived: full of enthusiasm and ambition to discover some great truth, his very sincerity and simplicity render him a [sic] easy prey to the clever schemer. I have seen him, after a test of a musical prodigy, clasp the child to his breast, with enthusiastic tears, whereas the audience had seen the mother's tricks. (Richet 1908, 98)

Richet offers a counter-version of the event with such detail of the number of distinct places Arriola had performed on this occasion, in different rooms, on different pianos, and always in full light, and observed by between twenty and thirty people, that he ends with the speculation that perhaps Scripture must have been referring to some other, and attacks with the same apparent benevolence demonstrated by his critic:

> Pour avoir cru que c'était Mme Arriola qui jouait du piano, et non son petit bébé de trois ans et demi, il faut vraiment que mon aimable et infortuné collègue M. Scripture ait eu devant les yeux le nuage épais d'une incrédulité stupéfiante. (Richet 1908, 98)

> [To have believed that it was Mme Arriola who played the piano, and not her little infant of three and a half, my good and unfortunate colleague M.

Scripture must have had a dense cloud of stupefying incredulity before his eyes.]

Despite the apparently different remits of the reviews involved in this exchange (Richet publishes in a purely scientific journal, is then attacked from another journal, albeit one dedicated to "psychical research", and is then rebutted from a journal whose name lays claim to the label of "scientific" for this area of activity, being the *Annales des Sciences Psychiques*) the distinctions between the publications are not entirely straightforward. Although the *Annales* contain the range of articles on spiritualism, mediums, general psychic phenomena, the occult, a clear demonstration of the concern with such affairs in the 1900s as signalled at the start of this paper, we also find, for example, on 1 February 1908, a quasi-scientific article by Lombroso on "Eusapia Paladino et le spiritisme" [Eusapia Paladino and Spiritualism]. It is also instructive to see its self-description as a journal that is a "Publication bi-mensuelle illustrée consacrée aux Recherches Expérimentales et Critiques sur les Phénomènes de TÉLÉPATHIE, LUCIDITÉ, PRÉMONITION, MÉDIUMNITÉ etc." [A Bi-monthly Illustrated Publication Dedicated to Experimental Research and Critiques of the Phenomena of TELEPATHY, SEERS, PREMONITIONS, MEDIUMS etc.]. It thus pins its spiritualist colours to the mast. But, although the original place of publication, the *Revue Scientifique*, is clearly scientific in the narrower sense, some of its contents do flag up for us the sort of broader concerns, hovering on the edge of accepted "hard" science, that attracted the attention of the scientific community of the time, and particularly, perhaps, that of Richet, in charge of the publication. The "Causerie bibliographique" [Biblographical Discussion] of this journal of 22 September 1900, for example, includes a review of H. Thulié's *Le dressage des jeunes dégénérés ou Orthophrénopédie* [The Training of Degenerate Young People or Orthophrenopedy], the neologism indicating yet another new science in the offing.

The Modern Story: Local Hero, Recuperation and Reflections

The modern story of Arriola, prompted in part by the fiftieth anniversary of his death in 2004, thus part of the 2000 noughties (his birth having occurred as the 1900 noughties dawned) is in many ways an attempt to reclaim him for himself, but also for the region that produced him. This includes a serious attempt to recuperate his musical history and activity as a composer. At the same time, and arguably quite characteristic of the

2000 noughties, the commemorative articles of a little remembered composer and performer published at this time have a sub-text of nationalism, in this case, the proud adoption of Arriola as a son of Galicia. In terms of the ongoing turbulence surrounding *memoria histórica* in Spain after the Civil War, examined by Ryan in chapter six, they also flag up new and old appropriations of excellence. This contrasts with the emphasis upon Arriola in the 1900s articles which concentrate upon the phenomenon of the prodigy.

The questions posed by Morán in the epigraph to this paper appeared in a brief piece published in *La Vanguardia* to commemorate the fiftieth anniversary of Arriola's death in Barcelona. If Morán cites Arriola as the "leyenda viva más importante de la música española" [the most important living legend of Spanish music], he is almost certainly exaggerating: the purposes of writing commemorative pieces of journalism virtually require such exaggeration. Yet even without the local and topical stimulus of such anniversary writing, the case of Arriola deserves re-examination as a case-history of cultural conflict and appropriation, of lionising and promotion, of personal story and public legend.

Morán argues that Arriola deserves his place among musical great names on the basis of his striking precocity. Comparing him with Pablo Casals and Saint-Saens, he argues that Arriola stands out given that he was performing in public before the age of four, while Casals got his renown at the age of twenty-two, and Saint-Saens when he performed in 1846 at the age of ten. He traces briefly Arriola's transfer from his native El Ferrol to Madrid with his mother, and notes how, in common with Casals, playing before the Queen Mother led to preparation for further success, with funds forthcoming for his musical studies in Germany.

Morán makes a brief but telling comment on Arriola's family background, with a reference to "su paranoica madre" [his paranoid mother]. In this he is referring to Josefa, the older sister of Aurora, and aunt to Hildegart. While it is not impossible that Josefa shared the paranoid and extreme tendencies of Aurora, it is also likely that Morán makes here an elision, conscious or not, between the two sisters, the one renowned as mad (for the murder of her daughter), and the other decried by the former as extreme in both temperament and conduct. Although he does not expound in detail on the role of Josefa, it is clear he views her as a parent who at least has managed and organised the success of her child.

The commemorative accounts of Arriola that emanate from his native Galicia are remarkably consistent in their vision of a child of a musical mother (his two siblings would show musical talent), and for the degree to which they stand apart from sensationalist nuancing of detail. Claiming

Arriola for his cultural contribution, for example, a set of programme notes for a commemorative concert on 1 February 2006, pictures him as the product of a cultured background, firmly set in the region: "El ferrolán Pepito Arriola nace no seo dunha familia de fondas raíces de tradición liberal e ilustrada da cidade, berce ou residencia de prominentes liberais vencellados á técnica, ás artes ou ás letras" [Pepito Arriola of Ferrol was born in the heart of a family deeply rooted in the liberal and educated tradition of the city, cradle or home of prominent liberals associated with technology, the arts and letters] (Mera Naveiras 2006). Aurora is absent from this picture, and his mother simply a companion. Thus Arriola is the subject who arrives in Madrid, with his mother alongside: "Pepito Arriola chega a Madrid na compaña da súa nai cuando aínda non cumprira os catro anos" [Pepito Arriola arrives in Madrid accompanied by his mother when he had not even reached the age of four]. Nor is she seen as the instrument for his performance at the Ateneo on 2 February 1900. In this account of Arriola's musical career, he is clearly the performing subject, and not the object created by another, whether his mother or his aunt. The use of the diminutive "Pepito" is of course appropriate for the four year-old that he then was, yet it would be used throughout his life. Mera Naveiras, however, reverts to referring to him as José Arriola later in this article, as does an article by Gaos cited by him, and both Pepito and José are used in the title of the programme notes. Yet the detail with which the account of his composition history opens is telling—at least for those with some idea of the family history. His first composition, at the age of three, was a *habanera*, entitled "Aurora", its title recording the name of his aunt. The next composition would not come until he was twenty-one, when he wrote his 1916 "Impresiones Argentinas" [Impressions of Argentina] (presumably prompted by his tour to Buenos Aires) (full details of compositions in Dopico Vale and Mera Castro 2003, 31-9).

A somewhat closer approach to the turbulent family background of Arriola is presented in *La Nueva España* on 26 October 2009, and responding to the questions of Morán about whether anyone now remembered this pianist. It reprints an interview by *Asturias* from La Habana with María Luisa Castellanos. Here at least it is noted that Aurora took care of the infant Arriola for some time, and commenting on the degree to which both sisters were capable of prompting fear in those around them, there is an instant displacement of Josefa for Aurora. While the article is on Pepito Arriola, and his mother is noted for having brought up three children to occupy the place of musical prodigies, the account suddenly swerves sideways as it recounts how Aurora brought *her* child up to be a major social reformer, particularly of woman's place in the world, murdering her when she judged Hildegart to be straying from the path appointed for her.

Conclusions

By a curious coincidence, unconsciously or consciously intentional, Hildegart would be born at almost exactly the same time of year as Pepito, that is, 9 December (1914). By a further curious coincidence, for some critics Arriola's success began to go into decline around 1913. But this is a sharply retrospective judgment, found in the *Faro de Vigo* in 1991, in an article by Manuel de la Fuente (Martínez López 2003, 65). The idea that Arriola was a prodigy who then somehow declined is arguably undermined by the perception that if he was a prodigy, he was not necessarily abnormal. As a child, Arriola was in some senses found in fact to be quite normal. Richet refers to him as a "joli enfant, fort intelligent, très gai" [a pretty child, highly intelligent, very cheerful] (Richet 1900, 433). If anything, the predominant view was of a child reluctant to accept discipline. Richet observes that "il est très rebelle aux leçons que sa mere veut lui donner, et il ne souffre pas qu'on le corrige" [he rebels strongly against the lessons his mother wants to give him, and he will not allow himself to be corrected] (Richet 1900, 434). By adolescence, and his Buenos Aires tour, this seems to have evolved into a style of playing notable for its emotional charge, something linked by Bianchi to his prodigy nature:

> Pepito Arriola se contiene muy pocas veces—deficiencia de la capacidad volitiva, no ausencia de comprensión. Y es posible que el defecto de los niños prodigios sea siempre este defecto de carácter, la indisciplina de los que no han vivido. (A. A. B. 1912, 97)
>
> [Pepito Arriola rarely keeps himself in check—a matter of lack of will to do so, not of understanding. And it is possible that the defect of infant prodigies is always this defect of character, the lack of discipline of those who have not lived.]

Whether he was a prodigy "naturally" produced, or fostered and encouraged into his phenomenal early achievement by either his mother or his aunt, remains in question. What is not in doubt is the degree to which he was perceived and used as a valuable object in the cultural self-promotion of others. His case clearly offered fuel for those fascinated by the exceptional in the 1900s, and for those looking for quality in the construction of national identities in the 2000s.

Works Cited

A. A. B. (Bianchi, A.) (1912). "Crónica musical", *Nosotros* vol. 6, no. 43, (November), 97-100.

Cal, R. (1991). *A mí no me doblega nadie. Aurora Rodríguez: su vida y su obra*. La Coruña: Ediciones do Castro.

Castellanos, M. L. (1918). Interview with Pepito Arriola for *Asturias* (La Habana), reproduced 26 October 2009 in *La Nueva España* (Asturias), http://www.lne.es/nueva-quintana/2009/10/26/maria-luisa-castellanos-entrevista-pepito-arriola/823354.html [Accessed 4 March 2010].

Cooke, J. F. (1913/1976). *Great Pianists on Piano Playing: Study Talks with Foremost Virtuosos*. Philadelphia: T. Presser, repr. New York: AMS.

Dopico Vale, J. and J. L. Mera Castro (2003a). "Entre la música y la intimidad de la familia Arriola", *Ferrol Análisis* no. 18 (separata): 7-11.

Dopico Vale, J. and J. L. Mera Castro (2003b). "Pepito Arriola, un músico de una generación", *Ferrol Análisis* no. 18 (separata): 13-46.

Fuente, M. de la (1991). "Se apaga la estrella de Pepito Arriola", *El Faro de Vigo*, 6 October, cited in Martínez López (2003) 65, 71.

Gordon, F. (2008). "Madeleine Pelletier: Psychiatry and Feminism", *History of Psychiatry* vol. 19, no. 2: 141-162.

Guzmán, E. and E. Endériz (1933). *Aurora de Sangre*. Repr. Madrid: G. del Toro (1972).

Hildegart (1931a/1977). *El problema sexual tratado por una mujer española*. Madrid: Morata [Gráfica Literaria]. Repr. Madrid: Morata.

Hildegart (1931b/1977). *La rebeldía sexual de la juventud*. Madrid, Morata [sucesores de Peña Cruz]. Repr. Barcelona: Anagrama.

Lombroso, C. (1908). "Eusapia Paladino et le spiritisme". *Annales des Sciences Psychiques* vol. 18, nos. 7-8, April, 97-101.

Martínez López, F. (2003). "De Pepito Arriola a Hildegart", *Ferrol Análisis* no. 18 (separata): 61-71.

Mera Naveiras, L. (2006). "A música e a intimidade da familia Arriola: José Arriola (Pepito Arriola) (1895-1954)", programme notes for a concert, 1 February 2006, Conselho da Cultura Galega, http://www.consellodacultura.org/xornadas/arriola/arriola.pdf [Accessed 20 June 2010].

Morán, G. (2004). "Homenajes imposibles. Pepito Arriola", *La Vanguardia*, 23 October, 28.

Ocampo Vigo, E. (2003). "Pepito Arriola: entre el mito y la realidad." *Ferrol Análisis* no. 18 (separata): 47-59.

Rendueles Olmedo, G. (1989). *El manuscrito encontrado en Ciempozuelos: análisis de la historia clínica de Aurora Rodríguez*. Madrid: Ediciones de la Piqueta.

Révész, G. (1925). *The Psychology of a Musical Prodigy*. London and New York: Kegan Paul.

Richet, C. (1900). "Note sur un cas remarquable de précocité musicale", *Revue Scientifique* vol. 14, no. 14, 432-35, 6 October, reprinted within Richet, C., "Des limites de l'incrédulité", *Annales des Sciences Psychiques* vol. 18, no. 7-8, 97-101.

—. (1908). "Des limites de l'incrédulité", *Annales des Sciences Psychiques* vol. 18, no. 7-8, 97-101.

Ruthsatz, J. and D. K. Detterman (2003). "An Extraordinary Memory: the Case Study of a Musical Prodigy", *Intelligence* vol. 31, no. 6, 509-518.

Scripture, E. W. (1908). "The Professor and the Medium", *Journal of the American Society for Psychical Research* vol. 4, 231-35.

Sinclair, A. (2007). *Sex and Society in Early Twentieth-Century Spain: Hildegart Rodríguez and the World League of Sexual Reform*. Cardiff: University of Wales Press.

Zamora, J. (1900). *Pepito Rodríguez Arriola: (apuntes para la biografía de este prodigioso músico)*. Carta-prólogo de Adolfo Luna. Madrid: Imp. del Asilo de Huerfanos del J. C. de Jesús.

Notes

[1] A *separata* of *Ferrol Análisis* 18 (2003), probably one of the best recent resources on Arriola, contains a family tree, as well as a number of significant articles on him. I am indebted to Paul Preston and Alison Zammer for facilitating my access to this material.

[2] The signatory to this article, A. A. B., is almost certainly Alfredo A. Bianchi, one of the two directors of *Nosotros*, the other being Roberto F. Giusti.

[3] Barrett, undeterred, would provide the preface in 1932 for A. Findlay, *On the Edge of the Etheric or Survival after Death Scientifically Explained*, (25th impression, London, Rider), cited by Jenny Hazelgrove, *Spiritualism and British Society Between the Wars*, Manchester University Press, 2000, 102. All of those listed here had established careers in science, but also were involved at some point in spiritualism, psychic research etc.

PART THREE

NEW—AND NOT SO NEW—BEGINNINGS

CHAPTER NINE

MIRRORING THE NEXT LIFE: JAUME ROIG'S MISOGYNY REASSESSED IN THE LIGHT OF HIS ESCHATOLOGY

LESLEY K. TWOMEY

Jaume Roig, a Valencian doctor, has been categorised as one of the most virulent misogynists of the medieval period because of his *Espill o llibre de les dones* [Mirror or Book of Ladies] which is the first-person account of a man who does not learn his lesson but keeps on marrying.[1] It is a story told for the most part by a narrator who is supposedly an old man looking back over his life and recounting how he has been embroiled in every problem that marriage brings. In the first part of this article, I discuss key aspects of eschatological thinking. In the second, I focus on how women are depicted first as mothers and then as wives. The final part of the article will explore some key aspects of eschatology in Roig's *Espill*, addressing how far these impact on the views of misogyny represented by the different narrative voices in the text.

Roig wrote in the second half of the fifteenth century, at a time when the plague had ravaged Valencia, causing its inhabitants to think that the end of the world was near. Hinted at in R. Howard Bloch's theorizing of women as evil or perfect is an underlying theme of salvation or perdition, a recognised element of misogyny but one with eschatological undertones (Bloch 1991, 91). Robert Archer (2005, 109) recognises the earnestness of the "defence of the ascetic position" in the *Espill*

> which advocates that a man who seeks wisdom should exclude women from his immediate domestic life, should direct his thoughts toward Christ, and should generally avoid women since they are the site of moral and physical disease.

Eschatology holds that all human beings face death and, in the *Espill*, death is a constant theme with an emphasis on final judgement, heaven, and hell.[2] The presence of the plague provides a backcloth to the narration, since the narrator claims he only has time to write because he is out of town to escape its ravages: "Trobant-m'en aquesta vall, / callosa, per los morts fuit" [finding myself in this rugged valley shunned by the dead] (*Espill,* 23).[3] Untimely death comes to two of the narrator's wives, as well as two of his sons, and an unborn child. Husbands poisoned by their wives (*Espill,* 127), daughters who kill their fathers and are punished for their acts (*Espill,* 42), guests killed and turned into tasty pies for others to relish by the Parisian pastry-cook and her daughters (*Espill,* 46), all serve as ever-present reminders of the brevity of mortal life. The range of punishments meted out, whether the gibbet or the bonfire, add to the concept of death as torture and judgement.[4]

Death, sin, and punishment are just one aspect of eschatology. According to Henning Graf Reventlow (1997, 170), eschatology contrasts two states of being, the present and future time, which will determine the final state of the world because "the present state of things and the present world order will come to an end and be superseded by another of an essentially different kind" (Mowinckel 1959, 125; cited in Reventlow 1997, 171). Reventlow's distinction provides a useful insight into the interface between narrative past and present time in the *Espill*, where the narrator looks back and interprets his past from the present. The shift between time frames also points to the future, with certain death and final judgement awaiting the old man.

Eschatology is also bound up with finality. It signifies the end of human history. According to C. H. Dodd (1963, 101), the *eschaton* "is such that no event could ever follow or need follow on it, because in it the whole purpose of God is revealed". Damian Thompson (1999) divides history into periods where end-time belief was particularly pronounced. He discusses the proliferation of end-time prophecies which marked the fifteenth century, following the schism in the Church, the emergence of an anti-Pope, and the arrival of the Black Death. The period saw a number of movements which Thompson identifies as millenarian, such as that of Girolamo Savonarola (1452-98) in Italy, the Taborite movement in Bohemia, and that of John Hus (1370-1415) and his followers. Reform movements and rooting out of evil behaviour were the order of the day in the late medieval period.

However, these manifest examples of the degeneracy of the present time could also be interpreted as the signs which accompany the end time. Albert L. A. Hogeterp (2009, 392) argues that an "inherent part of early Jewish apocalypticism is a perspective of revelation of the final age" and this is seen in signs, in trials, and in tribulations. Jürgen Moltmann (1969,

133-34) points out how, for apocalyptists, history "gradually unfolds a plan of God". He, and others, see this as rooted in the longing for the restoration of Israel which is part of Jewish thinking. Moltmann then notes the exhortation to endurance and to righteousness which mark the believer's response to eschatology. Hogeterp, like Victor Kossi Agbanou, notes the exhortations to "discernment, vigilance, and faithfulness" which are intrinsic to preparation for final judgement (Agbanou 1983, 205, cited in Hogeterp 2009, 165).

Eschatology also incorporates that dimension of theological thinking that deals with Christian hope, which includes death as a gateway to life, individual and universal judgement, heaven, hell, the resurrection of the body, and the destiny of the universe (Kelly 2006, 21). As Marjorie Reeves (1984, 41) argues, "apocalyptic expectation linked time with passing and nourished the hope of passing from the shifting sands of history to the eternal realm of beatitude". As a medieval writer, Roig presents the reader with death and judgement in the *Espill* but also with the old man's hope of attaining personal salvation. The vision of the last things in the *Espill* provides, as I will argue, a unifying force which has so far been unrecognised.

Most critics have focused on Roig's misogyny, seeking to justify or denounce it. According to Rosanna Cantavella (1992, 40), the very extent and variety of the attack on women in the *Espill* places it at the zenith of antifeminism: "amb el mestre Jaume Roig (1434-78) el vessant antifeminista arriba al seu màxim exponent" [with Master Jaume Roig the antifeminist current reached its peak]. She emphasises its clerical origins and the series of literary motifs which characterised literary and social debate in the late medieval period (Cantavella 2003, 45-46). Victorio Agüera (1975) points to the moralizing antifeminist style of the *Espill* as an early example of the picaresque. In his view, the antifeminist *exempla* are universalised, using stylistic multiple repetition. Michael Solomon (1997, 3) suggests that, as a general rule, "the act of composing treatises replete with discursive fragments that speak ill of women (...) is bound up in medical strategies for maintaining sexual well-being". He has argued that the main purpose of the *Espill* is to highlight the effects of *amor haereus* as a physical malady to which men can be prone when they are tempted by women. Solomon draws parallels between the *Espill* and a medical advice handbook, drawing out the close connection between the physical and spiritual aspects of disease. Jean Dangler (1998, 101) follows Solomon in considering that the main purpose of the *Espill* is to "ameliorate men's sexual well-being". She focuses on what she discerns as men becoming aware of pain's aetiology in women. Robert Archer includes an extract from the *Espill* in his anthology of misogynist texts from the classical period onward (2001, 215-66). He argues that "humour, deliberate or unintentional, latent or actual, occurs in the satire and ridicule of practically every period of negative writing about women since Juvenal, and its importance in the construction of a misogynist discourse would seem to be self-evident" (Archer 2005, 91). Both Antònia Carré (1994) and Anna Isabel Peirats (2003) study aspects of the comic in the *Espill*. According to Alcuin Blamires, in his anthology of western misogyny (1992, 12-13), and Archer (2005, 3), misogynist writing can be interpreted as no more than a game for the intelligentsia of the late medieval period. Taking a similar approach, Jordi Tiñena (1988, 33) has categorised the *Espill*'s pervasive misogyny as an example of medieval humour in the stamp of fifteenth-century Valencian satire, although he is forced to admit it is more "punyent i moralista" [sharp and moralizing] than the norm. Whilst there are elements of the Espill that can be taken as pre-picaresque, whilst moralizing antifeminism is extensively developed, and it is possible to read the *Espill* as a medical handbook, written by a practising doctor, there is more to it than any of these assessments have acknowledged.

Thus it is that in the early chapters of the *Espill*, different types of women are paraded before the reader and denigrated by the narrator, an old man, who we could take to be the author, Jaume Roig, looking back on his youthful exploits. The *Espill* is not just a series of vituperous vignettes about women, nor is it merely a set of instructions, essential for men's wellbeing, about how to keep out of their toils. Bloch has allied many of the stock elements of misogyny to early Christian theology. His discussion takes account of medieval French and English texts but could be applied to other European works, such as Roig's. [5] He examines the *molestiae nuptiarum*, as well as what he terms the aestheticisation of gender, in other words the close association of women with theologizing about the negative effects of care of the body, fashion, makeup, and hairstyles (Lacarra Lanz 1999). Bloch (1991, 65-91) explores the way that women are considered both gateway to hell and bride of Christ. Theologizing the problem of women is part of Roig's method.

The first group of women to be singled out for opprobrium is mothers. The narrator's own mother cast him out to make his own way in life (*Espill*, 35-37). She cut him out of his inheritance and remarried, thus presenting the narrator with an opportunity to castigate every woman who remarries, both for the bad end which will be their lot and also for their repulsive physical appearance: "La vella fembra del temps no's membra; / tendrà la pantxa ab plecs com mantxa, / ab semblant pell com terçanell (…)" [the old woman cannot recall time; / she will have a belly with folds like a blanket and with skin like slubbed silk] (*Espill,* 39-40).[6] Roig's narrator allies his personal experiences with accepted tenets of antifeminism particularly its negative opinions of old women, such as those in Jehan Le Fèvre's *Lamentations de Matheolus* (see selections in Blamires 1992, 177-97) and Giovanni Boccaccio's *Corbaccio* (see Cassell 1975). The young man undertakes a number of journeys, across France to Paris and across Spain on pilgrimage to Santiago, and this allows him multiple opportunities to observe the behaviour of other mothers and wives, providing grist to the antifeminist mill and enabling exploration of the *molestiae nuptiarum* topos (*Espill,* 41-47).

Young mothers are also castigated. In Book II, part IV, Roig's narrator describes how his young convent-educated wife neglects her maternal duties. Like his own mother, the young wife is a bad mother. The narrator describes the results of her refusing to suckle their child, which leads to its eventual death from the ministrations of wet-nurses. The young wife refuses because of pride in her personal appearance, since she does not want her breasts to sag. Of course, the narrator's view is contradictory, since he had earlier mocked the sagging breasts of elderly mothers:[7]

> Io novençana, no pel·licana,
> plaer vull pendre, no'm plau despendre,
> los pits nafrar per al fill dar
> la sang del cos. (*Espill,* 89)
>
> [I am a new young wife, not a pelican,
> and want to enjoy myself, and I don't like to make any sacrifice,
> damaging my breasts to give the child
> blood from my body.]

The key traits of the wives in the *Espill* contribute to an established corpus of information about women.[8] The description of the first wife is a mosaic of the characteristics regularly found in medieval misogynist writing. For example, Roig draws on stock anti-marriage *topoi*, to depict his first wife leaving the dinner to burn and overspending at every kind of shop (*Espill,* 57-58; 63). She is described as gluttonous because she eats heartily by night in her room: "en la cambreta, foguer, olleta, / ast hi tenia" [in her chamber she had a fire for cooking, a little roasting dish, and spit] (*Espill,* 57). She is a spendthrift: "Ab mi contava / l'especier, sastre, draper / e costurera, tapins, velera, / lo bruneter e confiter (…)" [the spice-merchant, the tailor, the dress-maker, the shoe-maker, the veil-maker, the bonnet-maker, and the sweet-maker all counted on income from me] (*Espill*, 63). She is a malingerer: "los jorns fainés / entre semmana mai era sana" [during the week, on work days, she never felt well] (*Espill*, 58). Her habits are disgusting: "mig any vestia una camisa (...) de sa divisa / gentil brodada" [for six months she had on a shift nobly embroidered with her emblem] (*Espill*, 56). Her choice of clothing, however, demonstrates pride in her lineage. She is unable to contain her sexual urges and warns her husband about the dangers of Lenten abstinence: "L'hom qui s'absté / d'axò en quaresma, a cinquagesma / cornut se troba" [he who abstains from doing it in Lent will be cuckolded by the Sunday before Ash Wednesday] (*Espill,* 61).[9] She is even physically incontinent: "sovint al llit / com s'orinava e fressejava / tant i sovint, lo llit podrint" [she often wet the bed and left so many skidmarks in it that it stank] (*Espill,* 56). Such excesses can be considered evidence of women's pathology and of why they spread disease, becoming a source of trouble for men (Solomon 1997, 78-79, Dangler 1998, 101).

Religious women fare no better and the narrator shows how nuns and Beguines use religion as a cover for seeking husbands and even for procuring sex, a theme found also in Boccaccio, who describes a widow using visits to Church as an excuse to prey on possible suitors. The none-too-innocent Beguine, whom the narrator has planned to marry, is a prime mover in using religion as a cover for sex.[10] Priests and friars are no better:

> Ab certs sofismes
> ells s'entenien; abdós venien
> al combregar davant l'altar
> de la capella; portava's ella
> sa tovallola, ell ab sa stola,
> idolotraven (...). (*Espill,* 76)
>
> [With a few wise words
> they made themselves understood and both went
> to communion at the altar in the chapel;
> she wore her veil and he his stole
> and they committed idolatry with each other.]

In Roig's misogynist universe, bad mothers (and, incidentally, their children too) come to a bad end (*Espill,* 86). The widow commits suicide and the narrator's last wife dies from a surfeit of wine before giving birth. Female physiology, menstruation, and childbearing underpin lengthy episodes in the *Espill.*[11] In describing his marriage to the widow, the narrator takes the opportunity to decry how far women will go to bear a child. Book II, part III, of the *Espill* is dedicated to the comeuppance the widow and her fellow conspirators receive for her false pregnancy and deceit of her husband: [12]

Déu los tenc presta
dolor e plor. La sua flor
entr'elles jeia. (...)
Dormint se giren,
qualsevol d'elles braç o mamelles
sus li posaren; mort lo trobaren,
ben acostat jus llur costat. (*Espill,* 86)

[God has sorrow and weeping ready for them.
Their little offspring
lay between them
and one or other laid their arm or breast
over him, and dead he was found,
snuggled under their rib.]

Women abandoning their children is a feature of misogynist writing being found, for example, in the story of Epia in Juvenal's Sixth Satire (2007, 322-23). The way in which all the different women deceive men, shows the old man-narrator that he has been mistaken in his pursuit of the perfect wife. He has after all been fooled by his mother, an innocent young girl, a nun, and a Beguine. Eventually, he resolves never to marry again. His decision chimes with the guidance given in the preface to the *Espill*. The prefatorial narrative voice had indicated, towards the end of the preface, that the *Espill*'s didactic purpose is to stop callow youths and old gallants, who should know better, from chasing after women.

Many of the punishments meted out to women are considered by the old man-narrator to be consonant with God's justice. They serve as a reminder to the reader of the nature of final judgement. God's righteous anger is a recurring topic:

car Déu irat fon molt placat
per la justícia d'aquella nícia
enrabiada qui degollada
fon lo jorn ans (...). (*Espill,* 119)

[for God's wrath was much appeased
by the justice of that stupid woman
who had her throat cut a day ago.]

This is a God who uncovers covert sin and punishes it. This at least is the view of the old man-narrator when he asserts that God discovers the wife's sin, investigates it, and castigates her:

> Mas Déu altisme,
> qui béns e mals e cominals
> tots investiga e los castiga,
> lo pus cobert fa pus ubert (...). (*Espill,* 85)
>
> [But Almighty God who investigates
> the good, the evil and the rest
> and punishes them,
> bringing hidden sins out into the open.]

Sin also leads to the death of others. The old man-narrator believes it is not by chance that his child dies. The wife's deceit is the cause because God prepares wailing and gnashing of teeth for sinful women: "Déu los tenc presta / dolor e plor" [God has sorrow and weeping ready for them] (*Espill,* 86).

The God depicted is the Old Testament judge of humanity, the "jutge just" [just judge] (*Espill,* 196), who exacts payment for wrongs committed, and who must be placated by sacrificing the evildoer. This is a God ready to punish those women who sin against nature by giving animal milk to their children. As noted above, doctors believed physical illness was a punishment for sin. In the *Espill*, women's postnatal breast abscesses are interpreted as a plague visited on them by God: "Déu les ne paga e dóna plaga / per tal nocura obrant natura" [God is not pleased with them and sends natural plague on them for such harm inflicted by human nature] (*Espill,* 138). In the original verse "paga" [pleased] and "plaga" [plague] rhyme.

The God portrayed by the old man-narrator is ready to utterly destroy the unrighteous. A bolt of lightning, interpreted as divine punishment, strikes the son of a woman who, led astray by his mother, has caused an innocent man to be condemned: "Del cel rajant, / llamp lo ferí e descobrí / sa malvestat" [lightning struck him from the sky and brought his wrong-doing out into the open] (*Espill,* 142). As in the case of the overlaying of the child by the mother or her bedfellow, women's offspring meet an untimely death because of their actions. Lest the reader wrongly interpret this event as an untoward accident, the word "descobrí" recalls "the parallel between 'cobert' [hidden] and 'ubert' [in the open]" (*Espill,* 85) and confirms the direct intervention of God in human affairs.

The narrator portrays a God ready to destroy not only individuals but even whole towns as punishment for sin. This is a God willing to raze Valencia to the ground, as a result of the impious behaviour of the fishwives (Cantavella 1992, 98-99). Valencia and the great fire which destroyed part of the city become contemporary examples of divine retribution:

> Per totes estes
> fer tals peccats, d'aquells veinats
> la pelleria, trenc, fusteria,
> fins mig mercat n'has vist cremat,
> any sis quaranta, pus de setanta
> cases, albercs. (*Espill,* 119)
>
> [since all these women had committed such sins,
> those neighbourhoods were destroyed,
> with the tanners, Trenc street, and the carpenters' shops
> and as much as half the market burnt down.
> In 1460 more than seventy houses and dwellings were burnt.]

The narrative voice clearly intends to accord biblical status to Valencia, since its destruction is on a par with similar divine penalties exacted from towns in ancient times, such as the destruction of Sodom (Genesis 13: 1-18). The same link to the destructive power of an avenging God is made in an eschatological discourse in Luke (17: 26-30) where the fire and sulphur raining from heaven is used to exemplify the "days of the Son of Man" (Bridge 2003, 39).

The reader is left in no doubt that the avenging God will strike them too and they should be justifiably afraid. The fate of Sodom prefigures the destruction of Jerusalem and is "an example of a narrative theme from Genesis whose interpretation has eschatological significance" (Hogeterp 2009, 159). The New Testament also predicts similar fates for a town that will not receive the Gospel (Matthew 11: 20-24, Luke 10: 12). The destruction of Valencia and the intervention of God to put an end to times of depravity can be seen as signs of the approaching *eschaton*.

Dualism is another key element of eschatology and in the *Espill* there is a dualism which is created as a frame for the main narrative. The parallel between one good woman, the Virgin Mary, and the rest of womankind is set out in the dedication to the "magnifich Mossèn Joan/ Fabra, cavaller valent" [the noble Mr John Fabra, a valiant gentleman] which accompanies the *Espill.* [13] The dedication's narrative voice, ostensibly Roig's own, calls on the reader to reject women, "les dones tener en vil", since they are "spines" [thorns] (*Espill,* 23).[14] Only one woman is to be loved, feared, and chosen, and she is the Virgin Mary. She is identified with the "flor de llir" [lily flower] (*Espill,* 23). She is the mirror, or "espill", who serves as a model for other women to follow in this life and beyond (Pérez de Tudela 1989, 65).

Dualism between good and evil underpins the contrast of the Virgin Mary, who is the only good mother, with the bad mothers already observed:

La humanal e paternal
mare parida, verge fon dida;
verge tendrera, verge lletera
verge nodrí, lo txic fadrí,
petit fillet. E ab la llet
celestial e virginal
pròpia d'ella, ab sa mamella
de cel umplida, fins que cumplida
hac la infantea, ab gran aptea
(...)
lo alletà. (*Espill,* 167-68)

[the human and fatherlike
mother who gave birth, gave suck;
tender Virgin, milk-giving Virgin
gave milk to her little boy, her tiny little baby.
And she fed him well with her virginal and heavenly milk
which she had within her breast,
giving a taste of heaven,
until he was weaned.]

Unlike the young convent-educated mother, who allowed her child to die, the Virgin breastfeeds her child, nourishing him with an exemplary kind of milk, which has the property to heal humanity's ills.[15] Significantly, she is not only the best of human mothers "humanal" but she is also "paternal" [father-like]. Perhaps the narrator accords her this epithet because she is in the father's entourage or perhaps, she is so good at providing for her children that she becomes like a father. She is associated with male characteristics, being fatherlike. In any case, she stands outside the ordinary and is unlike other "maternal" women. The old man-narrator's parallel between good woman and bad women is now transferred onto the eschatological plane. Following her Assumption into heaven, which marks the end of her sinless earthly life, the Virgin Mary displays her breasts in her intercession for humankind.[16] The breasts which have fed her holy child are now used to bring about the salvation of others:

mare humana
sos pits mostrant, d'ell impetrant
pels peccadós, sos oradós
fills adoptats (...). (*Espill,* 172)

[showing her breasts, pleading with him
for sinners, a human mother, for her petitioning
adopted children.]

The Virgin and her perfect lactation forms part of a theme of nourishment allied to salvation. The image of the pelican who tears open its breast and feeds its young on the blood is a figure of the Redeemer, who sacrifices himself, like the pelican, for others. The Redeemer-pelican provides the old man-narrator with another contrast to the young wife who refused to feed her child and renounced the role of pelican for herself:

(...) del cos la sang
ell, pelicà, sos pits nafrà
pels fills salvar e restaurar
scampant-la tota (...). (*Espill,* 196)

[he gave blood from his body
a very pelican, tearing his breast,
to save his sons and restore them,
ripping it from top to bottom.]

Good-evil dualism also underpins how the good wife, whose characteristics are outlined in Proverbs 26, is used to distinguish the Virgin from other women. She is unlike other women because she alone has the characteristics of the good wife. She sews and weaves: "Molt temps filava" [she used to weave for long periods] (*Espill,* 163) like the good wife in Proverbs who maintains her family by her industry. In contrast, the narrator shows how his first wife was unable to keep house and was incapable of sewing or weaving. When he comes to characterise the worthlessness of the Beguine, the old man-narrator alludes again to Proverbs when he asserts that they do not even know how to sew or spin: "no sap filar, / ni res cosir, ni menys llegir (...)" [she does not know how to spin, nor sew any garment, nor even read] (*Espill,* 206).[17]

Eschatological dualism points to who will be saved and who will be damned. The dualism of good wife/ bad wives, good mother/ bad mothers, would suggest the first are saved and the second unsaved. After all, the Virgin Mary, pure from the very beginning of her life in her mother's womb, was pre-redeemed and rose straight to heaven, after going to sleep in Christ. In a misogynist world view, it is to be expected that those women who have committed the unnatural crimes described in the *Espill* would be excluded from the ranks of the elect (see, for instance, Jehan Le Fèvre's *Lamentations*, in Blamires 1992, 197). Roig's vision of the coming of Christ, the *Parousia*, will now be explored to show whether he considers that women will be damned in his vision of the end of time.

The dualism of the elect and non-elect is given its greatest prominence in Book III of the *Espill*. Roig uses passages from the Gospels about the future establishment of God's kingdom to colour the warnings which the third narrator, Solomon, the Old Testament figure, author of Proverbs, and known for his great wisdom, provides for the old man (*Espill*, 202-03).[18] The first is the parable of the wedding feast (Matthew 22: 1-14), to which all are invited but not all come (*Espill,* 208). The second is the celebration following the return of the prodigal son (Luke 15: 11-32). In this case, it is the older brother who does not attend: "l'enfellonit / fora romàs" [the damned one did not come in] (*Espill,* 196). The third is the labourers who want to work by the sweat of their brow in the vineyard and receive their pay at the end of the day (Matthew 20: 1-16, *Espill*, 202).

The choice of parables as a vehicle for advice provided at the late stage of his protagonist's existence is illuminated by Mary Ann Beavis's explanation of the parable form (2001). The purpose of parables is to challenge the "deepest grounds of existential reality" and to cause the hearer to reassess "the very grounds of his being" (Perrin and Duling 1982, 417, cited in Beavis 2001, 18). Because of the way they cause the hearer to question perceived reality, the adapted parables provide the perfect vehicle for engineering a change in behaviour from the old man and from the reader.

In each of these reinterpreted parables, the Solomon narrative voice chooses to allude to the consequences of final judgement, pointing to those who will be among the saved and those who will be among the lost. One of the best known New Testament texts on final judgement is chapter 25 of St Matthew's Gospel, where the lost and the saved are portrayed as two flocks to be separated by the eschatological shepherd (Matt. 25: 31-46). The sheep will be saved and the goats will be condemned.[19] The narrator provides his own slant on the story of final judgement by showing the elect as a new flock, equated with those who follow the New Law, the Christians: "novell ramat, elet triat / anyells, moltons, barbuts cabrons / abandonant" [the new flock, chosen and selected, sheep, lambs, leaving aside the bearded goats] (*Espill,* 202). Those who follow the Old Law are lost: "barbuts cabrons / abandonant" (*Espill,* 202). In "barbuts" he refers to the long beards of the goats but also to the long beards of those who follow the Old Law, the Jews.

In the Gospel story, the saved and the unsaved are divided because of their actions. In the *Espill* interpretation, division of humankind at final judgement is based on religious creed. This division is made explicit a few lines later, when the narrator explicitly allies both the Jews and the Moors with the lost. The Jews have refused to recognise the fulfilment of their own prophecies and so are condemned:

Lo fre mordent
de dur cervell, sa odre vell
embotanat, desempegat,
jueu altiu, resta catiu
per culpa llur (...). (*Espill,* 202)

[biting the bit of his stubbornness
fastening up his old wineskin,
the haughty Jew is enslaved
by wrongdoing.]

The narrator uses the term "old wineskins" to associate the parallel established between old order and new order with the new wine of Christianity (Matthew 9:22). It means that he also weaves into the narrative an allusion to another wedding feast, that of Cana.

Immediately afterwards, the Old Testament story of the sacrifice of Isaac is used to prefigure New Testament eschatology. The two servants who accompany the father and son to the place of sacrifice are explicitly identified among the damned. They are representatives of other nations and worship other gods. In this version of the story of the sacrificial son, Isaac is a prefiguration of Christ's willingness to be bound over to death and only Isaac, prepared for sacrifice, is saved:

Són figurats
l'enterc hebraic, lo gentil laic,
pobles abdós, pels servidós
dos jovencells, l'ase ab ells
ensemps restats baix, no muntats
fer en la penya altar, ni llenya
pel sacrifici de Abram, inici,
començador de fe i amor.
Isac tercer lo poble ver
e cristià, qui creu e fa
lo que Déu vol; aquest tot sol,
lo u de tres, sols elet és (…). (*Espill,* 202-03)

[the stubborn Jew, the non-religious Gentile are both prefigured
by the servants, two young men
stayed down, the ass with them,
they did not go up to make the altar,

they did not bring wood for Abraham's sacrifice.
The person who began and instigated faith and love,
Isaac, is the third young man and represents the true people,
Christians, who believe and do what God wants.
There is only one group of the three
which is the elect.]

For Roig, belief is essential to salvation and wrong belief set to lead to damnation. In its original version, the parable of the labourers in the vineyard represents the reversal of rank which will be part of the End Times (Jeremias 1962, 35). In Roig's version it shows the divide between those who are and those who are not chosen by the owner of the vineyard. Those who are chosen will receive their divine pay, redemption. The other group takes its own decision not to work in the vineyard and these, condemned by their own actions, are the damned:

Los que, llogats, humiliats
obrar volran, e suaran
en les cavades, no fent llobades,
del divinal diner real
seran pagats. (*Espill,* 202)

[Those who are hired
and want to work with humility
digging the fields,
by the sweat of their brow,
making no false deals,
will receive their pay
in heavenly royal coin.]

In the *Espill*, the damned are those who, instead of being hired and being justified by God's mercy, are "enganats" [deluded], and "descaminats" [on the wrong track]. Unlike those who accept Christian belief, the Moors "romanen sclaus" [will stay enslaved]:

Los enganats
moros e atres, turcs, idolatres,
feroces, braus, romanen sclaus
descaminats. (*Espill,* 202)

[Those who are deluded,
Moors and such like,
Turks and the idolatrous,
ferocious and savage people,

will stay enslaved,
on the wrong track.]

Although at final judgement, Solomon, the advising narrative voice, does not portray women among the damned, the narrative voice used in the *entrada* took a different approach. There the Virgin Mary, represented by "lo llir" [the lily], is contrasted with the "spines, cards" [thorns, prickly weeds].[20] The dedication's reference to the lily among thorns in the *entrada*, suggests the contrast between the lily and the thorns from Song of Songs 2: 1, often interpreted as a prefiguration of the Virgin Mary: "As a lily among thistles, so is my Beloved among girls".

The prickly weeds symbolise all females other than the Virgin Mary: "lo llir corona / spines, cards crema" [he crowns the lily, and burns the thorns and prickly weeds] (*Espill,* 24). The "spines" [thorny plants] and the "cards" [prickly weeds] are to be thrown into the fire and burnt. The dualism explored between the perfect Virgin and other women is allied to final judgement through this parabolic allusion. In Matthew's Gospel, rotten trees, which cannot bear fruit, are cut down to be burnt (7: 19, 12: 33). According to Jeremias (1962, 224), the harvest and the fruitfulness of the fig tree is a symbol of the *eschaton*. Moreover, in another harvest parable, that of the wheat and the weeds, the weeds are thrown on the fire (Matthew 13: 20; McIver 1995, Jeremias 1962, 81-86 and 224-25).[21] Women are represented as non fruit-bearing plants, the non-elect, destined to be cast into the fire of damnation. Perhaps for this reason, in the second part of the prologue, the narrator asserts that all women alive today are "diablesses" [she-devils] and "dimoniesses" [female demons] (*Espill,* 29).

The *Espill's* principal narrative voice, the old man, also portrays women as thoroughly evil in their crimes. Picking up the condemnation of women as demonic from the preface, the old man-narrator shows women consorting with the devil and committing evil deeds.[22] Women are witches, sorceresses, handmaids of the Devil, "diablesses" (*Espill,* 146) who pact with the Devil, and even "dampnades" [damned] (*Espill,* 145). Making a pact with the Devil recalls the first woman, Eve: "ella soldà's / ab un dampnat apostatat" [she threw in her lot with an apostate who was damned] (*Espill,* 153). Presenting the history of salvation in Book III, Solomon, argues that sole responsibility for the Fall is Eve's: "ella peccà / de crim molt fort, digne de mort (...)" [she committed a very bad crime which merited death] (*Espill,* 153).[23] Her female descendants, daughters of Eve, share in the consequences of her crime, particularly pain in childbirth: "tostemps parís / no sens tristor, ab gran dolor" [she always bore children not without sorrow and with great pain] (*Espill,* 153).

If Eve were irredeemable, it should be expected that she should be the first to be cast into Hell, as a consequence of her actions. However, Roig's narrator depicts a different version of events. When Christ descends into limbo to meet with Adam, Eve, and all their descendants, they recognise Him and praise God. Only Cain is condemned forever:

Tos los del llim
o si d'Abram, Eva i Adam,
sos descendents Déu conexents,
de fet cobrà e se'n portà
tots Déu lloant, Caïm dexant
e tots los mals, perpetuals
habitadós en lo caós,
tots temps penant. (*Espill,* 198-99)

[all those in limbo,
If they knew of God as descendants of Abraham, Adam, and Eve,
came forth and went out
all praising God and leaving Cain and all the evil ones,
those perpetual dwellers in chaos,
to hard labour for all eternity.]

Despite the biting condemnation of women from the old man-narrator in the *Espill*, and despite their being condemned to damnation in the dedication, there is hope of salvation for women. They are advised in the *tornada* that, if they repent, they too can be saved:

Si lo contrari faran
del que d'elles ordit he,
ab la flor de llir també
les dones habitaran. (*Espill,* 24)

[If they do the opposite
of the tale I have spun about them,
then ladies too will dwell
with the Lily.]

When the old man is given advice by Solomon on preparing himself for final judgement, the holy examples he is to follow are all female saints. He is advised to give everything to the temple, like Sophia, the widow; he is to pour out rich ointments like Mary Magdalene, and model himself on Martha in doing good works (*Espill,* 180). At the very end of Solomon's counsels, there are other exemplary women on whom the old man should model himself, including biblical women like Sarah, Anna, Rachel, Esther, and Abigail, as well as saintly women like Tecla, Lucy, and Agnes (*Espill,* 212). In fact Roig's own wife is listed among the good women (*Espill,* 222-24). The narrator could have chosen to depict only male models of exemplary behaviour. Given that women have some hope of salvation and that there have been examples of good women, albeit in the past, and even one in the present time, it has to be concluded that the misogyny displayed in the *Espill* is not as intense as has often been argued.

The *Espill* incorporates different approaches to final damnation for women in the dedication, in the prologue and in the various parts of the narrative. Even though the most authoritative of the narrators, Solomon, permits women to be saved, the principal narrator, the old man, had shown that women were always to blame for men's damnation. In Matthew's version of the great feast (22:11-14), another metaphor for final judgement, it is those who have a field, those who have business to do, and those who seize and kill the son who are condemned. In Luke's version of the same parable (14:15-20), it is the man who has bought a field, the man who has bought a yoke of oxen, and the man who has taken a wife who are condemned. In the *Espill* version, the narrator conflates the two but only the man who has taken a wife is irrevocably cast into hell. The cause of the married man's damnation is that he rejects God and chooses searching for a wife over eternal salvation. The whole of the second book of the *Espill* with its desperate search for the perfect wife is, now, contextualised eschatologically: it becomes an extended image of the married man doomed to final damnation. The old man-narrator has been invited repeatedly to the eternal wedding feast and has refused to go because he has just married a new wife, meaning that the *Espill* becomes an eschatological interpretation of the effect of marriage.[24]

Through the humorous recounting of this moral tale, with its multiple perspectives, it can be discerned that salvation is a matter of choice. Each time he has searched for a wife, the old-man narrator has turned away from God. Inherent in the parable of the wedding feast, as in that of the hired labourers, is individual free will to make choices.

In the earlier sections of the *Espill*, it is the avenging aspect of God which is depicted in the narrator's tirades. God's hand has to be stayed by holy men like the Old Testament Jonah or St Vincent Ferrer (1350-1409), Roig's fellow-countryman. Jonah has eschatological significance as a sign to the people of Nineveh "living a careless life, heedless of the rumble of the approaching flood" (Hogeterp 2009, 186-87), but it can equally be argued that St Vincent serves the same purpose for the people of Valencia. His presence serves as a warning of the imminent final judgement for which they should be preparing:

Jutge final, en tribunal
cert quant seurà esclafarà
los reiatons, les nacions.
Déu poderós, hom piadós,
just jutjarà, caps cascarà
del terrenal. (*Espill,* 169)

[Judge of all time,
in the true court, when all will be revealed,
and the accused and the nations will clamour.
The powerful God will judge
the merciful, when the end of the earth comes.]

In the very last pages of the *Espill*, through the parabolic reconstructions, a different face of God is revealed. It is only as the old man-narrator approaches the end of his life that he begins to discover a God ready to save. The God of the final pages of the *Espill* is one who offers to save all, even women. Final judgement is reassessed: "Déu quants ha fets / vol ser salvats" [God wants all his created beings to be saved] (*Espill,* 203). Only those who "obrar volran" [want to work], only those who "creu e fa / lo que Déu vol" [believe and do what God wants] (*Espill,* 203), only those who willingly drink of the water freely offered by Christ to all believers can be saved.

Emphasis in the retold parable story of the wedding feast is on the individual believer and on his personal response to God. The excuse, whilst in harmony with misogynist theme of the *Espill*, is, however, incidental. The man who has married a wife is condemned because he has his eye fixed on the world and "the flesh" and not on the heavenly kingdom. For this reason, the narrator, with his repeated marriages, risks damnation. Roig emphasises the will of the old man who persists in seeking out women and refuses to accept salvation: "Tu bells ulls tens /e no hi vols veure, tornes e beure / lo vomitat" [you have fine eyes and you do not want to see, you turn and down what has been spewed up] (*Espill,* 112). The old man's lust for different types of young women is a misuse of his God-given free will:

Déu t'ha fet franc,
net e llibert; en lloc desert
te fas catiu, fuigs de Déu viu,
dexes senyor ton creador
omnipotent, fas-te servent
del teu pecat; Déu oblidat,
vas al diable. (*Espill,* 176)

[God made you free
clean and untrammelled;
you enslave yourself,
you flee from God
you leave your God and Almighty creator
and make yourself a servant of your sin;
since you have forgotten God, you are going to hell.]

In conclusion, the *Espill* can be read as an indictment of the female gender, as well as of the married state, and its vision of the world is one in which, women, with the exception of the Virgin Mary, and a small number of long-dead holy women, are shown negatively. However, the misogynist approach of the *Espill*, when combined with Roig's deep-rooted belief in a freely offered redemption, informed by his eschatological vision of judgement, leads to a slightly different conclusion. Eve is not subject to damnation at the *Parousia*. Although she was estranged from God as a consequence of sin, her alienation is not absolute.[25] She, like other women, can repent and be saved. Even marriage, when it is God's will, can be a means of salvation. Holy women have been saved in the past and provide examples of holy living for the narrator to follow. Redemption is available to all who do not turn away from God.

Roig's focus on eschatology informs his *Espill* from the dedication to the last pages and was entirely appropriate for a man writing at a time when civilisation was devastated by plague, an occurrence which focused the mind on death. He was writing when the end of time loomed, as the end of the century approached. The *Espill* should be read as an extended parable about pursuing lust over ensuring a right relationship with God. The eschatological message of the *Espill* was an important one for those facing the start of a new century with its endings and new beginnings. Living unselfishly and with moderation, as well as avoiding headlong pursuit of lust, were good counsels for those preparing themselves for the end of time.

Works Cited

Agbanou, Victor Kossi (1983) "Le discours eschatologique de Matthieu 24-25: tradition et rédaction", *Études Bibliques*, 2 (nouvelle série), 171-207.

Agüera, Victorio G. (1975) *Un pícaro catalán del siglo XV: el Espill de Jaume Roig y la tradición picaresca*. Barcelona: Hispam.

Allen, Prudence (1997) *The Concept of Woman: The Aristotelian Revolution 750 B.C. - A.D.1250*, 2nd edn. Grand Rapids, MI: Eerdmanns.

Archer, Robert (ed.) (1992) *Ausiàs March: A Key Anthology,* The Anglo-Catalan Society, Occasional Publications, 8. Sheffield: Interleaf.

—. (2001) *Misoginia y defensa de las mujeres: antología de textos medievales*, Feminismos, 63. Madrid: Cátedra.

—. (2005) *The Problem of Woman in Late-Medieval Hispanic Literature*, Colección Támesis, Serie A, Monografías, 214. Woodbridge: Boydell and Brewer.

—. and Isabel de Riquer (1998) *Contra la mujer: poemas medievales de rechazo y de vituperio*, La nueva caja negra, 24. Barcelona: Quaderns Crema.

Aston, Margaret (1993) *Faith and Fire: Popular and Unpopular Religion 1350-1600*. London: Hambledon.

Beattie, Tina (2007) "Mary in Patristic Theology", in *Mary: The Complete Resource*, Sarah Jane Boss (ed.), Oxford: Oxford University Press, 75-105.

Beavis, Mary Ann (2001) "The Power of Jesus' Parables: Were they Polemical or Irenic", *Journal for the Study of the New Testament*, 82, 3-30.

Blamires, Alcuin (ed.) (1992) *Woman Defamed and Woman Defended: An Anthology of Medieval Texts*. Oxford: Oxford University Press.

Bloch, R. Howard (1991) *Medieval Misogyny and the Invention of Western Romantic Love*. Chicago, IL: University of Chicago Press.

Bridge, Steven L. (2003) "Where the Eagles are Gathered": The Deliverance of the Elect in Lukan Eschatology", *Journal for the Study of the New Testament*, Supplement Series, 240. London: Sheffield Academic Press.

Cantavella, Rosanna (2003) "Debate on Women in *Tirant Lo Blanc*", in *The Querelle des femmes in the Romania: Studies in Honour of Friederike Hassauer*, Judith Bosch & Eva Cescutti (eds), Vienna: Turia & Kant, 45-56.

—. (1992). *Els cards i el llir: una lectura de l'"Espill" de Jaume Roig*. Barcelona: Quaderns Crema.

Carré, Antònia (1994) "L'estil de Jaume Roig: les propostes ètica i estètica de l'*Espill* de Jaume Roig", in *Intel·lectuals i escriptors a la baixa Edat Mitjana catalana*, Lola Badia & Albert Soler (eds), Barcelona: Publicacions de l'Abadia de Montserrat, Curial Edicions, 185-228.

Cassell, Anthony K. (ed. and trans.) (1975) *Boccaccio's The Corbaccio*. Urbana, IL: University of Illinois Press.

Cortijo Ocaña, Antonio (1995) "A propósito de *Medieval Misogyny and the Invention of Western Romantic Love* de R. Howard Bloch", *Revista de Filología Española*, 75, 351-58.

Dangler, Jean (1998) "Motherhood and Pain in Villena's *Vita Christi* and in Roig's *Spill*", *La Corónica*, 27, no. 1, 99-113.

Dodd, C. H. (1963). *The Apostolic Preaching and its Developments: Three Lectures with an Appendix on Eschatology and History*, 3rd edn. London: Hodder & Stoughton.

Ellington, Donna Spivey (2001) *From Sacred Body to Angelic Soul: Understanding Mary in Late Medieval and Early Modern Europe*. Washington, D.C.: Catholic University of America Press.

Flood, John (2002) "'Dentro del paraíso, en compañía de los ángeles formada': Eve and the Dignity of Women in Juan Rodríguez Padrón's *Triunfo de las donas*", *Bulletin of Spanish Studies*, 79, 33-43.

Ford, David (ed.) (1990) *The Modern Theologians: An Introduction to Christian Theology in the Twentieth Century*. Oxford: Blackwell, 1989, repr.

Graef, Hilda Charlotte (1963-65) *Mary: A History of Doctrine and Devotion*, 2 vols. London: Sheed & Ward.

Hogeterp, Albert L. A. (2009) *Interpretations of the End. A Comparative Traditio-Historical Study of Eschatological, Apocalyptic, and Messianic ideas in the Dead Sea Scrolls and the New Testament*, Studies in the Texts of the Desert of Judah, 83. Leiden: Brill.

St Isidore of Seville (1982) *Etimologías: edición bilingüe*, ed. José Oroz Reta & Manuel-A. Marcos Casquero, with introduction by Manuel C. Díaz y Díaz, Biblioteca de Autores Cristianos. Madrid: Biblioteca de Autores Cristianos.

Jeremias, Joachim (1962) *The Parables of Jesus*, 6th edn. London: SCM Press.

Juvenal (2007) *Sátiras*, Letras Universales, 394. Madrid: Cátedra.

Kelly, Anthony (2006) *Eschatology and Hope*, Theology in Global Perspective Series. Maryknoll, NY: Orbis.

Kramer, Heinrich and Jakobus Sprenger (1928) *Malleus maleficarum*, trans. & ed. Montague Sommers. London: n.p.

Lacarra Lanz, Eukene (1999) "Sobre la evolución del discurso del género y del cuerpo en los estudios medievales (1985-1997)", *Actes del VII Congrés de l'Associació Hispànica de Literatura Medieval (Castelló de la Plana, 22-26 de setembre de 1997)*, Santiago Fortuño Llorens & Tomàs Martínez Romero (eds), Castelló de la Plana: Universitat de Jaume I, 61-100.

McIver, Robert (1995) "The Parable of the Weeds among the Wheat (Matt. 13: 24-30, 36-43) and the Relationship between the Kingdom and the Church as Portrayed in the Gospel of Matthew", *Journal of Biblical Literature*, 114, no. 4, 643-59.

Mérida Jiménez, Rafael M. (1994) "Elogio y vituperio de la mujer medieval", in *La mujer: elogio y vituperio, Actas del IX Simposio de la Sociedad Española de la Literatura General y Comparada*, Esther Ortas Durand (ed.), 2 vols, Zaragoza: Universidad de Zaragoza, I, 269-76.

Moltmann, Jürgen (1969) *Theology of Hope: On the Ground and the Implications of a Christian Eschatology*, trans. James W. Leitch from the German. London: SCM Press.

Mowinckel, Sigmund (1959) *He that Cometh*, trans. G. W. Anderson. Oxford: Blackwell.

Ormerod, Neil (2007) *Creation, Grace and Redemption*, Theology in Global Perspective Series. Maryknoll, NY: Orbis.

Ortas Durand, Esther (ed.) (1994) *La mujer: elogio y vituperio, Actas del IX Simposio de la Sociedad Española de la Literatura General y Comparada*, 2 vols. Zaragoza: Universidad de Zaragoza.

Peirats, Anna Isabel (2003) "La comicitat de la moral o la moral de la comicitat", *Estudis Romànics*, 25, 251-77.

Pérez de Tudela y Velasco, M[a] Isabel (1989) "María en el vértice de la edad media", in *Las mujeres en el cristianismo medieval: imágenes teóricas y cauces de actuación religiosa*, Ángela Muñoz Fernández (ed.), Madrid: Asociación Cultural Al-Mudayna, 59-69.

Perrin, N. & D. C. Duling (1982) *The New Testament: An Introduction*, 2nd edn. New York: Harcourt Brace Jovanovich.

Reeves, Marjorie (1984) "The Development of Apocalyptic Thought: Medieval Attitudes", *The Apocalypse in English Renaissance Thought and Literature. Patterns, Antecedents, and Repercussions*, C. A. Patrides & Joseph Wittreich (eds), Manchester: Manchester University Press.

Reventlow, Henning Graf (1997) "The Eschatologization of the Prophetic Books: A Comparative Study", in his *Eschatology in the Bible and in Jewish and Christian Tradition*, *Journal for the Study of the Old Testament*, Supplement Series, 243. Sheffield: Sheffield Academic Press, 169-88.

Roig, Jaume (1978) *Espill o llibre de les dones,* ed. Marina Gustà, Les Millors Obres de la Literatura Catalana, 3. Barcelona: Edicions 62.

Rubin, Miri (2009) *Mother of God: A History of the Virgin Mary*. New Haven, CT: Yale University Press.

Sánchez de Vercial, Clemente (2005) *Libro de los exemplos por a.b.c*, ed. Antonio Baldissera, Pubblicazioni della Facoltà di Lettere e Filosofia dell'Università di Pavia, 114. Pisa: Edizione ETS.

Solomon, Michael (1997) *The Literature of Misogyny in Medieval Spain*, Cambridge Studies in Latin American and Iberian Literature, 10. Cambridge: Cambridge University Press.

Thompson, Damian (1999) *The End of Time: Faith and Fear in the Shadow of the Millennium*, 2nd edn. London: Vintage.

Tiñena, Jordi (ed.) (1988) *Llibre de les dones*. Barcelona: Laertes.

Wengst, Klaus (1997) "Aspects of the Last Judgement according to Matthew", in *Eschatology in the Bible and in Jewish and Christian Tradition*, Henning Graf Reventlow (ed.), *Journal for the Study of the Old Testament*, Supplement Series 243, Sheffield: Sheffield Academic Press, 233-45.

Wood, Charles T. (1981) "The Doctors' Dilemma: Sin, Death and the Menstrual Cycle in Medieval Thought", *Speculum*, 56, no. 4, 710-27.

Yoder, Christine Roy (1999) "A Woman of Substance: A Socioeconomic Reading of Proverbs 31: 10-31", *Journal of Biblical Literature*, 122, no. 3, 427-47.

Notes

[1] Jaume Roig, *Espill o llibre de les dones,* ed. Marina Gustà, Les Millors Obres de la Literatura Catalana, 3 (Barcelona: Edicions 62, 1978). All references to the *Espill* will be provided as page references in the body of the text.

[2] A partial framework for this overview of Roig's eschatology is provided by John Ford (1990).

[3] There is a play on words between "callosa" [rugged] and Callosa, a town 56 km northeast of Alicante.

[4] For an examination of the concept of fire in popular religion, see Aston 1993.

[5] This question is addressed in Antonio Cortijo Ocaña (1995).

[6] The description of the widow can be compared with that in Boccaccio's *The Corbaccio* (Cassell 1975, 55, cited in Archer 2005, 93-94). Jehan Le Fèvre writes in *Lamentations de Matheolus* of widows remarrying with undue haste (see selections, trans. Karen Pratt, in Blamires 1992, 187-88). For widows' remarrying, see, also, Cantavella 1992, 82-85.

[7] For commentary on abortions and infanticides, see Cantavella (1992, 87-88).

[8] See Blamires (1992) for an overview of European misogyny. Archer (2001) provides greater Hispanic focus. See, also, Archer and de Riquer (1998) for poems from the Catalan *maldit* tradition.

[9] The theme of sexual excess is included in the *maldit* addressed to Na Monboí and her lover En Joan, in Archer's anthology of Ausiàs March's poems (1992, 56-58). Blamires (1992, 26) traces this commonplace to its classical roots, citing Juvenal's Sixth Satire, which depicts the insatiable Empress (2007, 312-71). Juvenal describes the marriage bed (2007, 336-370). Stepping in a wife's urine in the morning is also mentioned (2007, 340-41). It can also be traced to the early Church Fathers. Isidore of Seville in his *Etymologiae* also depicts women as the more

lustful sex, according to Blamires (1992, 43; see St Isidore (1982)). For Catalan, as well as Castilian, antecedents, see Cantavella (1992, 72-73).

[10] For Beguines in misogynist literature, see Cantavella 1992, 81.

[11] For an overview of cultural representation of the female body through the ages, see Eukene Lacarra Lanz (1999). For a meticulous study of the adaptation of Aristotelian physionomy in the Middle Ages, see Allen (1997). Charles T. Wood (1981) has studied the fascination with and rejection of the female body. Dangler (1998, 103) suggests that Roig's concern is with the exclusion of husbands and fathers from a reproductive process which they nevertheless sought to control.

[12] Trickery practised by wives on husbands is a staple of many misogynist texts, including Clemente Sánchez de Vercial's *Libro de los exemplos por a.b.c* (2005). See Archer (2001, 206-10 and 191-92).

[13] On Mary as a key element of medieval faith, see Pérez de Tudela y Velasco (1989). On the tensions between the exaltedness of Mary and human lowliness, see also Donna Spivey Ellington (2001, 31-32) and Tina Beattie (2007). In contrast, Miri Rubin (2009, 256-68) shows how Mary was a source of inspiration and a model for female mystics and religious.

[14] Dangler (1998, 104), discusses how "gender, biology and lineage" are linked in the *Espill* so that women inherit their propensity to deceive from their foremother Eve.

[15] Ellington (2001, 58-59) discusses the way in which lactation was thought to be the result of original sin. She interprets the cult of the lactating Virgin as part of "late medieval preference for the sacramental and for symbols of bodily nourishment" (59).

[16] Ellington (2001, 122-25) discusses the eloquence of ritual bodily gestures by Mary, Christ's Mother, considering them an even more powerful form of intercession than her words. Her maternal gestures depend on her presence within the heavenly court.

[17] The perfect housewife, described by Solomon in Proverbs 31: 10-31, spins (31:19), makes clothes for her household (31: 21), and sells the cloths she has produced (31: 24). Christine Roy Yoder (1999) provides a study of the woman described in Proverbs 31 as a businesswoman.

[18] As author of several descriptions of wives and women both good and bad (Proverbs 5: 29, 6: 23-26, 7: 7-27, 9: 13-17, 12: 4, 31: 1-31, and Ecclesiasticus 25: 1-25, 26: 1-25), Solomon was considered an ideal counsellor on choosing a wife wisely.

[19] For a study of eschatology in Matthew's parables, see Wengst (1997) and Jeremias (1962, 33-206).

[20] The contrast between Mary as a "planta de llavor qualitativament diferent, resplendint en majestat per sobre d'unes comparses perilloses i miserables" [a plant with a qualitatively different seed, shining in majesty far above her dangerous and lowly companions] is expounded by Cantavella (1992, 121), who allies the contrast to Roig's defence of the doctrine of the Immaculate Conception. As Cantavella indicates, Roig holds that the doctrine elevates the Virgin Mary at the expense of other members of her sex.

[21] Jeremias (1962, 81) argues the traditional interpretation of the wheat as the saved and the tares as the unrighteous misses the point and that Matthew's purpose is to urge patience to his community who are faced with the delay in the timing of the *Parousia.*

[22] Wood (1981, 712) notes how, according to the Dominicans Heinrich Kramer and Jakobus Sprenger (1928) writing in 1486, in the *Malleus maleficarum*, witchcraft is a result of women's excessive carnal lust. See, also, Mérida Jiménez (1994).

[23] See Flood (2002) for a discussion of the relationship between Eve and other women. For the origins of the Eve-Mary parallel, see Graef (1963-65, I, 38-48).

[24] The Christian Church provides Roig with a plethora of documents which counsel against marriage. These begin with St Paul's celebrated injunctions in 1 Corinthians 7: 1-11. The early Church Fathers, such as Cyprian, Jerome, or Tertullian either decry marriage altogether, following St Paul, or promote virginity as the better option for women (Archer 2001, 73-86).

[25] See Neil Ormerod (2007, 165) on original sin; he draws out the inferences of Colossians 1: 20-22.

CHAPTER TEN

MILLENNIAL ENDINGS AND OLD BEGINNINGS IN JOSÉ SARAMAGO, H.G. WELLS AND JOHN WYNDHAM

MARIA MANUEL LISBOA

The noughties, the first decade of this new century, were also of course the first decade of the new millennium, with all the implications which that entails, culturally, psychologically and even pragmatically, at the most basic levels of daily life (prior to midnight on December 1999 it was thought possible that the world's computer systems might break down, with all the fearful consequences such an event would entail). Millenarianism, the belief in an impending major transformation after which the world will be changed is, as the name indicates, based on the logic of a one-thousand-year cycle, but on a reduced scale it is a disquiet that also prevails around the turning of centuries. In our living memory, of course (on 31 December 1999 or, for the mathematically pernickety, 31 December 2000), we witnessed the turning of both a century and a millennium. Transformative millenarianism goes hand in hand with a rise in cultural visions of Apocalypse, which is itself a term with gnomic possibilities: from its original etymology as discovery or epiphany (the revelation of something new and often better), to its current catastrophic, end-of-the-world usage in common parlance.[1]

In the Judaeo-Christian imagination, the key text for Millenarian preoccupations (the flip side of which is the conceptualisation of Apocalypse), is the book of Revelation, the last book of the New Testament, thought to have been written in 95 A.D., as the first century neared its end, by John of Patmos (according to some scholars the same person as John the Evangelist and the Apostle John). Other Apocalyptic texts are not necessarily so punctual in their turn-of-century manifestations: Snorri Sturluson pondered the end of the world in the Icelandic *Prose Edda* around 1220 (Sturluson 1916). Richard Wagner drew upon it during the third quarter of the nineteenth century, during which he composed the cycle of four operas, *The Ring of the Nibelung*, of which the last one, *The Twilight of the Gods* (*Götterdämmerung*), depicts the death of the Norse Gods and the end of the world (Wagner 1848-74). And nearer our time, the atomic bombs dropped on Hiroshima and Nagasaki in 1945—raising, as they did, the possibility that, for the first time in the history of humanity, the end of the world might be brought about by human agency—led to a mid-century wave of speculative and/or science fiction narratives in text and film which endures to this day. In the year 2000 the predicted millennium computer bug never materialised, and in 2008 the launching of the Large Hadron Collider did not after all rip open the fabric of the universe. On each occasion, however, speculation that they might was widespread, not just in the outer fringes of internet eccentricity but in serious scientific circles. At the time of going to press, there is abundant speculation in the former, if not in the latter, on the advent of Planet X, collision with which would bring about the death of planet Earth in 2012. We may sigh and shrug our shoulders, but possibly we should also wonder about the possible canonical status of these vagaries in two thousand years' time. No one accused John of Patmos of insanity when he warned that he had

> [H]eard a loud voice from the temple telling the seven angels, "Go and pour out on the earth the seven bowls of the wrath of God." (…) and a loud voice came out of the temple, from the throne, saying, "It is done!" And there were flashes of lightning, voices, peals of thunder, and a great earthquake such as had never been since men were on the earth, so great was that earthquake. The great city was split into three parts, and the cities of the nations fell, and God remembered great Babylon, to make her drain the cup of the fury of his wrath. And every island fled away, and no mountains were to be found; and great hailstones, heavy as a hundred-weight, dropped on men from heaven, till men cursed God for the plague of the hail, so fearful was that plague. (Revelation 16: 2-22)

Much closer to our time, with reference to the unleashing of global cataclysm, it is useful to consider figures as influential as Ronald Reagan, President of what was soon to be the world's only superpower, in the aftermath of the collapse of the Soviet Union. Reagan saw the Cold War as a cosmic struggle between Good and Evil and believed in the imminence and desirability of Armageddon as the preparation for the Kingdom of God on Earth. In 1971, the then-Governor of California stated:

> All of the other prophecies that had to be fulfilled before Armageddon can come to pass [sic]. In the thirty-eighth chapter of Ezekiel it says God will

> take the children of Israel from among the heathen where they'd been scattered and will gather them again in the promised land. That has finally come about after 2,000 years. For the first time ever, everything is in place for the battle of Armageddon and the Second Coming of Christ. (…). Everything is falling into place. It can't be too long now. Ezekiel says that fire and brimstone will be rained upon the enemies of God's people. That must mean that they will be destroyed by nuclear weapons. (Vidal 1989, 108-9)

Reagan, as his enduring popularity attested, was truly the voice of his people, or at least of a significant majority. He was also both the most powerful and only one of an estimated twenty million Americans who believe in the Rapture. A 1984 survey found that 39% of Americans believed that Biblical predictions of global destruction by fire referred to nuclear war (Crossley 2000, 57). And in a must-read essay pithily entitled "Armageddon," Gore Vidal describes how the belief in the need for a *tabula rasa* wipe-out prior to a new beginning was also espoused by such influential voices as James Watt, Reagan's Secretary of State for the Interior, as well as by Reagan himself, quoted above, his presidential finger at all times poised on the nuclear button. Vidal summarises the rationale whereby, as Watt explained to the American Congress in 1981, the end of the world could be relied on to happen sooner rather than later ("I do not know how many future generations we can count on before the Lord returns," (Vidal 1989, 192):

> Christ will defeat the anti-Christ at Armageddon (…). Just before the battle, the Church will be wafted to Heaven and all the good folks will experience Rapture (…). The wicked will suffer horribly. Then after seven years of burying the dead (presumably there will be survivors), God returns, bringing Peace and Joy, and the Raptured ones. (Vidal 1989, 103-4)

As recently as 1987, indeed, towards the end of his presidency (1981-89) Mikhail Gorbachev was so worried by the American President's happy supposition, upon becoming president, that "we may be the generation that sees Armageddon" (Dugger 1984, 4), that he was moved to administer a gentle reminder that "planet Earth was the only likely venue for the continuity of humanity and that it would be a pity to lose everything through war, or, more likely, accident" (Gorbachev cited in Vidal 1989, 111).

Often, in narratives of Apocalypse, from Genesis to the most recent Science Fiction, only hypothetical explanations are offered for the original disaster, broadly encompassed within what the entertainingly shared vocabulary of theology and insurance companies denominate "Acts of God" (with no liability accepted in either case). As is also often the case with these narratives, an initial raindrop quickly builds up to a flood, i.e. a widespread catastrophe. In what follows, three texts will be drawn upon to illustrate the process whereby what are initially small events escalate, in due course acquiring cataclysmic proportions with the capacity to unleash the kind of global disaster typically feared by the millenarian mind.

In José Saramago's *Ensaio sobre a Cegueira* [Blindness] (1995), the affliction in question begins with one isolated case, subsequently spreads to a few people and rapidly becomes generalised. In John Wyndham's *The Day of the Triffids* (1954), on the other hand, near-universal blindness is instantaneous, leading to the gradual revelation that only a small minority has been spared. In Saramago, disbelief, as well as failed attempts at explaining the origins of disaster, characterises the collective response, in both this novel and in an earlier work, *A Jangada de Pedra* [The Stone Raft] (1986). In the latter, the Iberian Peninsula breaks away from the rest of Europe and floats away into the Atlantic, in the process nearly colliding with the Azores. Ensuing events are conveyed from a multiplicity of viewpoints which include those of the characters experiencing them, a narrator reporting upon them to an unidentified audience and a third voice, possibly that of the author. The speakers address the reader, albeit with some appearance of scepticism regarding the reliability of their own narratives, thus introducing a dimension of uncertainty (nothing is now knowable or controllable) that commonly underpins the fear characteristic of much millenarian writing of Apocalypse. The discovery of something which under moonlight looks like a stone ship but in the light of day is just a pile of rocks is given a variety of explanations by different people, ranging from the geological to the fantastic, the effect being the ultimate dismissal of the possibility of ascertaining reality or truth in a world which in the past had taken them for granted. They, like the erstwhile Peninsula's geographical status (it is now an island of sorts) and location (it is not fixed to the seabed but floats) have now become uncertain. The world, at the most comically literal of levels, has become a moveable feast and what in the past was reality in the present no longer makes sense.

In *Ensaio sobre a Cegueira*, and with more than a coincidental whiff of a similarity to Camus's *La Peste* [The Plague] (1972) and Wyndham's *The Day of the Triffids* (1954), the disaster (blindness in Wyndham and Saramago, disease in Camus) which strikes a community and rapidly acquires many of the characteristics of standard pestilence (dead bodies, decay) offers no explanation, and only the possibility of a link, causal and/or punitive, to a more fundamental instability at the heart of the status quo. Either way, the effects are essentially similar in all three novels: in this not-so-brave new world, reality becomes meaningless and blindness/disease, literal rather than symbolic, becomes the unmanageable norm, in a world that no longer makes sense. In Saramago, as in other apocalyptic novels and films (*The Day of the Triffids*, already mentioned, popular culture narratives and films/television series such as *Earth Abides* (1973), *Survivors* (1975-77, 2008-10)) the onset of chaos is almost immediate, and is characterised by the swift arrival of the four horsemen of the Apocalypse: famine, since the blind cannot easily find or make food; war, as the result of competition for scarce resources; pestilence, as people die and bodies decompose; and death, which feeds on the effects of the other three. In Saramago, as elsewhere, the component of decay and the resulting stench become the primary objective correlatives of a problem that is literal but also symbolic (of political and social corruption). In each case the disaster not only unleashes violence and autocracy in a variety of forms but it also reveals that such tendencies were always already there, only latent. Camus's allegory of encroaching Fascism in *La Peste* is echoed in the prompt decision taken by the powers that be in Saramago's novel to control the contagion of blindness—that which defines these Others as "other"—by incarcerating them, appropriately, where dictatorships have traditionally confined that which is unorthodox: a disused psychiatric hospital. And why not? The label of madness is a solution which has been historically tried and tested by every human autocracy (whether defined by party politics, class or gender) since difference began (Foucault (1993), Showalter (1985), and Gilbert and Gubar (1984)). And it is perhaps apposite that, in the omnipresent stench that is the principal hallmark of the catastrophe in Saramago's novel, from the point of view of both the outside onlookers and those who cannot see but can still smell (the increasingly filthy and dehumanised prisoners themselves), the affliction renders its sufferers literally as well as ontologically abject (in Kristeva's sense of the term), for a variety of social and political exclusions: they are contagious, cast out, and dangerous.

> [O médico ...] sentiu uma forte necessidade de evacuar. No sítio onde se encontrava, não tinha a certeza de de ser capaz de chegar às latrinas, mas decidiu aventurar-se. Esperava que alguém, ao menos, tivesse tido a lembrança de levar para lá o papel higiénico que viera com as caixas da comida. Enganou-se no caminho duas vezes, angustiado porque a necessidade apertava cada vez mais, e já estava nas últimas instâncias da urgência quando pôde enfim baixar as calças e agachar-se na retrete turca. O fedor asfixiava. Tinha a impressão de haver pisado uma pasta mole, os

excrementos de alguém que não acertara com o buraco da retrete ou que resolvera aliviar-se sem querer saber mais de respeitos. (Saramago 1995, 96)

[[The doctor]…felt a pressing need to relieve himself. At the spot where he found himself, he was not sure that he would be able to find the lavatories, but he decided to take a chance. He was hoping that someone would at least have remembered to leave there the toilet paper which had been delivered with the containers of food. He got lost twice on the way and was in some distress because he was beginning to feel desperate and just when he could hold back no longer, he was finally able to take down his trousers and crouch over the open latrine. The stench choked him. He had the impression of having stepped on some soft pulp, the excrement of someone who had missed the hole of the latrine or who had decided to relieve himself without any consideration for others. (Saramago trans. Pontiero 1997, 88)]

And in *The Day of the Triffids* disease, contagion and epidemic death become apparent in the smell of decomposing bodies, even when, as is generally the case, people retreat indoors and hide to die:

The first thing I was aware of the next morning was the smell. (...) I am not going into details about [it]; those who knew it will never forget it, the rest of it is indescribable. It rose from every city and town for weeks, and travelled on every wind that blew. When I woke to it that morning it convinced me beyond doubt that the end had come. Death is just the shocking end of animation: it is dissolution that is final. (Wyndham 1954, 149)

Definitions of difference, otherness or alienation, of course, do not necessarily conform to expectation. It is curious, for example, although also surprisingly unimportant (as regards its effect on the community) that in H.G. Wells' "The Country of the Blind" (1982), the definition of orthodoxy (blindness as opposed to sight) is reversed without causing any significant change in overall effect. Normality, it soon becomes clear, is only what the majority declare it to be. In Wells, the hero, Nunez, is an educated man, traveller, explorer and philosopher, conqueror of both lands and ideas, who in the course of a mountain climbing expedition finds himself adrift in an imponderable new world. Arrival in the country of the blind is a plunge into the unknown, both literally (he falls down a ravine into the valley where that country is located) and rhetorically (he finds himself marooned in an upside-down world, where life is lived by night and sight is an unknown condition).

Exploration as both concept and practice usually has a double edge (knowledge and conquest, gnostic and material profit) and it is seldom a fair trade. Nunez's instinctive reaction on finding himself in a community where all are blind follows a standard formula, namely the desire for conquest in both senses of the word (conquest of power and conquest of love, Todorov 1984), based on the assumption that in the country of the blind the one-eyed man is king (and the two-eyed man, presumably, is master of that particular universe). In effect, however, as he soon discovers, the sighted man finds himself at a counter-intuitive disadvantage in a habitat set up for blindness, and in which sight is of no relevance.

In Wells, Nunez is eventually required to have his eyes gouged out as the pre-condition for being allowed to remain in the community and marry the girl he loves. It is neither sight nor blindness *per se*, therefore, only the value they are attributed in any given set of circumstances, that determine both the brutal aspects of majority rule and its criteria for defining who is predator and who is prey.

In these new worlds post-apocalypse, whether under relatively benevolent rules of government (*Survivors*, *Earth Abides*), or under the more savage ones of Saramago, Wells and Wyndham, any threat to the community (the diseased, anyone who is significantly different), is summarily dealt with by death, in the interests of a commonweal that must prioritise its own continuity above all. And in all three texts, generalised blindness encounters the immediate or eventual problem of opportunistic dictatorship (the one-eyed king): the newly arrived would-be conqueror in Wells, the diktat of authoritarian power that initially confines the first few victims of blindness to a make-shift leper colony in Saramago, and the triffids which with uncanny speed take advantage of near-universal blindness to begin an efficient takeover of the world:

> Those damn [triffids] have the drop on us. (...) there's more to them than we think. How did they *know*? They started to break loose the moment there was no one to stop them. [When we went blind] they were around this house the very next day. (...) They couldn't do that here until conditions made it possible. They didn't even try. But when they could, they did it *at once*—almost as if they *knew* they could. (Wyndham 1954, 235-6)

Something which, indeed, had been foreseen years before the catastrophe, by an earlier triffid expert: "If it were a choice for survival between a triffid and a blind man, I know which one I would put money on" (Wyndham 1954, 48); he continues, "A triffid's in a damn sight better position to survive than a blind man" (Wyndham 1954, 77).

In Saramago, the affliction of a minority leads to the implementation of a despotic, final-solution style bureaucracy, curtailed only by the subsequent onset of general blindness, which abolishes the definition of sightlessness as a minority condition and makes it the maladaptive norm. In Saramago, as in Wyndham, in the early stages of the epidemic the problem to be addressed regards the means whereby the status quo (the sighted) might control the alien (the blind and contagious Other), something reinforced by the bureaucratic language that describes the measures taken in response to this outbreak of difference:

> O Governo está perfeitamente consciente das suas responsabilidades e espera que aqueles a quem esta mensagem se dirige assumam também, como cumpridores cidadãos que devem ser, as responsabilidades que lhes competem, pensando que o isolamento em que agora se encontram representará, acima de quaisquer outras considerações pessoais, um acto de solidariedade para com o resto da comunidade nacional. (Saramago 1995, 50)
>
> O Governo lamenta ter sido forçado a exercer energicamente o que considera ser seu direito e seu dever (...). (Saramago 1995, 73)
>
> O exército lamenta ter sido obrigado a reprimir pelas armas um movimento sedicioso responsável pela criação duma situação de risco iminente, da qual não teve culpa directa ou indirecta (...). (Saramago 1995, 89)
>
> [The Government is fully aware of its responsibilities and hopes that those to whom this message is directed will, as the upright citizens they doubtless are, also assume their responsibilities, bearing in mind that the isolation in which they now find themselves will represent, above any personal considerations, an act of solidarity with the rest of the nation's community. (Saramago, trans. Pontiero 1997, 41)
>
> The Government regrets having to enforce to the letter what it considers its right and duty (…). (Saramago, trans. Pontiero 1997, 65)
>
> The army regrets having been forced to repress with weapons a seditious movement responsible for creating a situation of imminent risk, for which the army was neither directly nor indirectly to blame (…). (Saramago trans. Pontiero 1997, 81)]

In Saramago, then, blindness leads to dictatorial rule, whether by the sighted over the blind or by the ruthless over the meek (within the ranks of the blind). Similarly, in *The Day of the Triffids*, attempts to restore structures of social organisation in the aftermath of the disaster inevitably assume the character of "needs-must" dictatorial rule. And in H.G. Wells' "The Country of the Blind," blindness and sight, while demarcating difference, simply reverse definitions of supremacy and subalternity. The arrival of Nunez in the country of the blind is not the gnostic outcome of a scientific enterprise undertaken with deliberation, but an unintended plunge into the geographic and socio-political unknown. In this case, therefore, the journey of discovery was wrong-footed from the start, and the knowledge that is attained is troubling (in the country of the blind the one-eyed man is *not* king, and may in fact be forced to go blind in order to gain acceptance).

Is it possible, then, ever to learn one's lesson, or is it rather the case that any lesson can only ever be learnt after curiosity has already irreversibly killed the cat? If the loss of Paradise after knowledge was attained was the first Apocalypse, it is clear that after Eve, you can't go home again, not ever, not to any real pre-lapsarian state of unknowing innocence. There is no such thing as a born-again virgin or an un-fallen mother. In "The Country of the Blind" every parameter of understanding is destroyed by the immovable resistance of those who do not wish to be led to the light. In Wyndham, Science leads to Apocalypse (in the shape of the satellites whose possible malfunction resulted in the emission of light wavelengths that led to widespread blindness). At the end, it remains unclear whether the conquering spirit of Science will ultimately lead to humanity's restored dominion over the triffids which it created to begin with, or whether, if human rule is restored, what will ensue will be the cyclical repetition of the same mistake (unchecked scientific advancement) driven by hubris.

And in Saramago, too, knowledge comes with the flavour of the proverbial poisoned apple: as the world recovers its sight, it is left with the consciousness that all it took was the temporary removal of the restraining binds of civilisation for the primeval brute to re-surface in the average citizen. That knowledge, once acquired, will be impossible to relinquish. And in each case, therefore, the very concept of civilisation, which, to have meaning, requires belief in its superior merits, becomes untenable in the awareness of the ease with which it can be erased.

Common and unsettling patterns run through all the texts discussed: violent, misogynistic gender diktat (the rape of the women in Saramago; ownership of the female body in Wells), dictatorship and ostracisation (of the blind in Saramago and Wyndham; of the sighted in H.G. Wells), the imprisonment of the powerless (the sighted man in the valley of the blind, in Wells; the survivors from blindness corralled by the triffids into communities under siege, in Wyndham; the blind in the disused psychiatric hospital, in Saramago). In Wells, the Solomon's choice offered to Nunez (elective blindness) may in effect be a metaphor for the fact that whether your eyes work or not, there is always a power greater than that of the individual, and beyond that there is never really any choice. Theoretically, the one-eyed man's arrival in the country of the blind gives him a conquering advantage but no gnosis (what could one possibly learn from blind people who presumably live in darkness in all senses of the word?). The answer to this rhetorical question, as Nunez learns, in the end invalidates his status as a viable human being, because what the blind can teach him is something fundamental: the art of survival. In Saramago's *Ensaio sobre a Cegueira*, living in darkness—another double-edged expression which may also signify living in a particular state of mind, living in a state of obscurantism—is curiously not (or at least not literally) the fate of those afflicted by universal blindness, since their blindness is characterised by a sensation of bright white light. That sensation, habitually the correlative of either enlightenment, knowledge or arrival at Eternal Life (which is arguably the attainment of ultimate knowledge or understanding), however, here betokens spiralling despair. The ophthalmic and existential darkness of the inhabitants of the country of the blind, on the other hand, is literal (they only see darkness, they live by night and sleep during the day when it is too hot to work), but it does not represent their existential reality. In the past, progressive but *gradual* generational blindness had resulted in the evolution of a community with a blind-friendly, perfectly structured and organised habitat in which life is prosperous and productive, and sight is an irrelevance or even a drawback (the rules of communal existence being determined *by* the blind *for* the blind). To see or not to see, that is not the question. In the end, like the triffids who have no sight or indeed any other sense apart from touch, the usual human definition of fitness is not necessarily meaningful in the survival stakes, or in gaining mastery, in these differently-arranged universes.

In these texts two clusters of potential survival emerge: the first composed of those who, having been blind from birth, know how to get by without sight (everybody in "The Country of the Blind," the relatively happy few in *The Day of the Triffids* and one single man in *Ensaio sobre a Cegueira*); and the second composed of those who for various reasons escaped the near-universal blight. And within these set-ups, noticeably, while adjusted modes of existence quickly emerge, the radically altered circumstances unhelpfully show signs of reproducing the intellectual, moral and social defects that arguably provoked the present disaster. Or, in other words, the seed of a recycled end already lies at the heart of the brand new beginning.

Violence, including gender violence, is always ready to manifest itself in texts of the post-Apocalypse, including the three discussed here: the intended blinding of the foreigner in exchange for the possession of the desired female in H.G. Wells; the gang rape of the women in exchange for food, and the retaliatory murder of the ring leader of the rapists by the doctor's wife in Saramago; the proposed reinstatement of oppressive, quasi-feudal, would-be seigneurial law, including enforced polygamy, as a means of re-establishing order and re-populating the world in Wyndham. Whether with good or bad intentions, it all comes down to the fact that, post-Apocalypse, brave new worlds, more often than not, come already equipped with a hell pre-paved with those intentions and with some recognizable traits of the old order. If heroes are ordinary people asked extraordinary things in terrible circumstances and delivering (Mo 2002, 404), post-Apocalypse there may be some heroes, but not necessarily enough and often they are outnumbered by villains, with women as one of the automatic recipients of unavoidable violence. Whatever the causal components of catastrophe, be they war, scientific hubris or natural cataclysm, the common factor in the aftermath of Apocalypse may be that the two categories of humanity—defined, within the ethical parameters of the text, broadly speaking, as good and bad—are at best evenly matched. And this, in its turn, opens the possibility that in the near *tabula rasa* that follows global disaster, the problems that brought about that cataclysm in the first place, become part of the new equation. Faced with the unimaginable, what we are able to articulate in its aftermath will almost certainly be just another version of what we already know: "Humanity in its essence (…) is what these apocalypses unveil" (Berger 1999, 10).

With variations, as will now be argued, a similar logic often informs texts on both utopia and dystopia, (millenarian or otherwise): namely the end—or almost the end—of the world (dystopia), followed by a post-cataclysm set-up involving an authoritarian despot or ruling power which saves humanity from itself and sets about creating a new, supposedly better—perfect—world (utopia); the price being acceptance of a panoptical control that in various ways dehumanises it.

Millenarian fear and desire both involve the ability to imagine cataclysm: in the case of the former, as the cause of the end; and in the case of the latter, as a means to it. As regards the latter, some examples may usefully illustrate the point. Long before the global cleansings envisaged to precede either the rise of American Fundamentalist Rapture or, much earlier, the New Testament's glimpse of the New Jerusalem, Plato's Utopia of the ideal Republic had already required the exclusion (by unspecified means) of numerous categories of undesirability (artists, poets, the sick, the ugly and the non-conformists, to list but a few). And in envisioning his New Republic, H.G. Wells, not now in the guise of purveyor of Science Fiction but in his self-appointed role as philosopher-architect of the future, argued in all seriousness that Utopia could only become a reality by means of state regulated birth control ("wifehood [being] the chief feminine profession," "the efficient mother who can make the best of her children [... being] the most important person in the state," Wells 1999[1901], 174); and, more dramatically, by means of radical measures implemented beyond the specific concerns of gender or birth control: for example, large-scale eugenics or genocide:

> It has become apparent that whole masses of human population are, as a whole, inferior in their claim upon the future to other masses (…). [T]he men of the New Republic will hold that the procreation of children who, by the circumstances of their parentage, *must* be diseased bodily or mentally (…) is absolutely the most loathsome of all conceivable sins. (…) And how will the New Republic treat the inferior races? How will it deal with the black? How will it deal with the yellow man? How will it tackle that alleged termite in the woodwork, the Jew? Certainly not as races at all. (…) It will tolerate no dark corners where the people of the Abyss may fester (…). And (…) those swarms of black, and brown, and dirty-white, and yellow people, who do not come into the new needs of efficiency?
>
> Well, the world is a world, not a charitable institution, and I take it they will have to go. (…) [I]t is their portion to die out and disappear.
>
> The men of the New Republic will not be squeamish (…). They will have an ideal that will make killing worth the while; like Abraham, they will have the faith to kill. (Wells 1999 [1901], 163-78)

H.G. Wells' selective utopias, both in "The Country of the Blind" and *Anticipations*, like Saramago's and Wyndham's dystopias, bring us back to starting point of this discussion: end-of-century, end-of-millennia, end-of-time cultural mind sets, which, by way of more or less bloody epiphanies, undertake the enterprise of imagining sometimes unwelcome, new but also already previously-rehearsed beginnings.

Works Cited

Berger, James (1999) *After The End: Representations Of Post-Apocalypse*, Minneapolis: University of Minneapolis Press.

Camus, Albert (1972), *La Peste*, Paris: Editions Flammarion.

Carey, John (1999), *The Faber Book of Utopias*, London: Faber and Faber.

Crossley, Robert (2000) "Acts of God", in David Seed (ed.), *Imagining Apocalypse: Studies in Cultural Crisis*, London: Macmillan Press.

Dugger, Ronnie (1984) "Does Reagan Expect a Nuclear War?" in *Washington Post*, 8 April, C1, 4.
Huxley, Aldous (1977) *Brave New World*, London: Grafton.
Foucault, Michel (1993) *Madness and Civilization: A History of Insanity in the Age of Reason*. London: Routledge.
Gilbert, Sandra and Gubar, Susan (1984) *The Madwoman in the Attic: The Woman Writer and the Nineteenth-Century Literary Imagination*. London and New Haven: Yale University Press.
Ketterer, David (1974) *New Worlds for Old: The Apocalyptic Imagination, Science Fiction and American Literature*, Bloomington: Indiana University Press.
Kristeva, Julia (1984) *Powers of Horror: An Essay on Abjection*, Columbia University Press.
Mo, Timothy (2002) *The Redundancy of Courage*. London: Paddleless Press.
More, Thomas (1980) *Utopia*, Harmondsworth: Penguin.
Plato (1987) *The Republic*, trans. Desmond Lee, London: Penguin Classics.
Rees, Martin (2003) *Our Final Century*, London: Arrow Books.
—. (2003) *Our Final Hour*, London: Arrow Books.
Saramago, José (1986) *A Jangada de Pedra*, Lisbon: Caminho.
—. (1995) *Ensaio sobre a Cegueira*, Lisbon: Caminho.
—. (1997) *Blindness*, trans. Giovanni Pontiero, London: Harvill Press.
Sontag, Susan (1979) "The Imagination of Disaster", in *Against Interpretation and Other Essays*, London: Penguin Classics.
Showalter, Elaine (1985) *The Female Malady: Women, Madness and English culture, 1830-1980*. London: Virago.
Stewart, George R. (1973) *Earth Abides*, London: Corgi.
Sturluson, Snorri, *Prose Edda*, trans. Arthur Gilchrist Brodeur (1916), Available: http://www.sacred-texts.com/neu/pre/ [Accessed 8 July 2010].
Survivors, Series 1 (1975-77), dir. Terry Nation, UK: BBC Television.
Survivors, Series 2 (2008-10), dir. Adrian Hodges, UK: BBC Television.
Todorov, Tzevetan (1984) *The Conquest of America: The Question of the Other*, trans. R. Howard, New York: Harper and Row.
Vidal, Gore (1989) "Armageddon?", in *Armageddon? Essays 1983-1987*, London: Grafton.
Wagner, Richard, *Götterdämmerung (Twilight of the Gods)* (1848-74).
Wells, H.G. (1982) "The Country of the Blind" in *Selected Short Stories*. Harmondsworth: Penguin, 147-53.

—. (1999)[1901] *Anticipations of the Reaction of Mechanical and Scientific Progress upon Human Life and Thought*. New York: Dover.
Wyndham, John (1954) *The Day of the Triffids*. Harmondsworth: Penguin.

Notes

[1] The Greek term *apokalupsus* implies an unveiling either of future events or of the unseen realms of heaven and hell. James Berger (1999) identifies three meanings of the term Apocalypse: first, eschaton, referring to the actual imagined end of the world as presented in the Biblical book of Revelation (for more on this, see chapter nine in this volume), in millenarian movements and in visions of nuclear or environmental Armageddon; second, catastrophes or rupture points which mark the end of something within clear limits, such as for example the Holocaust, Hiroshima, 9/11; third, Apocalypse as an uncovering or revelation leading to something new and different.

CHAPTER ELEVEN

DIGITAL BRAZIL: OPEN-SOURCE NATION AND THE META-RECYCLING OF KNOWLEDGE

MARGARET ANNE CLARKE

> In the Information Society, the defence of digital inclusion is fundamental not only for economic motives or employability, but also for socio-economic reasons, principally to ensure the inalienable right to communication…It is not sufficient to have a free mind if our words cannot circulate like the words of others. The majority of the population, on being deprived of access to communication via a computer, is simply being prevented from communicating in the most flexible, complete and extensive means. This digital apartheid represents a breakdown of a basic formal liberty of universal liberal democracy. (Amadeu quoted in Warschauer 2004,13)

These words were spoken at the beginning of the first decade of the millennium by Sérgio Amadeu da Silva, the president of the National Institution of Information Technology in the administration headed by President Inácio Lula da Silva (2003–2011). They were to signal a key direction and focus for this regime as it sought to consolidate the stabilisation and economic reform established in the late 1990s, while simultaneously cultivating a broad alliance for political support. But by the end of this decade, according to Leslie Bethell, "Brazil's sense of itself has undergone a deep change" (Bethell 2010, np). This new-found self-confidence is due partly to the present and future promise of economic prosperity enabled by two decades of relatively stable economic growth and democratic consolidation; the nation's present position as the world's eighth largest economy means that Brazil now regards itself, and is regarded, as "an emerging global power—or, at least, a regional power with global influence and aspirations" (Bethell 2010, np). The emphasis has thus shifted throughout the Lula administration to the full attainment of the "liberal democracy" referred to by Amadeu, and the quest for a new model of development, aimed at the social inclusion of the majority of the nation's populace through the redistribution of resources. But this quest has also evolved in tandem with the intensification of the profound structural shifts brought about by the transition from the industrial economy to the global networked economy, powered by electronic and communications technologies (ICTs). In the digital age, "resources" are not now defined solely as material: they consist also of knowledge goods of all kinds, and the human capital, skills and capabilities enabled by ICTs.

The terrain on which Brazil has chosen to assert itself as a developmentalist state is precisely the principle of free dissemination of these knowledge goods and the "inalienable right to communication" through technological means. Social inclusion, democratic participation and development are now indivisible from "digital inclusion", a goal which has informed the numerous measures taken by the Brazilian state to combat the alienation of the nation's populace from physical access to and use of ICTs; as Gilberto Gil, Brazil's Minister of Culture from 2003 to 2008, put it:

> The margins of Brazilian society getting access to the digital world. The creative impulses of the people getting access to the digital world. The repressed intelligence of the Brazilian poor, the Brazilian middle class, getting access to this intelligence-empowering tool that is the digital world. (Dibbell 2004, 4)

This goal is also shared by Brazilian civil society: the coalition of media activists, volunteer communities, non-governmental organisations and other associations who have taken up the cause of access to information and communications technologies as both a civic right and as an organising principle for popular mobilisation and education (Albernaz 2002, 3). Over the course of the noughties, a synergy has developed between the technological infrastructure provided by the state, and the methodologies developed for using this infrastructure by community initiatives within civil society, with the aim of generating technological development based on the agency and creative potential of Brazilian citizens and communities. Thus, as the decade has progressed, a unique "institutional ecology" has evolved, based on public access to and communal use of ICTs. In the process, the concept of "digital inclusion" has gradually been transformed from the mere availability of networked technologies for public consumption into a model of production which integrates these networks with the human resources, skills and cultures that communities in Brazil already possess.

Moreover, as the nation has gained in importance in different areas of the international arena, so it has become an active partner for development within the various blocs and alliances comprising the "Global South". Brazil has also asserted a new global leadership role as a "voice" for this bloc in crucial international debates, and in particular, those debates which concern legal, policy and practical issues surrounding the ownership and distribution of knowledge in the information society. Within the contemporary politics of globalisation, knowledge of all kinds may constitute commercial merchandise and a source of profit; or it may be regarded as public goods that benefit from state intervention to ensure effective universal access. Brazil's assertion of the latter as a basis for national sovereignty and development is the means by which it has sought to assert its unique identity and forge international alliances with emerging nations. According to Dibbell, "Sooner or later some country was bound to square off with the intellectual property empire and be the first to insist, as a matter of state policy and national identity, on an alternative" (Dibbell 2004, 1).

Brazil's alternative has focussed to a great extent the assertion of free and open-source software systems (FOSS) as both a pragmatic and symbolic means of implementing its development policy and effecting democratic inclusion. The politics of software revolve around the question of access to what is arguably the most critical layer of the networked society (Stalder 2010, 1), the source code, programming language which manages the internal function of computers and other ICTs, and also specific data processing tasks.[1] Free and open-source software is based on the liberty to share and modify this source code, and distribute it freely without sanctions and restraints. The unfettered distribution of the software ensures a process of continual dissemination and change, as each modification of the source code is made publicly available and subsequently improved on (James 2003, 77). A broader community and global movement of developers and users has evolved, based on the principle of free access to these codes. In contradistinction to the closed monopoly of intellectual property represented by proprietary software corporations, the movement generated by FOSS systems and their use signifies a business model focussed on open collaboration in solving shared problems, combined with a system of free licensing that guarantees user freedom instead of producer control. In Brazil, the commitment to the implementation of FOSS systems throughout the Lula administration has symbolised the nation's attempts to assert national sovereignty over the nation's social and economic infrastructures; to attain a distinctive model of technological autonomy and development; and a core principle in domestic strategies to combat digital exclusion.

This chapter will trace the particular ways in which the emerging global software system enabled by FOSS has been adapted in Brazil, within three interrelated contexts. I will begin by describing the role that Brazil's engagement with the distinctive political economy of free and open-source software has played in the nation's foreign policy and diplomatic strategies, in alliance with other nations of Latin America, and the Global South; then, on a national level, the related practical and ideological role of FOSS within the Brazilian government's implementation of policies aimed at combating digital exclusion. Finally, the chapter will outline one example of the methodologies developed by grass-roots digital activists based on the adaptation of FOSS systems in uniquely Brazilian contexts: *Metareciclagem*, or Metarecycling. This methodology is described by one of its founders, Felipe Fonseca, as "...a typically Brazilian yet globally replicable way to reflect on and bring about human-centred technology development" (Fonseca, 2007, np) and points toward a future ideal of the conversion of ICTs into a means of genuine empowerment for individual citizens and communities.

Brazil on the International Stage: Multilateral Initiatives and the Global Open-Source Alliance

One consequence of Brazil's new-found self-confidence and sense of direction has been considerable activism on the world stage, within three broad pillars of Brazilian international diplomacy: firstly, what Lievesley and Ludlam (2009, 2) have termed a "new continentalism": that is, a new form of regional integration within Latin America and a marked distancing from the United States and the "Washington consensus". Related to these traditional alliances is the forging of links between the nations of the "Global South", as reflected, for example, in the launch of the alliance in 2003 between the Southern powers India, Brazil, and South Africa with the aim of increasing trilateral cooperation, and achieving greater impact by uniting their voices in the global arena. Brazil has also promoted itself as an emerging global actor in the international development system, which actively pursues multilateral initiatives in international organisations such as the UN and its different agencies, the WTO and the OECD. Brazil's initiatives within all these platforms have been consistently focused on the "global digital divide", that is, the starkly differential extent to which information and communications technologies benefit western industrial countries as opposed to developing ones. The divide is also reflected by a heavy concentration of global research and development in the former, a percentage that even in 2003 amounted to some 96% of the world's total (James, 2003, xi). Thus the risk becomes ever greater that nations who lack the technologies through which knowledge goods are transmitted will be unable, or less able, to make the investments required for building "knowledge societies" (Mansell and Wehn 1998, 1). As the material property on which the industrial era was based has given way to an economy based on intellectual property, profound global divisions have emerged. Corporate interests, heavily protected by copyright and patent law, have expanded their developments in electronics, biotechnology, pharmaceuticals, electronic information and, of course, software; Western industrialised nations have assisted these developments by expanding intellectual property rights in the name of maximising national competitiveness in a global market place (Heong 2004, np). In this context, antipathy to corporate information technology monopolies has also been a strong feature of the Brazilian government's discourse, especially those corporations such as Microsoft, whose codes are kept hidden from the consumer, and whose prices are kept artificially high through the enforcement of artificial scarcity and vendor lock-in.[2] The facilities provided by this type of proprietary software are out of reach of much of the world's populace, which accounts for the very low level of individual computer ownership in developing countries, and exacerbates the structural dependency and indebtedness, both financially and technologically, to Western countries (Story 2008, 6). For Gilberto Gil, Brazil's Minister of Culture from 2003 to 2008, the model of democratic development that Brazil wished to promote is fundamentally opposed to corporate proprietary software, which represents "the fundamentals of absolute property control…a world opened up by communications cannot remain closed up in a feudal vision of property" (Dibbell 2004, 3). The implementation and use of FOSS systems are therefore a prerequisite for the full collaborative model of development envisaged by Brazil and its regional and international partners: there can be no "digital inclusion" without access to the codes that create knowledge. Access to these codes also symbolises alternative models of democracy, precisely because, in the information society, a code accessible to all is a prerequisite for transparency of governance, participation and auditing at all levels. According to Lula:

> In a world dominated by competitiveness and search for profit at any cost, the free software movement shows that space still exists for the democratisation of knowledge… what we are discussing is the means of access to development. (Barreto and Caminhada 2005, 1)

The rejection of corporate monopolies of knowledge is not a uniquely Brazilian stance, and a consensus has been building throughout the decade among economically developing nations that open-source technology is the only option for establishing an inexpensive reliable information infrastructure, essential for autonomous development, good governance and democratic accountability (Weerawarana and Weeratunge 2004, 4-5). The outline of an international open-source alliance dedicated to achieving these aims has emerged, led by numerous Brazilian initiatives. For example, a joint document was submitted by Brazil and Argentina to the 2004 General Assembly of the World Intellectual Property Organisation (WIPO) asserting "the need to integrate the 'development dimension' into policy-making on intellectual property protection" (WIPO 2004, 2). In this context, the document went on, "in order to tap into the development potential offered by the digital environment, it is important to bear in mind the relevance of open access models for the promotion of innovation and creativity" (WIPO 2004, 3). More recently, the International Congress for Free Software and Electronic Government (CONSEGI) hosted in Brasilia in 2010, brought together representatives from twelve governments around the world[3] to form an alliance based on the use of an Open Document Format (ODF) to enable transparency and access to all state and legal documents, for better governance and democratic accountability (Tiemann 2010, np).

Brazil's Domestic Policy: Digital Inclusion and Public Access

The internationalist discourse on free software has also been integrally linked to the domestic aim of digital inclusion, a dominant thread in the Lula administration's national development strategy. Fundamental to the Program for Digital Inclusion, initiated in 2003, was the radical change that took place in the patterns of consumption of software within the nation's public and commercial institutions. As the Brazilian government was responsible for half of all the purchases of information technology in the country, it was able to use this power to effect the transition to FOSS systems on a national scale. Major companies and industries, such as the Banco do Brasil, Petrobrás, the state-controlled oil company, the postal services, and government ministries and agencies all switched to systems running on Linux. Brazil was also the first country to require any company or research institute that received software to license it as open-source (Benson 2005, 2).

A number of motives informed the decrees issued throughout the decade mandating the use of FOSS. Partly, these were pragmatic: one aim was to reduce the government's extensive financial expenditure on software licensing fees, which amounted to $1.1 billion in 2002 (Schoonmaker 2009, 554). Another justification was the need to develop an autonomous national software and information technology industry, a condition for which was the ability of domestic programmers to customise software for local business, research and development needs. But, on a much wider scale, the installation of FOSS was regarded by the nation's governance as "an affordable way to bring technology to the people" (Knight Ridder Washington Bureau) and proprietary software was seen, simply, as unaffordable: according to Marcelo D'Elia Branco, coordinator of the government's free software project in 2004: "Every license for Office plus Windows in Brazil—a country in which 22 million people are starving—means we have to export 60 sacks of soybeans" (Dibbell 2004, 10). While the adoption of FOSS in Brazil has not necessarily been universal or accepted,[4] numerous government-sponsored programmes aimed at furthering public access to information technology have been implemented by the government. According to Grassmuck (2005, 12) these digital inclusion projects, in their first phase, were top-down initiatives aimed at furnishing Brazil's populace with computers and hardware: tax incentives and payment plans to enable the working poor to purchase computers at an affordable price; and the development of low-cost computers. The second phase of digital inclusion has been focused on extending public access to the Internet. The principal strategy for accomplishing this since 2003 has been the implantation of community Internet centres, or *telecentros*, running on Linux platforms, and where local residents can access the Internet or take computer courses free of charge, or at low cost. The *telecentros* have been the principal agents in establishing a model of public access to information and communications technologies, which has continued to accelerate throughout the decade. In 2009, for example, use of digital inclusion points of all kinds accounted for more than 50% of the Internet access in the country, which had increased by 39% in that year alone (Horst 2009, 3).

Nonetheless, the initiatives taken by the Brazilian government to extend physical access to information technologies have been a target for criticism, principally among grass-roots media activists working for the same objective of "digital inclusion", but with the aim of effecting more fundamental transformations in the nation's structures of power. While the Brazilian government had indeed partly realised its more ambitious aims of democratising consumption of computers, free software and the Internet among Brazil's poor, this remained a philosophy of consumption, and not one of adaptation, appropriation or production of technology according to the diverse needs of communities in Brazil. As one activist put it: "So what if it's run on Linux if all the visitors do is chat and go to Globo websites or porn?" (Garcia 2004, 11). While the implementation of FOSS systems was a profoundly symbolic gesture on the part of the Brazilian state towards the democratic inclusion of its citizens, it would remain symbolic without alternative strategies and a praxis which would effect a radical transformation in the "hierarchies of access" to information technologies (Rodman 2003, 33), enabling Brazilian citizens to freely control and use technological affordances for their own purposes and for development of their communities.

Metareciclagem: A Brazilian Praxis of Open Source

One particular praxis is *Metareciclagem*, which originated with a mailing list Metá:fora, created in mid-2002. In less than three months, the list, described by Felipe Fonseca as "an incubator for collaborative projects" (Fonseca 2010, np) had hosted a dozen social inclusion projects inspired by the free software movement, all led by new media groups with roots in free radio, hardware hacking, media art and alternative journalism, who had begun to converge from many different points.[5] *Metareciclagem*[6] arose from the need to provide a physical infrastructure for the projects generated by Metá:fora, using donated computers, and the fundamental objective was the following:

> We would transform the technology, using the software to help people in need. To restore computers which were broken or obsolete, put them to running Linux and donate the machines to social organisations. That was the basic aim. (Rinaldi n.d., 2)

A methodology evolved from this preliminary work which one founder, Dalton Martins, described as taking place in three stages: appropriation of the "obsolescent" technology, adapting it via deconstructive tasks in a specific location and reality, to reinventing it within its local context (Grassmuck 2005, 15). The computers are repaired and reconstructed: then the machines are transferred to spaces in community centres, and new *telecentros* are created in order to train local groups in recycling technology: from the disassembling of the original computers to the construction of new ones, "laboratories of recycling" are transformed into local centres of professional education. The computers are customised and painted, becoming cultural artefacts, and an expression of the communities which have created them. The *telecentro* is the basis for the organisation of a cooperative enterprise, capable of linking to other networks for collaboration and exchange.

For *Metareciclagem*'s activists, that the newly created machines are also put to running Linux and other FOSS applications is essential to this praxis. The choice of software, according to Felipe Fonseca, was not only due to ideological considerations: it was based on the needs of the hardware which had been constructed through recycling. Donated, old or reconstructed machines have low processing power, and need lighter and more flexible software; the groups sponsored by *Metareciclagem* are also protected from accusations of software piracy. But, on another level, the choice of FOSS over proprietary software also heals the breach between developers and users. The closed or proprietary model

> tends to divide people into two distinct groups: the software developers and the end users. If the developers wish to learn what the end users require of the software, then specific channels of communication must be set up between the two groups. In contrast, the effect of the open source's bazaar approach is to merge these two groups of people. The end users are themselves the developers. (James 2003, 73)

Metareciclagem takes this process one step further by uniting once more the hardware and the source code which makes the computer meaningful and functional. It is also a practice which reverses the consumerist cycle of the individual purchase of computers. Ever more sophisticated proprietary software programs installed on these machines require constant upgrades in hardware, and, as a corollary of the process, the purchaser's computer becomes obsolete with great speed. Thus hardware must be replaced with ever increasing frequency, which explains how a digital divide can coexist with a situation where millions of computers are discarded each year (James 2003, 62). The process of recycling effected by *Metareciclagem* represents a symbolic reversal of the classic pattern of dependency on the part of developing nations and peoples on large multinational corporations.

Yet recycling is also a philosophy which has acquired additional meanings in Brazil itself: it is not solely carried out for environmental purposes, but is, for the poor, a question of survival and a means of subsistence, and anything at all is of value. According to one *Metareciclagem* participant: "Garbage is only garbage because it's in the wrong place. Things in their right places have value. To some, it's nothing…to others…it's an inversion of values" (Rinaldi n.d., 6). Another tactical media protest group, Recicle1Político, who recycle the waste left on the street left by election propaganda, had already defined the meanings accruing to recycling in Brazil. Their aim is "To recycle, to return raw material to the productive cycle, to take advantage of the residues, to add meanings, to intervene, to recombine" (Brunet 2005, 5). Recycling can be a means of subsistence, protest or resistance. It can create a new functional object, or it can be a means of aesthetic creation.

Thus *Metareciclagem* is founded on a unique form of ecological consciousness which is based on the specificity of Brazilian culture, characterised "by improvisation and by the reappropriation and transformation of what comes from abroad" (Fonseca 2007, np). In the words of Gilberto Gil, it is "no longer a mere submission to the forces of economic imperialism, but a cannibalistic response of swallowing what they gave us, processing it and making it something new and different" (Dibbell 2004, 3). In the new context of the networked society, and the digital age, these profound cultural responses to the legacy of colonial and neo-liberal domination have been integrated with the free and open-source software movement's ideals of decentralised and emergent development, of the creation and distribution of knowledge through collaboration and change. The "tropicalisation" of these ideals in a Brazilian context is summed up in the title of *Metareciclagem*'s archive, "Mutirão da Gambiarra". *Gambiarra* is a uniquely Portuguese term for the informal use and improvisation of technology, which is, according to Fonseca, a widespread cultural practice in Brazil, consisting of all kinds of improvised solutions for everyday problems with any material to hand; "... exploring the indetermination of technology...less a solution than a process: on the boundary of 'temporary' and 'definitive' solutions, it is always about trying, observing, learning and trying again, an unstable condition which allows for a great deal of ad-hoc innovation" (Fonseca 2008, np). Thus *Metareciclagem* posits one solution to what has been identified as an overriding challenge for the nation's developmentalist goals: that of "making technology match the country's social reality" (Albernaz 2002, 3) which can ultimately only be brought about by generating technological development from the innate skills, literacies and cultural identities of Brazil's pluralistic society. Indeed, during the movement's nine years of existence, *Metareciclagem* has become a national point of reference for the elaboration and implementation of many other forms of Brazilian cultural practice; some of these have been large-scale projects supported by the infrastructure provided by the Brazilian state. As early as 2004, *Metareciclagem* was adopted by the government as part of several infrastructure programmes: *Casas Brasil*, for example, which involved the construction of ninety *telecentros*, all with their own recycling laboratories. The best-known example, and one which has now begun to be diffused on an international level, is the programme *Cultura Viva* [Living Culture]. This programme was created by the Ministry of Culture in 2004 under the auspices of Gilberto Gil. *Cultura Viva* aims to target groups that are already active in cultural production in Brazil's peripheral communities, such as hip-hop, *capoeira* and samba schools, providing these groups with multimedia studios configured with FOSS software tools, supported by workshops enabling the production of digitised culture and its distribution and exchange on a regional and national level.[7] At the end of the decade, these collaborations have signalled a new phase in the nation's democratic institutional development, effecting closer relationships between the state and grass-roots civil activist movements, all with the common aim of shifting the axes of power in Brazil to a new equilibrium. More than this, at least since the establishment of the Culture Points, the concept of "digital inclusion" is gradually, through the course of the decade, being reformulated to one of "cultural diffusion", that is, transforming Brazilian citizens and their communities into active protagonists in their technological "development" and creators of knowledge goods, and, in the process, asserting Brazilian culture itself in its full heterogeneity as an agent of social change and democratic participation within the information economy.

Conclusion

By the end of the decade of the noughties as we have seen, Brazil's new-found "sense of itself" alluded to by Leslie Bethell has been fostered not only by the promise of present and future prosperity and increasing global influence; this sense has also been profoundly informed by the quest for an autonomous paradigm of technological, social and cultural inclusion, not only on behalf of Brazil's own citizens, but its international allies in Latin America and the Global South. As the Information Society has gained ever greater momentum in the first decade of this millennium, so it has become clearer that a country such as Brazil must develop an alternative strategy for building a national infrastructure based on the production, dissemination and use of knowledge. Software is the fundamental driver of these strategies: the global convergence and spread of FOSS systems and the movement associated with these has opened up opportunities for Brazil to serve its development goals. As we have seen, this movement is also a concept around which the long struggle for full democracy in Brazil may be reconfigured and consolidated in the digital age.

Brazil has chosen to stake its present identity and future status on the investment in the possibility of a global information order in which knowledge is distributed freely, unfettered by intellectual property rights and the monopoly interests of large corporations. The numerous initiatives to turn this vision into reality by the Brazilian state and civil society, from the platforms of international diplomacy to the most diverse local communities in Brazil, point towards at least the possibility of radical innovation within the global information society, and also represent Brazil's establishment as an open-source nation: the "natural knowledge economy" of the twenty-first century.

Works Cited

Albernaz, A. (2002) "The Internet in Brazil: From Digital Divide to Democracy?". Available from: http://www.aaplac.org/library/AlbernazAmi03.pdf (accessed 19 September 2010).

Amadeu da Silva, Sérgio. (2001) *Exclusão Digital: a miséria na era da informação*. São Paulo: Fundação Perseu Abramo.

Barreto, Elzio, and Caminhada, Carlos. (2005) "Brazil Extends Microsoft Challenge with Global Group", *Bloomberg News*. Posted 11 May 2005. Available from: http://bloomberg.com/apps/nes?newsarchive&sid=aJ08rWTOnQsk&refernce.html (accessed 2 September 2010).

Benson, Todd. (2005) "Brazil: Free Software's Biggest and Best Friend", *The New York Times*, 29 March. Available from: http://www.nytimes.com/2005/03/29/technology/29computer.html (accessed 20 August 2010).

Bethell, Leslie. (2010) "Brazil: Regional Power, Global Power", *openDemocracy*. Posted 8 June 2010. Available from: http://www.opendemocracy.net/leslie-bethell/brazil-regional-power-global-power (accessed 20 August 2010).

Brunet, Karla Schuch. (2005) "Do-it-yourself as free culture practices: Perspectives of Brazilian network projects". Available from: http://members.multimania.co.uk/sonhotipico/ai/pdf/artigos/brunettext.pdf (accessed 20 July 2012).

Dhanapalan, Sridhar. (2007–8) "Introduction to Linux, Free Software and Open Source", *linux australia*. Available from: http://linux.org.au/linux#CostNothing (accessed 20 July 2012).

Dibbell, Julian. (2004) "We Pledge Allegiance to the Penguin", *Wired* 12.11. Available from:

http://www.wired.com/wired/archive/12.11/linux_pr.html (accessed 25 March 2010).

Fonseca, Felipe. (2007) "Mutirão da Gambiarra", *Bricowiki*. Available from: http://wiki.bricolabs.net/index.php/Mutirao_da_Gambiarria (accessed 31 March 2010).

—. (2008) "Metareciclagem", *Mutirão da Gambiarra*. Posted 27 March 2008. Available from: http://mutirão.metareciclagem.org/fonte/Success-stories-metareciclagem (accessed 31 March 2010).

—. (2010) "PropostalInterface", *Metareciclagem*. Posted 8 March 2010. Available from: http://rede.metareciclagem.org.wiki/PropostalInterFace (accessed 31 March 2010).

Fried, Ina. (2008) "Brazil's Love of Linux", *Cnet News*, 28 August. Available from: http://news.cnet.com/2009-11397_3-6245409.html?tag=txt (accessed 3 July 2012).

Garcia, David. (2004) "Fine Young Cannibals, of Brazilian Tactical Media". Posted 10 September 2004. Available from: http://pub.descentro.org/fine_young_cannibals_of_brazilian_tactical_media (accessed 13 July 2007).

Grassmuck, Volker. (2005) "Tactical media in Brazil – Submidialogia conference report by Volker Grassmuck", *Wang Sarai Exchange Platform*. Available from: http://waagsarai.waag.org/ (accessed 13 July 2010).

Heong, Chee Yoke. (2004) "Putting the brakes on intellectual property rights", *Asia Times*. Posted 15 October 2004. Available from: http://www.atimes.com/atimes/Global_Economy/FJ15Dj01.html (accessed 30 August 2010).

Horst, Heather. (2009) "New Media Practices in Brazil, Part II: The Internet", *Futures of Learning*. Posted 11 March 2009. Available from: http://futuresoflearning.org/index.php/Firda_08/comments/new_media_practices_in_brazil_part_ii_the_internet/ (accessed 2 August 2010).

James, Jeffrey. (2003) *Bridging the Global Digital Divide*. Cheltenham: Edward Elgar Publishing.

Knight Ridder Washington Bureau. (2005) "Brazil Has Become a Trailblazer in Computer Use", *redOrbit*. Posted 25 September 2005. Available from: http://www.redorbit.com/news/technology/250691/brazil_has_become_a_trailblazer_in_computer_use/ (accessed 20 August 2010).

Latin America Bureau. (2009) "Cultural Hotspots – an anthropological 'do-in'?" Available from:

http://www.lab.org.uk/index.php/cultures/263-culture-points (accessed 19 September 2010.

Lievesley, Geraldine and Steve Ludlam, eds. (2009). *Reclaiming Latin America: Experiments in Radical Social Democracy*. London: Zed Books.

Mansell, Robin and Wehn, Uta. (1998) *Knowledge Societies: Information Technology for Sustainable Development*. Oxford: Oxford University Press.

Rinaldi, Bia. (n.d.) "Metareciclagem". Available from: http://philipe.files.wordpress.com/2007/09/metarec_bia_tudo.pdf (accessed 26 August 2010).

Rodman, G.B. (2003) "The Net Effect: The Public's Fear and the Public Sphere", in B. Kolko (ed.), *Virtual Publics: Policy and Community in the Electronic Age*. New York: Columbia University Press, 11-48.

Schoonmaker, Sara. (2009) "Software Politics in Brazil", *Information, Communication and Society*, vol. 12, no. 4, 548-565.

Stalder, Felix. (2010) "Digital Commons", in Keith Hart, Jean-Louis Laville and Antonio David Cattani (eds), *The Human Economy: A World Citizen's Guide*. Cambridge: Polity Press. Also available from: http://felix.openflows.com/node/137 (accessed 30 March 2010).

Story, Alan. (2008) "Study on Intellectual Property Rights, the Internet, and Copyright". University of Kent: Commission on Intellectual Property Rights.

Tiemann, Michael. (2010) "Report from CONSEGI Conference", *Open Source Initiative*. Posted 9 July 2010. Available from: http://www.opensource.org/node/545 (accessed 19 September 2010).

Warschauer, Mark. (2004) *Technology and Social Inclusion: Rethinking the Digital Divide*. Cambridge, MA: The MIT Press.

Weerawarana, Sanjiva and Weeratunge, Jivaka. (2004) "Open Source in Developing Countries" SIDA: Swedish International Development Agency. Stockholm: Edita Suerige AB. Available from: http://www.sida.se/publications (accessed 19 September 2010).

WIPO. (2004) Proposal by Argentina and Brazil for the Establishment of a Development Agenda for WIPO. WIPO General Assembly: Thirty-First (15th Extraordinary) Session, Geneva, September 27 to October 5, 2004. Geneva: World Intellectual Property Organization. Available from: http://www.wipo.int/edocs/mdocs/govbody/en/wo_ga_31/wo_ga_31_11.pdf (accessed 30 August 2010).

Notes

[1] "Free Software" as a concept emerged from the software development of the late 1980's. At that time, the notion of software as a standardised product for mass markets was still relatively new, established by proprietary commercial companies such as Microsoft. To combat the artificial separation between producers and users brought about by the restricted access to the software's source code, a dedicated "Free Software" movement was founded by Richard M. Stallman to realise four essential freedoms: the freedom to run the software for any purpose; the freedom to change the program without restrictions; the freedom to distribute copies of the program to help others; and the freedom to distribute changes so that others might benefit (Stalder 2010, 2). Linux, the operating system most identified with free software, was developed in the early 1990s. Open Source was coined in 1998 as a more "business-friendly" concept.
[2] Also, many proprietary software packages are sold at far above the cost of their production. Microsoft Windows, for example, has for many years been sold at a profit margin of 85%. A mere 15% is spent on marketing, packaging, shipping, and development of the product (Dhanapalan 2007–8, 2).
[3] These governments were: India, Malaysia, Indonesia, South Africa, Argentina, Chile, Cuba, Ecuador, Peru, Paraguay and Venezuela, in addition to Brazil.
[4] Many of the country's technology leaders are more pragmatic than ideological; according to Fried (2008, 16), some of the most important digital inclusion projects such as the Campaign for the Democratisation of Information work in partnership with Microsoft, and a large percentage of Linux PCs are transferred to Microsoft shortly after they leave the store where they are purchased.
[5] Some examples of these were: IP://Interface, Pública, Re:Combo, ContraTV, Centro de Mídia Independente, Sampa.org and the festival MídiaTática Brasil.
[6] A complete archive of *Metareciclagem's* history (with some material available in English) can be found on the site "Mutirão da Gambiarria", which, according to Felipe Fonseca, is "a collaborative attempt to collect, organise and publish the documentation generated throughout the Brazilian *Metareciclagem* network (Fonseca 2007, 1). Available from:
http://wiki.bricolabs.net/index.php/Mutirao_da_Gambiarria.
[7] At the time of writing, there are more than 800 of the "Culture Points" active in Brazil, and the number is targeted to increase to 2,000 over the next five years. During the II Congress of Ibero-American Culture held in São Paulo, nineteen countries from Latin America and the Iberian Peninsula pledged to adopt the *Cultura Viva* approach as part of their country's own public policy (Latin America Bureau 2009, np).

EDITORS

Kathy Bacon is the author of *Negotiating Sainthood: Distinction, Cursilería and Saintliness in Spanish Novels* (Oxford: Legenda, 2007). She has a doctorate from the University of Cambridge, has held a Post-Doctoral Fellowship at the Institute for Advanced Studies in the Humanities, University of Edinburgh, and has taught Spanish, translation, and Spanish literature at Heriot Watt University and the University of Stirling. Her research currently focuses upon the appropriation of St Teresa of Ávila in the service of discourses of gender and nationhood in Spain from the seventeenth to the twentieth centuries. She has published articles in the *Forum for Modern Language Studies* and *Antes y después del Quijote: en el cincuentenario de la Asociación de Hispanistas de Gran Bretaña e Irlanda* (Valencia: Biblioteca Valenciana, 2005), as well as book reviews for *Modern Language Review*, the *Bulletin of Hispanic Studies*, and the *Bulletin of Spanish Studies.*

Niamh Thornton has been a senior lecturer in Spanish Language, Latin American Culture and Film Studies at the University of Ulster since 2004. She is currently head of Film Studies and coordinator of Spanish at Coleraine. Before joining the University of Ulster, she previously worked as a lecturer in Spanish at Waterford Institute of Technology (1999-2002, 2003-2004), Dublin City University (2002-2003) and University of Dublin, Trinity College (2003-2004). While at Waterford, she co-founded, and continues to be an editor of the journal *Film and Film Culture*. She is the president of Women in Spanish and Portuguese Studies and the conference secretary of the Association of Hispanists of Great Britain and Ireland. Her primary area of research is contemporary Latin American and Mexican narrative and film, and is currently completing a monograph on the war story in Mexican film. She has published a monograph, *Women and the Novela de la Revolución in Mexico,* (New York and Lampeter: Edwin Mellen Press, 2006) and two co-edited books, *Transcultural Encounters: Film, Literature, Art*, co-edited with Pat O'Byrne and Gabriella Carty (Newcastle-Upon-Tyne: Cambridge Scholars Press, 2010) and *Revolucionarias: Gender and Revolution in Latin America*, co-edited with Par Kumaraswami (Bern: Peter Lang, 2007). In addition, she has previously co-edited a special section for the *Bulletin of Latin American Research.* She has also published several chapters on film, literature and cyberculture, as well as articles in journals such as *BLAR*, *BHS*, *FFC*, and *Transnational Cinemas.*

CONTRIBUTORS

Margaret Anne Clarke graduated from the University of Liverpool with a PhD in Brazilian culture. Her research interests include contemporary Brazilian digital culture and writing, and the use of computer and multimedia applications for language learning. She has published articles and book chapters in all these areas. She is a senior lecturer in Portuguese at the University of Portsmouth, UK.

María Donapetry is currently a lecturer in Spanish at Balliol College and faculty member of the Women's Studies Programme at Oxford University. She completed her doctoral studies at the University of Oviedo where she lectures regularly. She has published widely on cinema and on women's issues in academic journals in the US, UK and Spain. Her books *La otra mirada* (New Orleans: University Press of the South, 1998), *Toda ojos* (Oviedo: KRK, 2001), and *Imaginación* (Madrid: Fundamentos, 2006) comprise different feminist analysis of Spanish and Spanish American cinema. Donapetry's current research interests centre on ethical issues of film-making and reception.

Paula Jordão is an assistant professor at the University of Utrecht. Her teaching and research fields are Brazilian and Portuguese contemporary literature and Brazilian contemporary cinema. She is the editor of volume three (Spring 2010) "Identity and Memory in Lusophone Cinema" of the electronic review *P: Portuguese Cultural Studies* (http://www2.let.uu.nl/solis/PSC/P/VolumeTHREE.htm). She is also the author of: "Da Memória e da Contra Memória em *O Vento Assobiando nas Gruas*". *Para um leitor ignorado. Ensaios sobre a ficção de Lídia Jorge*. Ana Paula Ferreira (org.). Lisboa: *Texto*. 2009. 243-262; "O cruzamento do desejo e da memória em "O Belo Adormecido" e "Assobio na Noite" de Lídia Jorge. *Bulletin of Hispanic Studies*, Vol. 86, issue 4, 2009, 565- 574; "As Mulheres de Tijucopapo and A Hora da Estrela – from diaspora to a nomadic identity in the work of Lispector and Felinto", *CLCWeb: Comparative Literature and Culture*, Issue 11.3 (September 2009), 2-9. http://docs.lib.purdue.edu/clcweb/vol11/iss3/8/. She is currently working on a research project on the representation of gender as expression of otherness in Brazilian cinema (1984-2004).

Susana Lorenzo-Zamorano teaches and coordinates Spanish language at departmental level at the University of Manchester. She is also an Associate Lecturer for the Open University. Her area of specialisation and the focus of her doctoral thesis, which she completed in 2001, is contemporary Spanish theatre with special attention to women playwrights and issues of performance, gender and language. Susana's research interests also include intercultural pedagogy, kinetic manifestations, theatre and dramatic forms in the teaching of Spanish as a foreign language, enquiry-based learning and interdisciplinarity. Recent publications include "Corrupción, enfermedad y censura en el teatro español contemporáneo", in A. Davies, P. Kumaraswami and C. Williams (eds.), *Making Waves Anniversary Volume: Women in Spanish, Portuguese and Latin American Studies*, 2008, II, 25-42 and "Cross-Faculty Interdisciplinary Work or How to Work with the Others", in B. Chandramohan, S. Fallows (eds.), *Interdisciplinary learning and teaching in higher education: theory and practice*, London, Routledge/Taylor & Francis Inc, 2008, 66-75.

Abigail Loxham holds degrees from the University of Cambridge, has worked as a lecturer at the University of Hull and is currently a postdoctoral researcher in the Centre for Critical and Cultural Studies at the University of Queensland, Australia. Her research interests include Hispanic Cinemas, European Directors, Documentary Cinema and Film Theory. She completed her doctoral thesis on peripheral identities in the cinema of Spain and has published articles on Julio Medem and Bigas Luna. The preliminary research for this chapter was funded by the Dorothy Sherman Severin Fellowship awarded by the AHGBI and WISPS and is part of a new project on memory and hispanic visual culture.

Maria Manuel Lisboa is Professor of Portuguese Literature and Culture at the University of Cambridge and is a Fellow of St. John's College, Cambridge. Her teaching covers Portuguese, Brazilian and Lusophone literature from the nineteenth century to the present and also aspects of the visual arts (the work of Paula Rego). She is the author of articles in all these areas and has published four monographs: *Machado de Assis and Feminism: Re-reading the Heart of the Companion* (1996); *Teu Amor Fez de Mim um Lago Triste: Ensaios sobre Os Maias* (2000); *Paula Rego's Map of Memory: National and Sexual Politics* (2003); and *Uma Mãe Desconhecida: Amor e Perdição em Eça de Queirós* (2008). She is currently working on a book on themes of Apocalypse in fiction and film.

Susanne Meachem was born in Vienna, Austria in 1960. She moved to Tenerife, Canary Islands in 1982; a move that sparked a passionate interest in Hispanic culture, history, and politics. She then met her future husband, an Englishman she married in 1997, and has been living in England since 1996. She completed her BA in Spanish and European Studies in 2003 at the University of Wolverhampton, followed by a PGCE (in Post-Compulsory Education) at the same institution in 2004. In July 2010 she was awarded a PhD by the University of Birmingham on "Women's Actions, Women's Words: Female Political and Cultural Responses to the Argentine State". Her research interests include: interdisciplinary approaches to Argentina, gender in Latin America, Feminist theory, Social theory, and Literature by women. She has been a member of WiSPS since 2004.

Lorraine Ryan is a lecturer in Hispanic Studies at the University of Birmingham. She received her masters and doctorate in the University of Limerick. Her research interests centre on the sociology of memory; the family in Spain; Contemporary Spanish Literature; and Spanish cultural and collective memory. Her articles have appeared in *Memory Studies*, *History of the Family: An International Quarterly*, *Hispanic Research Journal*, *Modern Language Review*, *Romance Studies* and the *International Social Science Journal*, as well as in various edited collections.

Alison Sinclair is Professor of Modern Spanish Literature and Intellectual History at the University of Cambridge, and Fellow of Clare College, Cambridge. Her research and teaching covers nineteenth-century and early twentieth-century Peninsular literature, culture and intellectual history. Her publications include *Valle-Inclán's "Ruedo ibérico": a popular view of revolution* (1977), *The Deceived Husband* (1993), and *Dislocations of Desire: Gender, Identity, and Strategy in "La Regenta"* (1998). More firmly in the history of ideas is her book *Uncovering the Mind: Unamuno, the Unknown, and the Vicissitudes of Self* (2001). Two further monographs provide some background to the paper in this collection: *Sex and Society in Early Twentieth-Century Spain: Hildegart Rodríguez and the World League for Sexual Reform* (2007), and *Trafficking Knowledge in Early Twentieth-Century Spain: Centres of Exchange and Cultural Imaginaries* (2009), in addition to co-edited collections of papers on the interface between ideas, practices and discourses on the mind and body in contemporary Spain (2004) and on comparative eugenics (2008). She is currently Principal Investigator on an AHRC-funded research project on

"Wrongdoing in Spain, 1800-1936: Realities, Representations and Reactions" (2011-2014).

Laura Soler González holds a B.A in Catalan philology and a second B.A. in English philology from the Universitat Autònoma de Barcelona. She has taught Catalan, Spanish and English at secondary school level in Spain and she also taught Catalan language and literature at the University of Oxford for four years (2006-2010). She received an MPhil degree in Medieval and Modern Languages (Spanish) in 2009 from the University of Oxford. At present, she has a double appointment at the University of Bristol and Cardiff University where she teaches Catalan language, literature and culture. She also teaches Spanish at the Foreign Languages Centre at the University of Bath. She is currently working on her PhD thesis in Catalan Studies at Queen Mary, University of London on the Catalan author Pere Calders. Her research interests are in Catalan and Latin-American fiction, with a particular focus on modern short stories. She has also given papers on women's writing and gender studies and participated in the WISPS X conference held at Lady Margaret Hall (Oxford) in 2010. She has recently published chapters in *Metanarrativas hispánicas* (Lit Verlag) and *Exilio e identidad en el mundo hispánico* (Biblioteca Virtual Miguel de Cervantes), has co-edited a forthcoming volume of essays *The Limits of Literary Translation: Expanding Frontiers in Iberian Languages* (Edition Reichenberg) and has also contributed to the new edition of the *Oxford Pocket Catalan Dictionary*.

Lesley Twomey is Principal Lecturer in Hispanic Studies at Northumbria University and Programme Director for the Design History team in the Department of Arts. Her main research interests are Marian liturgy and religious literature, and medieval material culture. She has published books and articles on religious literature, including *The Serpent and the Rose: The Immaculate Conception and Hispanic Poetry in the Late Medieval Period*, Studies in Medieval and Reformation Tradition, 132 (Leiden: Brill, 2008), her edited *Faith and Fanaticism: Religious Fervour in Early Modern Spain*, (Aldershot: Variorum, 1997) and "Sor Isabel de Villena and the *Vita Christi* as Immaculist Writing", *La Corónica*, 32 (2003): 89-103, as well as her forthcoming co-edition of *La Corónica* (Fall 2013) with Andrew M. Beresford, *Visions of Hagiography*. She edited a comparative study of contemporary culture in France and Spain: *Women in Contemporary Culture: Roles and Identities in France and Spain* (Bristol: Intellect, 2000). More recently she has developed an interest in the material culture of medieval Valencia and written on medieval clothing and textiles ("Poverty and Richly Decorated Garments: A Re-evaluation of their Significance in the Vita Christi of Isabel de Villena", in *Medieval Clothing and Textiles*, ed. Robin Netherton & Gale R. Owen-Crocker [Woodbridge: Boydell & Brewer, 2007], III, pp. 119-34) and on perfume ("On the Scent of Mary: The Power of Perfume in the *Espill*", *Catalan Review*, 20 [2006]: 337-45). Her monograph *The Fabric of Marian Devotion in Isabel de Villena's Vita Christi*, a study of a Valencian nun's exceptional approach to devotion to the Virgin Mary, is to be published in early 2013 with Boydell and Brewer in the Tamesis series.